# Chicken Soup for the Soul®

# Stories of Faith

Our 101 BEST STORIES

*Chicken Soup for the Soul: Stories of Faith*
*Inspirational Stories of Hope, Devotion, Faith, and Miracles*
by Jack Canfield, Mark Victor Hansen & Amy Newmark

Published by Chicken Soup for the Soul Publishing, LLC www.chickensoup.com



The publisher gratefully acknowledges the many publishers and individuals who granted Chicken Soup for the Soul permission to reprint the cited material.

*Cover photos courtesy of © Radius Images/Alamy, iStockphotos.com/sunnyfrog. Interior illustration courtesy of iStockphoto.com/Vjom*

*Cover and Interior Design & Layout by Pneuma Books, LLC*
For more info on Pneuma Books, visit www.pneumabooks.com

Distributed to the booktrade by Simon & Schuster. SAN: 200-2442

**Publisher's Cataloging-in-Publication Data**
*(Prepared by The Donohue Group)*

Chicken soup for the soul. Selections.
Chicken soup for the soul : stories of faith : inspirational stories of hope, devotion, faith, and miracles / [compiled by] Jack Canfield [and] Mark Victor Hansen ; [edited by] Amy Newmark.

p. ; cm. -- (Our 101 best stories)

ISBN-13: 978-1-935096-14-6
ISBN-10: 1-935096-14-1

1. Faith--Literary collections. 2. Christian life--Literary collections. 3. Faith--Anecdotes. 4. Christian life--Anecdotes. I. Canfield, Jack, 1944- II. Hansen, Mark Victor. III. Newmark, Amy. IV. Title. V. Title: Stories of faith
PN6071.F17 C55 2008
810.8/5/02/0382022 2008935337

PRINTED IN THE UNITED STATES OF AMERICA
on acid∞free paper
16 15 14 13 12 10 09 08 01 02 03 04 05 06 07 08

Inspirational Stories of Hope, Devotion, Faith, and Miracles

Jack Canfield
Mark Victor Hansen
Amy Newmark

Chicken Soup for the Soul Publishing, LLC
Cos Cob, CT

Chicken Soup for the Soul®

# Contents

**3**

## ~Comfort from Heaven~



**4**

## ~Answered Prayers~



**5**

## ~The Power of Love~

6

## ~Family~



7

## ~Making a Difference~

8

## ~Special Moments~



9

## ~Miracles~

## 10
## ~Celebrating Life~

Chicken Soup for the Soul®

# A Special Foreword

## by Jack and Mark

For us, 101 has always been a magical number. It was the number of stories in the first *Chicken Soup for the Soul* book, and it is the number of stories and poems we have always aimed for in our books. We love the number 101 because it signifies a beginning, not an end. After 100, we start anew with 101.

We hope that when you finish reading one of our books, it is only a beginning for you too — a new outlook on life, a renewed sense of purpose, a strengthened resolve to deal with an issue that has been bothering you. Perhaps you will pick up the phone and share one of the stories with a friend or a loved one. Perhaps you will turn to your keyboard and express yourself by writing a Chicken Soup story of your own, to share with other readers who are just like you.

This volume contains our 101 best stories and poems about faith, hope, miracles, and devotion. We share this with you at a very special time for us, the fifteenth anniversary of our *Chicken Soup for the Soul* series. When we published our first book in 1993, we never dreamed that we had started what became a publishing phenomenon, one of the best-selling series of books in history.

We did not set out to sell more than one hundred million books, or to publish more than 150 titles. We set out to touch the heart of one person at a time, hoping that person would in turn touch another person, and so on down the line. Fifteen years later, we know that it has worked. Your letters and stories have poured in by the hundreds of thousands, affirming our life's work, and inspiring us to continue to make a difference in your lives.

On our fifteenth anniversary, we have new energy, new resolve, and new dreams. We have recommitted to our goal of 101 stories or poems per book, we have refreshed our cover designs and our interior layout, and we have grown the Chicken Soup for the Soul team, with new friends and partners across the country in New England.

We have chosen our 101 best stories and poems of faith from our rich fifteen-year history to share with you in this new volume. We know that your connection and relationship with God are important to you, and we are confident that you will enjoy these stories as much as we did. These true stories about the power of faith, prayer, and devotion will move you, amaze you, and enlighten you.

We hope that you will find these stories inspiring and supportive, and that you will share them with your families and friends. We have identified the 33 *Chicken Soup for the Soul* books in which the stories originally appeared, in case you would like to continue your personal journey among our other books. We hope you will also enjoy the additional books for Christians, families, and women in "Our 101 Best Stories" series.

With our love, our thanks, and our respect,
*~Jack Canfield and Mark Victor Hansen*

# Stories of Faith

## God's Healing Power

*For by grace you have been saved through faith,*
*and that not of yourselves, it is the gift of God.*
*~Ephesians 2:8*

# My Network

*One doesn't know, till one is a bit at odds with the world, how much one's friends who believe in one rather generously, mean to one.*
*~D.H. Lawrence*

I have always known that building a strong connecting network was the secret to my career and business success, but I never knew it would help save my life.

On a Thursday at 5:00 P.M., my doctor called. "Sarah—the routine chest X-ray you had this morning revealed a tumor—between your heart and lung—it's the size of an orange—you need to have a CAT scan ASAP."

A fear I had tried to deny seized me. Twelve years ago my brother had died of Hodgkin's disease. Four years later, my mother died of it, and on the day of her funeral my sister was diagnosed with the same cancerous demon. All three had tumors in their chest—like me.

My panicked mind raced as fast as my fingers on the phone pad. Knowing we'd need pre-approval, my husband, Fred, and I spent the entire next day, Friday, trying to convince my insurance company to approve this desperately needed test.

They finally agreed at four o'clock and we rushed to get it done that evening, only to be told that the radiologist couldn't read it for a day or so. We wouldn't know anything until Monday morning.

I knew that these lymphatic tumors could double in size in seven days! Waiting three was not an option. I did the only thing I knew to do in times of crisis. I prayed. "Please, God, connect me with the right people to help me."

Suddenly, a friendly client came to mind whose stepfather repaired radiology equipment for the hospital where my CAT scan was done. I knew it was a long shot. But after one phone call, he drove fifteen miles in a blizzard to meet us at the hospital and introduce us to the doctor, who then spent an hour showing us the scans of my fast-growing tumor. He said I needed a vascular surgeon to perform the biopsy confirming the cancer type. There were only a handful of these surgeons in town.

On our fourth call, we found one who took my insurance and agreed to do it on Wednesday. Our relief was short-lived—twenty-four hours later I was bumped off his schedule for a week due to an open-heart case that took priority.

Once again we turned to my network for help. We called an old friend and colleague of my husband's, an internal medicine doctor in Denver whom we hadn't talked to in five years. She immediately called a vascular surgeon, who agreed to see us that afternoon. Forty-eight hours later, I was on the operating table having my biopsy. However, again it was a Friday—no results until Monday afternoon.

Yet again, we turned to my network for help. We called a friend in San Antonio who had a friend who was a pathologist in Arkansas who told us what to say and do to get the on-call pathologist to come in and meet with us.

Forty-five minutes later, on a snowy, cold Saturday morning, Fred and I were looking through a microscope with the pathologist showing us my tissue biopsy confirming classic Hodgkin's lymphoma.

When we met with my doctor on Monday morning, we told him what my cancer was... he hadn't even seen the report yet!

After three surgical procedures, a nuclear PET scan and several other diagnostic staging workups, three weeks after my diagnosis, my chemotherapy began.

For five months, over seventy people in our network—including clients, coworkers, colleagues, friends, neighbors and parents of my children's classmates—brought meals to our home during my chemo weeks. I'm the only person I know who gained twelve pounds on chemo!

My two daughters decorated a three-ring binder to hold over 250 cards, e-mails and letters I received from my vast network. The cover simply read, "Mom's Cancer Blessings." I dragged this thirty-pound book with me to chemo every week for five months to read the inspiring and uplifting words from my network of encouragement.

My network also connected me to over one hundred prayer chains throughout the world. I will never really know how many people prayed for my recovery, but I can tell you I felt the power of prayer. I'm convinced I would not be in remission and completely cancer-free today without them—and my Divine Connector!

~Sarah Michel
*Chicken Soup for the Christian Soul 2*

# Forgiven

*Nurses—one of the few blessings of being ill.*
*~Sara Moss-Wolfe*

The real power of healing is not about curing diseases. This was revealed to me by a male nurse who spent a lot of time with a woman in a nursing home who hadn't been able to walk for six years. Edward lifted her in and out of her chair or into the bed, depending on her schedule.

She always wanted to talk about God and forgiveness. Because Edward had had a near-death experience, he felt comfortable doing this.

One night it was so late that Edward slipped out without being the one to put her to bed. He was heading for his car in the parking lot when he heard her call, "Edward!" He snuck back inside and into her room.

"Are you sure God forgives us for everything?" she asked.

"Yes, I'm sure, from my own experience," he said. "You know the gospel song that tells us, 'He knows every lie that you and I have told, and though it makes him very sad to see the way we live, he'll always say "I forgive."'"

She sighed. "When I was a young woman, I stole my parents' silver and sold it so I would have enough money to get married. I've never told anyone and no one ever found out. Will God forgive me?"

"Yes," Edward reassured her. "God will forgive you. Good night."

When Edward returned to work the next morning, he was told

to see the administrator who asked what he had told the woman the night before.

"As usual," Edward explained, "we talked about God and forgiveness. Why?"

"At 3:00 A.M. the woman came out of her room and, with no help, walked the entire length of the nursing home, put her Bible and teeth on the nurse's desk and said, 'I don't need these any more.' Then she turned and walked back to her room, laid down and died."

This is what the soul of nursing is all about, the reason God created a world where we can all be nurses by showing our compassion and empathy for the wounded.

~Bernie Siegel
*Chicken Soup for the Nurse's Soul*

# The Visit

Slowly I walked down the aisle of the empty church. It had been a while since I'd stopped by for a visit. After many years of attending Catholic schools I'd slipped into the category of "lapsed." Whatever spiritual juice I'd felt as a young boy growing up had evaporated years ago.

I looked around before slipping into a pew and kneeling down. It was pretty much the same as I remembered. I glanced up toward the altar and noticed the flickering candle that symbolized God was present, though invisible. "So," I whispered, "maybe you're here and maybe you aren't. We'll see." Somewhere along the line I'd lost faith in whatever had sustained me in my earlier days.

I blessed myself, sat back on the hard wooden pew, gazed ahead and continued to address the God whose presence I doubted. "Anyway, if you're really here, I need your help. I've tried everything I can think of. Nothing works. I feel totally helpless. I have no idea what else I can do. I'm thirty-three, healthy and fairly successful. You probably know all this. But I'm lonely. I have no one to share my life with, no special woman to love, no one to start a family with. My life feels empty, and I have nowhere else to go. I've taken eighteen seminars in as many months, learned how to access my feelings, release past hurts, complete old relationships, communicate my needs, understand and respond to what my partner wants. But still I'm alone. I can't seem to find the right woman, the one who feels right deep inside. What am I missing?"

I sat still, listening. There was no reply to my question, no still small voice. Just the occasional car horn outside, or the sound of a bus passing by. Just silence. I shrugged. Continuing to sit quietly, I let the silence wash over me.

Day after day, I repeated this routine. I sat in the same pew, on the same hard bench, uttering the same plea to a flickering candle, in the same silence. Nothing changed. I was as lonely as I had been on day one. There were no mystical answers, no hidden messages.

I continued to live my life, managing to laugh and have some fun. I went on dates and enjoyed myself, whether I was dining out, dancing or at the movies. I also prayed. Day after day, I took an hour away from my regular activities, emptied myself and asked the same questions again and again.

One morning about six weeks later, I awoke and knew that something had shifted. I looked around. Something about the slant of light through the clouds, the fragrance of newly bloomed jasmine, the warm beach breeze, was different. I couldn't quite put my finger on what it was, but I felt it. On my way home that afternoon, I stopped by the church as usual. Instead of my usual whining, I knelt and smiled at the candle.

Then I conveyed my thoughts to God. "I'm not quite sure what happened, but I feel different. Something has shifted inside. I don't feel lonely anymore. Nothing's changed 'out there,' but it all feels completely different. Would you happen to know anything about that?"

Suddenly, I was struck by the foolishness of the question, and I laughed out loud. My laughter echoed off the high ceilings and the stone walls, and then there was silence once more. But even the silence felt different. It no longer conveyed a feeling of emptiness and desolation. On the contrary, it radiated a wonderful serenity and tranquillity. I knew in that moment that I had come home to myself. I felt full, complete inside. I bowed my head, took a deep breath and exhaled.

"Thank you," I whispered. "I have no idea what you did but I feel this happiness comes from you. I know that. I haven't done anything new or different. So I know it's not from me. Who else could it be from?"

I continued to sit in the silence, alone, content, happy. Then I spoke again to God. "I surrender to not knowing. I surrender to you being in charge. I surrender to my life being an expression of your will instead of my will. And I thank you for this feeling, this change or transformation or whatever it is."

In the days and weeks that followed, my sense of fulfillment grew and expanded. I looked at everything from an entirely different perspective. Rather than looking for my "missing piece," I simply enjoyed life. Gone was the angst, the stifling urgency to find the "perfect woman" for the rest of my life.

The shift in my viewpoint expanded into other areas as well. Instead of trudging through life, I glided. I embraced being single. It felt wonderful. As long as I maintained my connection with my inner self, I brimmed over with happiness, excitement, joy, fulfillment. There was nothing to fear. If it was God's will that I should marry, then I would. If not, that was fine, too. I no longer held onto any preconceived notions of how my life should turn out. Every day was a new and wonderful adventure.

Four months later, I bumped into Kathy—again. We'd met years ago, but I'd forgotten all about it. She was sweet, bubbly, cute and lots of fun. We hit it off instantly. Her marriage was over and she was still mourning its passing, even though her brown eyes twinkled whenever we got together. There was something powerful that I couldn't ignore about this bright Irish lass.

Her laughter was infectious, her heart as big as the endless sky. Every time we were together, time stood still. We finished each other's sentences, giggled like school kids, brimmed over with excitement and delight. I felt protective of her. She was everything I'd ever dreamed of, everything that I'd stopped looking for months ago.

Once again, I surrendered to something so much more powerful than myself. We were in love.

One afternoon on my way back from the beach, I made a quick visit to the church. It was still just as silent, and the wooden bench was as hard as ever. The candle still flickered on the empty altar. Full of joy and mirth, I raised my eyes.

"Thanks," I whispered. "Again. For bringing us together. For helping me let go of all the baggage I was carrying, all the stuff that prevented me from seeing what was already there inside. Thanks for showing yourself to me in her smile, in myself, in the summer breezes, the cool evening sky, the curling waves, the seagulls, the sun and the rain. I couldn't have done it without you. But you always knew that, didn't you? I was the one who had to learn. Thanks for not giving up on me like I had on you. Thanks for hanging in there with me. I promise I'll never forget."

~C. J. Herrmann
*Chicken Soup for the Single's Soul*

# The Healing Power of Forgiveness

*To forgive is to set a prisoner free and discover that the prisoner was you.*
*~Lewis B. Smedes, "Forgiveness—The Power to Change the Past,"*
Christianity Today, *7 January 1983*

I thought about her. I dreamed about her. I saw her in every woman I met. Some had her name—Cathy. Others had her deep-set blue eyes or curly dark hair. Even the slightest resemblance turned my stomach into a knot.

Weeks, months, years passed. Was I never to be free of this woman who had gone after my husband and then, following our divorce, married him? I couldn't go on like this. The resentment, guilt and anger drained the life out of everything I did. I blamed myself. I went into counseling. I attended self-help classes, enrolled in seminars and workshops. I read books. I talked to anyone who would listen. I ran. I walked the beach. I drove for miles to nowhere. I screamed into my pillow at night. I prayed. I did everything I knew how to do.

Then one Saturday I was drawn to a daylong seminar on the healing power of forgiveness held at a church in my neighborhood. The leader invited participants to close their eyes and locate someone in their lives they had not forgiven—for whatever reason, real or imagined. Cathy. There she was again, looming large in my mind's eye.

Next, he asked us to look at whether or not we'd be willing to forgive that person. My stomach churned, my hands perspired and my head throbbed. I had to get out of that room, but something kept me in my seat.

How could I forgive a person like Cathy? She had not only hurt me, but she'd hurt my children. So I turned my attention to other people in my life. My mother. She'd be easy to forgive. Or my friend, Ann. Or my former high school English teacher. Anyone but Cathy. But there was no escape. The name, and the image of her face, persisted.

Then a voice within gently asked, "Are you ready to let go of this? To release her? To forgive yourself, too?"

I turned hot, then cold. I started to shake. I was certain everyone around me could hear my heart beating.

Yes, I was willing. I couldn't hold on to my anger any longer. It was killing me. In that moment, an incredible shift occurred within me. I simply let go. I can't describe it. I don't know what happened or what allowed me at that moment to do something I had resisted so doggedly. All I know is that for the first time in four years I completely surrendered to the Holy Spirit. I released my grip on Cathy, on my ex-husband, on myself. I let go of the rage and resentment—just like that.

Within seconds, energy rushed through every cell of my body. My mind became alert, my heart lightened. Suddenly I realized that as long as I separated myself from even one person, I separated myself from God. How self-righteous I had been. How arrogant. How judgmental. How important it had been for me to be right, no matter what the cost. And it had cost me plenty—my health, my spontaneity, my aliveness.

I had no idea what was next, but it didn't matter. That night I slept straight through until morning. No dreams. No haunting face. No reminders.

The following Monday, I walked into my office and wrote Cathy a letter. The words spilled onto the page without effort.

"Dear Cathy," I began. "On Saturday morning..." and I proceeded to tell her what had occurred during the seminar. I also told her how I had hated her for what she had done to my marriage and to my family, and, as a result, how I had denied both of us the healing power of forgiveness. I apologized for my hateful thoughts. I signed my name, slipped the letter into an envelope, and popped it in the mail, relieved and invigorated.

Two days later, the phone rang. "Karen?"

There was no mistaking the voice.

"It's Cathy," she said softly.

I was surprised that my stomach remained calm. My hands were dry. My voice was steady and sure. I listened more than I talked—unusual for me. I found myself actually interested in what she had to say.

Cathy thanked me for the letter and acknowledged my courage in writing it. Then she told me how sorry she was—for everything. She talked briefly about her regret, her sadness for me, for my children and more. All I had ever wanted to hear from her, she said that day.

As I replaced the receiver, another insight came to me. I realized that as nice as it was to hear her words of apology, they didn't really matter. They paled in comparison to what God was teaching me. Buried deep in the trauma of my divorce was the truth I had been looking for all my life without even knowing it. No one can hurt me as long as I am in God's hands. Unless I allow it, no one can rob me of my joy.

~Karen O'Connor
*Chicken Soup for the Christian Woman's Soul*

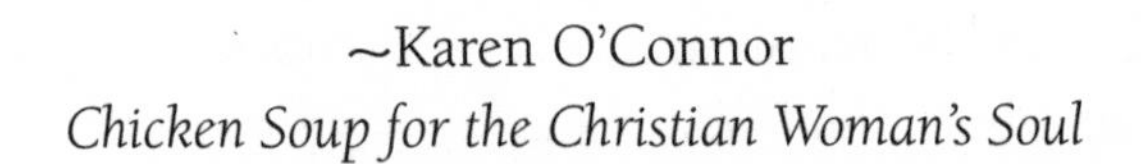

# Medically Impossible

*He shall give his angels charge concerning thee:*
*and in their hands they shall bear thee up,*
*lest at any time thou dash thy foot against a stone.*
~Matthew 4:6

I remember it was almost Christmas because carols softly played on the radio in the nurses' station. I walked into Jimmy's room. A small seven-year-old, he seemed dwarfed by the big, indifferent, mechanical hospital bed with its starchy white sheets.

He looked up at me through suspicious eyes, hidden in a face puffed up from the use of steroids to control his kidney condition. "What are you gonna do to me now?" they seemed to ask. "What blood tests are you gonna order? Don't you know they hurt, Doc?"

Jimmy had a disease called nephrotic syndrome, and it was not responding to any therapy we had tried. This was his sixth month with the illness, his second week in the hospital. I was feeling guilty—I had failed him. As I smiled at him, my heart felt even heavier.

The shadow of defeat had dulled his eyes.

"Oh no," I thought, "he's given up." When a patient gives up, your chances of helping that patient lower dramatically.

"Jimmy, I want to try something."

He burrowed into the sheets. "It gonna hurt?"

"No, we'll use the intravenous line that's already in your arm. No new needles." What I planned I had tried a few weeks earlier without success. I gave him intravenous Lasix, a drug that is supposed to "open up" the kidneys.

This time I planned a new twist, which the nephrologist said probably would not work but was worth a try. A half hour before I injected the Lasix I would inject albumin, a simple protein that would draw water from the bloated cells into the bloodstream. Then, when I gave the Lasix, the water flooding the bloodstream might flow into and open up the kidneys. The problem was, if it didn't, the "flooded" blood vessels could give Jimmy lung congestion until his body readjusted. I had discussed this with his parents. Desperate, they agreed to try.

So I gave albumin into his intravenous line. A half hour later I came back to give the Lasix. He was breathing harder and looked scared. I had an idea. I never believed in divine intervention, but Jimmy came from a very religious family.

"You pray a lot?" I asked.

"Yes, "he answered. "I pray every night. But I guess God don't hear me."

"He hears you," I replied, not knowing in all honesty if God did or didn't, but Jimmy needed reassurance. And belief. "Try praying as I give this medicine to you. Oh, and I want you to pretend you see your kidneys—remember all those pictures of them I showed you awhile back?"

"Yes."

"Well, I want you to picture them spilling all the extra water in your body into your bladder. You remember the picture of your bladder I showed you?" I figured I might as well try visualization. This was in the early 1970s. Some articles had been written about visualization and some evidence existed that it worked—in some cases, anyway.

"Yeah."

"Good. Start now. Concentrate on your kidneys." I placed my hands there and shut my eyes, concentrating—just to show him how, you understand. Then injected the Lasix.

Jimmy closed his eyes and concentrated, and mouthed a prayer.

What the heck. I also prayed, even though I knew it wouldn't work. I did not believe in divine intervention. When I died I would have a few choice questions for God about why he allowed certain terrible things to happen to certain children. One of my friends suggested that when I did die, God would probably send me the other way just to avoid me. But in for a penny, in for a pound.

"How long will it take to work?" the nurse asked as she adjusted the dripping intravenous line. I motioned for her to step from the room.

"In a person with normal kidneys, maybe twenty minutes—fifteen minutes tops," I replied. "With Jimmy, I'm hoping a half hour. But I have to tell you, it's a real long shot. Stay with him. If he has trouble and needs oxygen, call me. I'll be at the nurses' station writing all this down."

I sat down and opened Jimmy's cold, metal-jacketed chart, almost cursing the irony of the Christmas carol on the radio: "Oh Holy Night." Before I had scribbled one sentence, the nurse stuck out her head from Jimmy's room. "A half hour to work?" she asked.

"For normal kidneys."

"Otherwise fifteen minutes 'tops,' right, Doc?"

"That's what I said."

"Well, the floodgates have opened: He's urinating like crazy. Within just two minutes he asked for the urinal. I've got to go get another."

Two minutes? Impossible. I went to the room as fast as my cane would allow me to walk. Jimmy had already filled the plastic yellow urinal. The nurse rushed in with another two. He grabbed one and started filling that one, too. He grinned at me, the light back in his blue eyes.

I left the room, a numbness coursing through my mind and body. It couldn't be. If he diuresed—if his kidneys opened up—he was on the way to a cure. No, it just could not happen that fast. Impossible. Medically impossible. And yet...

Was it sheer pharmacology and physiology breaking the rules? Was it the visualization?

I could clearly hear a fragment of a carol on the radio. I felt goosebumps: "Fall on your knees, oh hear the angel voices..."

A paraphrase of the last line from *Miracle on 34th Street* came to me: "And then again, maybe I didn't do such a wonderful thing, after all."

~John M. Briley Jr., M.D.
*A 5th Portion of Chicken Soup for the Soul*

# We Almost Lost Her

New York City, April 20, 1996. It is Parents' Day at Columbia University's College of Physicians and Surgeons. About three hundred professors, medical school students, and proud parents gather in Bard Hall, waiting for the luncheon speaker. We've spent the morning touring the facility. We're delighted that our children are learning at a school so obviously dedicated to excellence.

It is hard for me to believe today that more than twenty-four years have slipped by since our daughter came into the world. I remember her first year of life so vividly. How could I not? We almost lost her....

My mind quickly skips backward across the years. It is 5:00 A.M. on April 8, 1972. Gordon and I suddenly awaken in the predawn hours to a sharp cry coming from the crib in the corner of our bedroom. It is uncharacteristic of our six-month-old daughter to announce her needs with such urgency, so I jump out of bed. As I approach her, Valerie throws up and begins to cry.

"Now don't you worry, Mrs. Jones," comes the calm voice of Valerie's pediatrician over the telephone line. "Little babies often throw up very hard when they have the stomach flu. It's going around, you know, but it's nothing to be concerned about."

So I cradle Valerie in my arms, trying my best to emulate the attitude of her thoroughly unalarmed pediatrician. But her face, usually relaxed and smiling, reflects a mixture of anxiety and discomfort.

By lunchtime, I'm even more alarmed. "The baby is throwing up blood!" I exclaim in a second phone call.

"That's perfectly normal," says the unruffled physician. Just keep giving her fluids."

"But she doesn't want to nurse anymore."

"Well, that's all right. After all, when we have the flu, we're not usually very hungry, are we?"

My heart continues to sink when, a few hours later, I put Valerie on the changing table and see traces of blood in her diaper. As a first-time mother, am I overreacting?

And so it goes throughout the day, with me calling the doctor, then waiting for the doctor to return my calls. Valerie finally is admitted to our neighborhood hospital late that afternoon when the pediatrician decides she will improve quicker with the help of intravenous fluids. When we arrive, emergency-room personnel cut deep gashes in her chubby little ankles to insert needles when they can't find her veins. Valerie reacts with admirable stoicism to these painful procedures, refusing to cry in spite of the obvious miseries.

By 9:00 P.M. that night, Gordon shares my concern. "She's not doing very well at all," he frowns. Turning to the pediatrician, who remains unruffled, he underscores my observations. "My wife says she's been throwing up ever since she got here."

"And I still see blood!" I add.

"The capillaries are still acting up, are they?" the doctor says. "When the spasms stop, the capillaries will heal."

"Now go home and get a good night's sleep," he adds, stepping aside to let us pass. "There's nothing you can do sitting here. Valerie needs her mom and dad to be fresh and rested when she checks out tomorrow!"

Early the next morning, I am shocked into consciousness by a ringing phone.

"I don't want to alarm you, Mrs. Jones," says the pediatrician, "but I thought it best for me to talk to you first. Valerie had a little setback during the night."

"A setback?" I echo, bolting up in bed.

"It's nothing serious, I assure you," he continues. "She had a seizure, but it's completely under control now, and she's resting peacefully."

"A seizure?" I exclaim, feeling the blood rise to my face. "Why?"

"Well, it's easy to explain, really. The IV caused a slight imbalance in her blood chemistry. It's not at all unusual."

"I want to be with her," I tell him. "I'm coming right away."

I arrive to find Valerie drowsy. I am told it's because of the heavy dose of medication prescribed to prevent further seizures.

After Gordon leaves for work, I spend the day hounding the nurses. Are they still taking blood tests to determine the level of her electrolytes? Why is she so restless? Why does she seem so much sicker than the other babies in the flu ward? How long had the seizure lasted? What is wrong with my baby?

By nighttime, Valerie cannot get comfortable. No matter how much she twists and turns, she cannot find a position that satisfies her.

"Can't I hold her on my lap?" I ask one of the nurses. The tolerant nurse decides that the easiest thing is to let me have my way.

But after about an hour helping Valerie find a comfortable position, I realize her abdomen has distended noticeably. Though I want to go to the nurses' station to report my findings, Valerie is hooked to two separate IVs, and there is no way I can get her back to bed without help. I sit there, trapped and horrified, watching her abdomen continue to grow, until a nurse materializes.

"Look!" I cry. "Look at the size of my baby's abdomen! And how could it distend so quickly? I don't understand!"

"The doctor will answer your questions in the morning, Mrs. Jones."

"But I want to know right now!" I insist.

"The doctor can't be disturbed," says the nurse. "He's at home."

"I'll call him," I say. "He can't fire me! What's his number?"

"I'm sorry, Mrs. Jones, but we can't give out that information."

"Then you call him!" I plead. "If he gets mad at you, just blame me. Tell him I threatened to report him to the chief of pediatrics!"

"Mrs. Jones, he is the chief of pediatrics," the nurse replies, smiling pleasantly, turning and walking briskly away.

I sit there for an hour, frustrated and scared. Suddenly, the door bursts open.

"I decided to call the doctor after all," says the nurse. "He told me to get Valerie to X-ray immediately!"

As Valerie is moved straight to X-ray, a group of doctors, including the pediatrician, gathers and examines the results. Gordon slips his hand into mine as we listen to the doctors.

"How could you have missed it?" says one, looking angrily at the chief of pediatrics. "Haven't you heard of an intussusception?"

"It never occurred to me!" he replies. "She didn't fit the statistics! She's a girl, for one thing. This usually happens to boys! She's only six months old, and that puts her on the low end, age-wise. And besides, I did not know she was in pain! She never even cried!

Suddenly, the doctors turn and see us. The chief of pediatrics turns pale.

"Mr. and Mrs. Jones," he says in a trembling voice, "there's no time to waste. Valerie's life is in the balance. She must have an operation right now. It's up to you to decide whether you want my colleague to do it here, or whether you want to risk sending her to Columbia Presbyterian in New York, an hour away. I can't guarantee that she'll live for another hour, but they have the best pediatric surgeons in the world there."

"He's absolutely right," says one of the other doctors, a general surgeon. "The physicians at Columbia Presbyterian are highly trained specialists. I've never operated on a baby before, but I'll do the best I can if you want me to go ahead. It's your call. You have to decide right now, though."

"We want the best for our baby," says Gordon. "Send her to Columbia. She's a fighter. She'll make it there."

"What exactly is wrong?" I ask.

"It's called telescoped bowel," explains the pediatrician. "By some fluke, the large intestine managed to catch a piece of the small intestine at the valve where they meet, and began sucking it down."

"Why is her abdomen so distended?" I ask, fearing his answer.

"Her abdomen," the doctor replies, "is swollen with gangrene."

There is no time for grief, panic or tears. The surgeon and the pediatrician, feeling there is nothing more they can do, go home. Gordon and I wait anxiously for the ambulance. We hound a kind resident who repeatedly picks up the phone and checks on the ambulance; it's a good thing. The driver gets lost, and the resident directs him the rest of the way via telephone.

Thirty minutes later, the paramedics come running down the corridor.

"What do you think you're doing?" says one of the paramedics as I climb inside the ambulance.

"I'm going with you!"

"No, you're not," he shouts, pulling my arm. "It's against regulations!"

But I protest, digging in my heels and holding on to a bar on the wall. "Let's go," I tell them. "We don't have time for this!"

"All right," he says finally, "but if the baby starts to fail, we may have to resuscitate. So I'm warning you, lady, if you interfere in any way, I'll knock you out!"

"It's a deal," I say. "Let's go!"

Once we arrived at the hospital, Gordon and I say goodbye to Valerie as we are ushered to a waiting room.

We anxiously wait there for the pediatrician. Finally, a young blond man enters the room and moves toward us, a clipboard clutched in his left hand. This can't be the surgeon, I think. They must have sent a medical student.

"Mr. and Mrs. Jones?" says the fair-haired youth, extending his right hand. "I'm Dr. John Schullinger. We don't have much time, so forgive me if I come straight to the point. The prognosis for your baby is extremely poor. The truth is, she is moribund. It would be unfair of me to give you any real hope that she'll survive. If she does live, she may very well suffer serious brain damage, and she'll almost certainly have intestinal problems for the rest of her life. I'm deeply sorry to have to be the one to bring you this news, but you have every right to know the facts. And now, if you'll excuse me, every minute counts."

I've given my baby into the care of a boy, I think with sudden alarm.

Now, there is nothing to do but sit on the couch in the waiting room and cry. I sob until I hear Gordon.

"Stop," he is saying in a pleading voice. "I can't stand it! You must stop crying."

Grief is a feeling that is hard to share, even with loved ones. Gordon seems in another world, far away and out of reach. I feel walled in by a cocoon of pain, hollow silence and unbearable loneliness. We are completely alone together. The only thing I can do for him now, the only gift I can give him, is to stop crying.

I pray to God for the first time. Like many other supposedly self-sufficient people, I have waited until I am overcome with grief and helplessness before it occurs to me to turn to God for comfort. I have often heard it said that God is merciful and is, in fact, love itself. Indeed, those words come to life for me in the barren, silent waiting room at the Babies and Children's Hospital, a room that surely witnessed the bitter tears of countless other parents.

I peek out the door of the waiting room several times during the night, wishing there were someone I could ask how the operation is going, but the halls are dark and the nurses' station is empty. Then I hear the squeak of crêpe soles coming down the corridor. I open the door and see a nurse putting her shoulder bag on the desk.

"Could you please call the operating room and find out how my baby is?" I cry breathlessly.

"Okay!" she says wearily, picking up the phone. "What's the name of the patient?"

"Valerie Jones."

"And the surgeon?"

"Dr. John Schullinger."

"Dr. John Schullinger?" she repeats. "You have no worries. He's the best there is. I'm sure your baby is just fine."

"No, you don't understand! He doesn't think she'll make it! She is moribund!"

The nurse holds up her hand to silence me as she speaks to someone on the line.

"She's doing just fine," says the nurse in a matter-of-fact tone as she replaces the receiver. "She's in intensive care now. I told you that we don't lose babies here!"

New York City, April 20, 1996: The voice of the Parents' Day program coordinator brings me back to the present. Gordon and I, meanwhile, look with astonishment as Dr. John Schullinger rises from his chair at the head table. As he makes his way to the podium, I quietly approach a professor and ask if I might make a short speech after Dr. Schullinger's address. When I explain what I want to say, she agrees.

When the doctor takes his seat after speaking, I keep my words brief. I say to the smiling audience, after recounting that unforgettable night twenty-four years ago, "I am delighted to have this opportunity to thank Dr. Schullinger publicly. I now know that God was guiding his hand that night. Who could have predicted our daughter would end up being mentored by the very man who saved her life?

"In retrospect, it is obvious that you save babies here at Columbia-Presbyterian so you can train them to become doctors who will save other babies in turn. Isn't this, after all, what medicine is all about?"

I take my seat as the audience erupts with the applause Dr. Schullinger so richly deserves.

Valerie Jones has completed her second year of medical studies at Columbia. She continues to enjoy life free from symptoms or complications.

Dr. Schullinger is no longer "the boy" I first met, but he seems perenially young.

And God? He's the same yesterday, today and tomorrow.

~Sonia Jones
*Chicken Soup for the Christian Family Soul*

# "I Am," I Said

The young physical-therapy aide at the rehabilitation center chattered endlessly while we prepared for my session. I'm embarrassed to admit I was too caught up in my troubles to listen to her. As I watched the other patients struggling with their crutches and wheelchairs, my spirit was overcome by a sense of loss.

So much had changed. Only weeks had passed since bone cancer stole my left leg. Recently healed from surgery, I could barely sit in a chair for an hour at a time. Now I faced the difficult task of learning to walk with a prosthetic limb, a process complicated by an old back injury. The slightest activity sent scalding "phantom" pain into my nonexistent foot. As if that weren't enough, chemotherapy had robbed me of my hair and my strength. A wide range of emotions drained my remaining energy: fear, anger and grief, topped off by a huge dollop of self-pity. Worst, though, I was unable to care for my father who had Alzheimer's disease. I had no choice but to place him in a nursing facility and leave with a load of guilt.

When faced with overwhelming problems, we often escape by focusing on minor ones. People are funny in that way. In this instance, I fretted over the loss of my nursing career and the income it provided. Thankfully, my husband handled the finances. Every time the huge bills arrived, we thanked God that our insurance was adequate. Nevertheless, I missed the rapport with my patients and my colleagues. I'd always enjoyed the teaching aspect of nursing and loved seeing the glow of relief when a patient was able to understand his or her illness. It was such fun when the couples in my childbirth classes proudly showed me their new babies, gushing, "Shirley, it happened just like you said it would."

How I longed to believe I would someday return to nursing. The yearning left me feeling ashamed of my selfishness.

I argued, first with myself, then with God. There were so many reasons for gratitude. Countless people had prayed for me. I was still alive, still a child of God, a wife, a mother and a grandmother. I tried to keep a sense of perspective by telling myself that nursing was only a career; it wasn't my identity. "But, Lord, you led me into nursing and gave me a love for it. It's my calling, and I feel the loss deeply. Why have you taken it from me?"

I paid scant attention to the aide's words as I watched an elderly stroke victim attempting to operate a can opener. Nearby, a middle-aged man recovering from knee surgery drooped in despair. Across the room, a handsome airline pilot practiced walking again, following a severe spinal-cord injury. His cheerfulness puzzled me. I wondered what determined a patient's response to loss. What spurred some on when others were easily defeated? Was it merely an inborn character trait, like a strong personality or a deep-seated tenacity? Was it faith? Whatever it was, I wanted it myself.

I'd like to think I fashioned a prayer that touched God's heart. But in truth, I muddled through a jumble of emotions and came up with nothing but a scrambled plea that meant, "Lord, I need help." I expected no reply.

The aide, still valiantly trying to cheer me up, said, "I understand you used to be a nurse."

A fresh load of anger welled up inside my chest. Used to be? I felt like asking her what she thought I was now. Before my mind could form a sarcastic response, words came from my mouth. "Yes, I am a nurse." Somehow I felt different, stronger, but I wasn't sure why.

Later, still feeling insulted, I mentally conducted a one-sided quarrel with the aide who had reminded me of who I "used to be." Wait a minute. I'm everything I've ever been. I have one less leg, but

I still have my brain and my heart. I'm not a has-been! God doesn't have any has-beens.

I carried that thought in my head until the day a familiar scripture came to mind. I located it in my Bible concordance, then turned to Acts 17:28 and read aloud. "In him we live, and move, and have our being." Three words stood out from the rest: "live," "move" and "have." It didn't say that we had our being; we have it. My life isn't in past tense. I still am. I am!

No sudden or dramatic change occurred, but gradually that passage influenced my attitude. It fanned a tiny ember of faith that lay buried under my negative emotions. Over a period of months, that faith grew to the flame it had once been. I gained strength, and with it a sense of my own potential.

A year and a half after my surgery, I returned to the hospital where I had worked for eighteen years. Physically unable to resume my previous role, I became the manager of the hospital's new home-health agency. Though I could work at my own pace, I found that making home visits was painful and difficult. In our rural area, many homes have no sidewalks or handrails at the steep doorsteps. Carrying a heavy bag while walking with a prosthetic leg was not easy, even with a cane. Once inside, I struggled to keep my balance as I bent over low beds to perform sterile procedures. And I loved it.

Though nothing lessened the joy of being a nurse again, I often doubted whether I could continue this work while we waited for the census to grow enough to hire more staff. But the growth was rapid and steady. Soon I hired other nurses to visit the patients while I managed the office. Once again, I was teaching patients, this time by phone. Friendships developed between us, though many of us never met in person. The nurses, aides and therapists formed a great team, and when I retired, the agency was thriving.

At my retirement party, a doctor and colleague of many years announced, "I'm astonished at Shirley's accomplishment in this community." I'm sure he knows, as I do, that God had a hand in making the agency the blessing it is to this day. Isn't it strange how God uses the things we focus on, rightly or wrongly, to get our attention? In my case, he used my anger and my love of nursing to draw me closer to him. Now, when I hear Neil Diamond sing that song titled, "I Am... I Said," I smile inside. It was God who brought me from "I Was," to "I Am." Who but he could know the value of one little word?

~Shirley McCullough
*Chicken Soup for the Nurse's Soul*

# A Heart to Give

As I lay in bed on Thanksgiving Day 1989, my body wracked with pain, I found little to be thankful for. Some months earlier, I had broken my foot. Having been a world-champion steer wrestler on the rodeo circuit in my early years, I certainly didn't worry over broken bones. The main problem was the inconvenience of the cast. But as the weeks went by, I began to experience intense pain. Finally, the cast was cut away, and the source of pain revealed. Somehow, the cast had cut the bottom of my foot, and since I was a diabetic, gangrene had quickly set in. After several days of intravenous antibiotics, I went home, but the wound never healed. The searing, throbbing pain was unbearable, and my temperature escalated. I knew what the next step would be.

The following morning, an emergency surgical team prepared to amputate my right leg, just below the knee. Though I had protested in the beginning, now I just wanted to live and to be out of pain. After the surgery, I gradually moved from a wheelchair to crutches and often hopped around on my good leg, until a blister appeared on my foot. Six months later, I was a forty-four-year-old double amputee. I had felt sorry for myself after the first amputation, but it was nothing compared to the anger and rage I experienced with the second.

When I was a youngster, I had joined a little country church and thought that took care of my religion. I didn't talk to God the way some people claim to. I took care of myself and figured most folks would be better off if they did the same. What I learned about God growing up was that He was to be feared, and I had experienced enough fear in my own home. I certainly didn't need more from some deity.

But now, as a grown man trying to cope with two "stubs" instead of legs, I even lost my fear of God. As I sat in the middle of the bathroom floor, unable to raise myself up, I cursed God violently. So what if He struck me with lightning, could that be much worse? Maybe I wasn't the best person in the world, but I didn't deserve this.

Eventually, I was fitted with two prostheses and spent time in rehabilitation learning to walk again. By 1995, I was back to a fairly normal lifestyle, with a good job, wife and family. Then, I began having chest pains. The pain was familiar. When I was thirty-one, I had quintuple heart bypass surgery. Years later, stents were placed in the arteries. What else could they possibly repair? Increasing pain and total exhaustion forced me into the hospital. Finally, the doctor recommended a heart transplant, even though my medical problems posed a great risk. Having been a gambler in my rodeo days, I didn't like the odds they were giving me, but I saw no other option.

Being accepted by a transplant team was no easy task. As a diabetic and double amputee, some teams wouldn't even consider me. And even if I was accepted, I would have to go on a waiting list, which could take months or years. Even if I got lucky and received a heart, there were no guarantees that the surgery would work.

When I had the bypass surgery years earlier, I was put on a heart-lung machine to keep my heart pumping during surgery, and then an electrical impulse restarted my heart to function on its own. But this time, someone else's heart would be placed in my body. It didn't take a genius to figure out that the only One who could make a brand new heart start beating was Almighty God, and I figured I had alienated Him completely the day I cursed Him. I was tired of the anger and bitterness, and didn't want to live what life I had left raging against my circumstances. So, I made my peace with God.

Eventually, I was accepted as a transplant candidate, and on the day after Christmas, I went into the hospital with hope and apprehension to wait for a new heart. It was like living with life and death at the same time. One minute I thought of being healthy again; the next minute the reality surfaced that I might die.

Finally, on January 22nd, the doctor told me a heart had been located. I gathered my family together. As they prepared me for surgery, I felt complete peace.

Suddenly, the doctor came in and told us there was a problem. Hesitantly, he said, "We have a seventeen-year-old boy on a ventilator who probably won't make it through the night without a heart." He paused awkwardly. "I don't know how to ask you this, but would you consider giving him the heart?" He emphasized that the heart was originally intended for me, and it was my choice. I could keep it, since there was no way of knowing when another heart would become available or how long my body would make it without one.

From the moment I was notified a heart had been donated, I had gone from disbelief to elation, to apprehension to acceptance, and now I wasn't sure what I was feeling. How do I choose who lives or dies?

The tough part was knowing what my family would go through if I didn't receive another heart. I didn't want to make my wife a widow. I wanted to live and see my grandchildren grow up. The easy part was knowing who needed the heart most.

It was the toughest and the easiest decision I ever made.

The young man survived the surgery, and one week later I received my new heart, an even better physiological match for my body than the previous one. Several months later, one of the doctors told me that he knew of no one in medical history who had chosen to give up a donor heart to someone else.

That was seven years ago. Today, it takes extra energy for me to walk, but I enjoy going places and meeting people. I wear shorts everywhere I go, no matter what the season or weather. I want people to see my prostheses and ask questions, so I can tell them about my medical miracles. When they ask, I tell them that God gave me new legs so I could walk with Him. Then, I explain how He gave me two new hearts—this physical heart transplanted into my chest cavity and a spiritual one deep in my soul, which overflows with His love.

~John Patterson as told to Louise Tucker Jones
*Chicken Soup for the Caregiver's Soul*

# Soaring with Eagles

*Though no one can go back and make a brand new start,*
*anyone can start from now and make a brand new ending.*
*~Author Unknown*

John and I strained forward as if to assist his worn Army surplus Jeep, inching up a steep hill blanketed with loose sliding rock. A heartbeat later, I was hurled to the ground. The Jeep's wheels pointed skyward, spinning dizzily. I screamed for John; then I screamed again. My cries were met with silence.

We had first become acquainted as pen pals. I so admired his struggle to become a doctor and to serve his people with no thought of personal gain. It was not just a profession for John, it was a calling. So when he invited me to spend the summer with him as an assistant and traveling teacher, on vacation from my regular teaching job, I could barely contain my excitement. Many of the families he treated lived in remote areas that often lacked roads, and the small children had no benefit of schooling.

Our first meeting at the airport held no awkwardness—John offered a warm embrace as if we'd been friends forever. Early the next morning we were off on rounds, leaving dusty white whirls behind the Jeep. Abruptly, I cried out: "Stop, John! Stop!"

Alarmed, he slammed on the brakes. "What's wrong?"

"Look up there!" I shouted. "Look, an eagle! Oh! It's my very first one." Overcome by its beauty and majesty, I wept.

He leaned to brush away my tears with gentle fingers. "My city girl has heard her first call of the wild," he said quietly. "From this moment on, you shall be known as 'Little Eagle.'

In that moment we fell in love.

Each morning after that, John would call, "Come, Little Eagle, it's time to soar. The children need you."

Whenever we pulled up to a cluster of tiny houses, children would run to hug us. Shouts of "Dr. John and Little Eagle are here!" were a symphony to my ears. How I loved this work. John treated his patients with respect and compassion. He listened before he spoke, and his patients' smiling eyes mirrored the trust he had earned.

I often assisted John until the children tugged at my jeans for their lessons, which I disguised as games. Their eyes grew wide when I brought oranges and cut them into fractional parts. At the end of the lesson, we sat in a circle, sang a numbers' song and ate every fraction.

John and I cared for their bodies, minds and spirits. Our pay was a shared meal, a heartfelt hug or a handshake. Grateful mothers offered to patch our threadbare jeans with bits of colorful cloth. With the small stipend we received from the government, we purchased upgraded medical supplies and nourishing treats for the children.

In a few short weeks, our friendship blossomed into a spiritual bond bred of shared service. Our hearts became one. Whenever unpredictable medical emergencies delayed our departure, we would camp out, as traveling after dark on makeshift roads was impossible. Sleeping in John's arms beneath billions of stars in the South Dakota sky was the closest thing to heaven I have ever known.

By mid-August, I called home to tell Mom and Dad that I would be staying on.

"If it makes you happy," said Dad, clearing his throat, "then I share your happiness."

Mama whispered into the phone, "I know you're young and in love, but it pains me to think you'll be dirt poor for all your life."

"Oh, no, Mama, we'll never be poor. You cannot imagine how rich we are."

These are the memories that sustained and tortured me once

my dreams were shattered. John was dead and my career was over, because none of the city schools were wheelchair accessible. My principal had offered to build a ramp, but his request to have me return was denied.

In the hospital, I cried myself to sleep.

I awoke one night to see John sitting on my bed, and I heard his gentle voice as if he were whispering in my ear: "The Little Eagle that I know and love would not give up so easily," he scolded. "You have to help yourself soar again—the children need you."

"Oh, John, I can't. It's just too much. Take me with you, please!"

"That is not to be," he said. "The city children need you. Imprisoned by concrete, they know nothing of the joys of nature. Share your joy with them; bring it into the classroom. You have the gift, Little Eagle. Don't throw it away."

Then he was gone.

For the next two months, I worked feverishly in physical therapy. Every muscle and bone in my upper body screamed, but I would not stop. Struggling to hold myself erect on parallel bars, I swung my legs ahead or dragged them behind me, refusing to acknowledge their numbness.

My doctor entered the therapy room and sat down, "You've given it all you've got, Toni, but there's no improvement. I'm discharging you tomorrow."

"I will walk. I know it."

Cradling my face in his hands, my doctor said, "Sweetie, you're in denial; at some point you'll be better off accepting your reality."

Reality, I thought, as I drifted to sleep that night.

About 3 A.M. a voice awakened me. "Come, Little Eagle—it's time to soar." John was standing over my bed, smiling. "Push your legs over the edge and stand up." John's softly glowing image kneeled at my feet and gently rubbed my legs until they tingled. I swear I could feel his hands touching me. Then he stood with hands outstretched and backed away. "Walk with me now."

With hesitant, shuffling steps, I followed him out of my room and into the hall. My eyes were riveted on John, coaxing every step. A stairway loomed ahead.

"One step at a time, Little Eagle. You can do it."

The sensation in my legs was almost unbearable, as I climbed one step, and then another. Suddenly, from the stairwell door, the excited voices of the resident intern and head nurse carried up the stairs.

"I'll always be with you," John whispered. With a kiss on my cheek, he was gone.

For the next two hours, doctors poked and prodded; they mumbled to each other about "spontaneous something or other," and finally left. When all was quiet, a nurse came in and sat on my bed.

"I saw the young man leading you up the stairs," she said quietly. "Is he your guardian angel?"

"Yes, he is."

"I've often heard patients speak of seeing angels. Did he tell you his name?"

"Yes," I nodded. "His name is John."

Two months later, I returned to my teaching job with a gait sorely lacking in feminine grace, but propelling me nonetheless. My classroom is now filled to bursting with all the wonders of nature. The walls are covered from ceiling to floor with colorful sights from the wild.

Many teachers bring children to my room to view live creatures firsthand. In each child's eyes, wide with wonder, I see my beloved John, smiling.

And in the quiet of night, when my day is done, my spirit soars with him in velvet skies on the wings of eagles.

~Toni Fulco
*Chicken Soup to Inspire the Body & Soul*

# Stories of Faith

## Divine Intervention

*Nothing is or can be accidental with God.*
*~Henry Wadsworth Longfellow*

# Just Two Tickets to Indy

*There is no telling how many miles you will have to run while chasing a dream.*
*~Author Unknown*

We had talked about the possibility and its ramification for months as test after test failed to confirm or deny the diagnosis. But now we sat in my office crushed by the reality that it was true: John had ALS, Lou Gehrig's disease. The insidious affliction strikes the muscular system of its victim, eventually draining the body of all strength to support even breathing and a beating heart.

John had been my business partner, my friend, my mentor for many years. He was the kind of friend who pushed you beyond what you thought you could do. John always saw you not for what you are but for what he thought you could be, and then he never let you accept anything less. He told me one time, "I wouldn't really be much of a friend if I let you settle for what you think is your best."

We sat in the office crying and holding hands like two adolescent children, realizing that the crippling death sentence would not allow John to live for more than two years. I asked him to think about the one thing he had always dreamed of doing that he hadn't done. Was there some event he would like to see, such as the running of the bulls in Spain, or would he prefer to take Bonnie, his beloved, to the Great Wall of China or the Wailing Wall?

His response was predictable. As a lifelong car-racing enthusiast, John had always wanted to go to the Indianapolis 500. Unfortunately, it seemed that the tickets for the event were tied up in corporate commitments or fans who handed their seats down through the family as a legacy.

However, I confidently told John it would be no problem. Many of my clients had connections to the automobile industry, from tire makers to parts suppliers; someone was bound to have access to tickets. But my confidence was misplaced. Time after time, I was told that even though the request was noble, the corporate allotment was predetermined for years in the future. The 1996 Indy came and went and I was unable to get the tickets for Bonnie and John.

I took advantage of my position for fifteen months as a speaker and asked over one hundred audiences for the tickets. My hopes were sagging as the months passed and the 1997 Memorial Day classic loomed nearer. While John's faith remained and his hopes drove him on to lead a normal life, his body declined and his strength weakened. He would often say, "This disease thinks it has me, well little does it know I got it and it ain't seen anything like me."

For all of his positive faith, I knew in my heart that 1997 would be John's last chance to see the event. By the time I became desperate enough to call them, even the scalpers were out of tickets. In a depression for weeks because I failed to act sooner, I could barely face John and Bonnie. I had failed to make his wish come true. John reassured me that he appreciated my efforts but said, "You are going to die worrying about this ticket thing before I die of ALS."

Then two weeks before the event, the telephone rang and Peggy Zomack of Cooper Power in Pittsburgh asked the question that stopped my breathing.

"Rick," she asked, "are you still looking for those Indy 500 tickets?" Then she had to ask, "Rick, are you still there?"

I couldn't say anything. My voice was paralyzed. Eventually, I got the words out and through tears assured her that she was heaven sent. She put the tickets in overnight mail, and I called Bonnie.

"Bonnie," I said. "Tomorrow, before 10:00 A.M., I will have in my hands tickets to the 1997 Indy 500 for you and John." She and I rejoiced for several minutes through bouts of more tears. Then a horrifying thought struck me, "Bonnie, I don't know if you will be able to find a room. The 500 is just a couple of weeks from now."

"Oh don't worry about that," she replied, "I paid for the room almost a year ago. I knew if I showed enough faith, God would provide the tickets somehow."

~Rick Phillips
*Chicken Soup for the Christian Family Soul*

# Like an Angel

*It is not known precisely where angels dwell—*
*whether in the air, the void, or the planets.*
*It has not been God's pleasure that we should be informed of their abode.*
*~Voltaire*

Returning to work as a nurse after an illness of six months was an ordeal in itself, but now the bitter cold and intense winds added to my stress. The employee entrance to the hospital was on the west side of the old brick building. The parking lot was on the east side across the street, so I'd have to cross the vast expanse to reach the entrance, with the unrelenting wind pushing me along.

My recent bout with pneumonia and the subsequent asthma attacks made me doubt if I could survive the walk on this subzero morning. After parking my car, I crossed the street and carefully battled the elements as I started for the entrance. Within seconds, I realized it was hopeless. My weakened condition and the penetrating cold took my breath away. The icy winds blowing off Lake Michigan pierced my lungs like shards of crystal. My chest tightened. I realized I would soon be in distress and unable to make the distance. I looked back at the warm car and contemplated whether to return to it or risk going ahead. The early morning darkness seemed to close in on me, and wafts of icy snow blew around my legs.

At that moment a shaft of light opened in the shadows on the side of the building, spilling light from a small doorway onto the pavement ahead of me. A tall, lean figure in a long, threadbare woolen coat and knit cap stood silhouetted against the amber light from the doorway. He stood holding the door against the frigid air and waved for me to come in.

I could see the boiler room inside, an area prohibited to nursing personnel. I didn't want to be in trouble for being in a restricted area, but it was predawn, dark and cold, and I could barely breathe. My mind raced. The elderly black man raised his arm and motioned me toward him for the second time. I thanked him for getting me out of the cold and followed him past the steaming pipes of the boiler room. I had a sense of deep calm and peace as he spoke in soft tones and led me through the maze of pipes. As if he were trying to reassure me, he talked about the cold, the old pipes and cautioned me to watch my step. He opened a doorway and I was directly in front of my time clock.

I quickly punched my time card, then turned to thank him and to tell him that he had probably saved my life, but he was gone. As mysteriously as he came, he'd left.

In the weeks that followed, I looked for him, but no one knew who he was. I had many questions for him: How did he know I was out there in the dark, since there were no windows on the door or on that side of the building? Why did he risk his job by giving me access to a restricted area? How did he know which was my time clock since various departments used different clocks? And why did no one know him?

The memory of that figure silhouetted against the light, motioning for me to follow, reminds me that angels come in many forms.

~Naomi Follis
*Chicken Soup for the Christian Soul 2*

# A Perfect Mistake

*A miracle is a work exceeding the power of any created agent, consequently being an effect of the divine omnipotence.*
*~Robert South*

Grandpa Nybakken loved life—especially when he could play a trick on somebody. At those times, his large Norwegian frame shook with laughter while he feigned innocent surprise, exclaiming, "Oh, forevermore!" But on a cold Saturday in downtown Chicago, Grandpa felt that God played a trick on him, and Grandpa wasn't laughing.

Mother's father worked as a carpenter. On this particular day, he was building some crates for the clothes his church was sending to an orphanage in China. On his way home, he reached into his shirt pocket to find his glasses, but they were gone. He remembered putting them there that morning, so he drove back to the church. His search proved fruitless.

When he mentally replayed his earlier actions, he realized what happened. The glasses had slipped out of his pocket unnoticed and fallen into one of the crates, which he had nailed shut. His brand new glasses were heading for China!

The Great Depression was at its height, and Grandpa had six children. He had spent twenty dollars for those glasses that very morning.

"It's not fair," he told God as he drove home in frustration. "I've been very faithful in giving of my time and money to your work, and now this."

Several months later, the director of the orphanage was on furlough in the United States. He wanted to visit all the churches that supported him in China, so he came to speak one Sunday night at my grandfather's small church in Chicago. Grandpa and his family sat in their customary seats among the sparse congregation.

The missionary began by thanking the people for their faithfulness in supporting the orphanage.

"But most of all," he said, "I must thank you for the glasses you sent last year. You see, the Communists had just swept through the orphanage, destroying everything, including my glasses. I was desperate.

"Even if I had the money, there was simply no way of replacing those glasses. Along with not being able to see well, I experienced headaches every day, so my coworkers and I were much in prayer about this. Then your crates arrived. When my staff removed the covers, they found a pair of glasses lying on top."

The missionary paused long enough to let his words sink in. Then, still gripped with the wonder of it all, he continued: "Folks, when I tried on the glasses, it was as though they had been custom-made just for me! I want to thank you for being a part of that."

The people listened, happy for the miraculous glasses. But the missionary surely must have confused their church with another, they thought. There were no glasses on their list of items to be sent overseas.

But sitting quietly in the back, with tears streaming down his face, an ordinary carpenter realized the Master Carpenter had used him in an extraordinary way.

~Cheryl Walterman Stewart
*Chicken Soup for the Christian Family Soul*

# The Hand of God

In 1966, during the earliest days of kidney transplantation, I witnessed a series of events where I could clearly see the hand of God touching a man's life.

I was a member of the transplant team in a very large, busy hospital. The plan was in place for a man named Don to donate a kidney to his younger brother, Ray, on Wednesday.

On Monday morning , Ray was beginning his scheduled kidney dialysis four floors below the surgery suite. Monday was a heavily scheduled day for surgeries. I was assisting a surgeon in one room, while another nurse re-sterilized the transplant equipment used over the weekend.

At the same time, a man in his mid-thirties entered the emergency room in cardiac arrest. The intern, who had just spent the previous month as part of the kidney transplant team, recognized the man as Don. He had worked with this donor just the week before. When his frantic efforts to save Don failed, the intern continued CPR, hoping to save the kidney until his younger brother was located. His staff called our surgery suite and was stunned to learn that not only were there two surgery rooms suddenly available, but the younger brother was in the building undergoing his weekly dialysis.

The responsibility fell on the nurses in the dialysis unit to explain to Ray that his brother had fallen gravely ill at work and was not able to be revived. With the two brothers side by side in adjoining operating rooms, the kidney was removed from Don and successfully implanted into Ray.

In a big-city hospital, only by the grace of God could two surgical suites be empty on a busy Monday morning, the kidney transplant team be in the OR, the kidney recipient be in the hospital, and the intern recognize the donor at the time of his death.

That day each team member felt they were a part of implementing God's will on this Earth.

~Jo Stickley
*Chicken Soup for the Nurse's Soul*

# The Dime

*Success seems to be largely a matter of*
*hanging on after others have let go.*
*~William Feather*

One day I visited a businessman's office, and while we talked, I noticed that he constantly twirled a small paperweight with a dime in it. Curious, I asked him about it.

He said, "When I was in college, my roommate and I were down to our last dime. He was on a scholarship, while I had earned my tuition by working in the cotton field and a grocery store. We were the first two members of our families to ever attend college, and our parents were extremely proud of us. Each month they sent us a small allowance to buy food, but that month our checks hadn't arrived. It was a Sunday, the fifth of the month, and between us we had one dime left.

"We used the solitary dime to place a collect call to my home five hundred miles away. My mother answered. I could tell from her voice that something was wrong. She said that my father had been ill and out of work, so there was simply no way they could send any money that month. I asked if my roommate's check was in the mail. She said that she had talked with his mother. They also couldn't raise the extra money that month either. They were sorry, but it looked like we'd have to come home. They had put off telling us, hoping for some solution."

"Were you disappointed?" I asked.

"Devastated. We both were. We had one month remaining to finish the year, then we could work all summer to earn our expenses. My grades were excellent, so I had been guaranteed a scholarship for the next term."

"What did you do?"

"When I hung up the telephone, we heard a noise and dimes started pouring out of the pay phone. We were laughing and holding out our hands to catch the money. Students walking down the hall thought we were crazy. We discussed taking the money and using it. Nobody would know what happened. But then we realized we couldn't do that. It wouldn't be honest. You understand?"

"Yes, but it would have been tough to return it."

"Well, we tried. I called the operator back and told her what had happened." He smiled, remembering. "She said that the money belonged to the telephone company, so to replace it in the machine. We did, over and over again, but the machine wouldn't accept the dimes.

"I finally told the operator that the dimes kept falling back out. She said that she didn't know what else to do, but she'd talk to her supervisor. When she returned she said that we'd have to keep the money, because the company wasn't going to send a man all the way out to the school just to collect a few dollars."

He looked over at me and chuckled, but there was emotion in his voice. "We laughed all the way back to our dorm room. After counting the money, we had $7.20. We decided to use the money to buy food from a nearby grocery store and we went job hunting after class."

"Did you find a job?"

"Yes, we told the manager of the grocery store what had happened as we paid for our purchases with our dimes. He offered us both jobs beginning next day. Our money bought enough supplies to last until our first paycheck."

"You were both able to finish college?"

"Yes, we worked for that man until we graduated. My friend went on to eventually become a lawyer." He looked around him and said,

"I graduated in business, then went on to start this company which today is a multi-million-dollar corporation. My own children have attended college, as have my roommate's, but we were the first."

"Is that one of your original dimes?"

He shook his head. "No, we had to use those, but when I got my first paycheck I saved a dime, which I carried all the way through college. I've kept it to remind me where I came from. When I count my blessings, I remember that once in my life, a single thin dime stood between me and the poverty my parents faced every day of their lives."

"Did you ever meet the telephone operator or tell her how much that money meant to you?"

"No, but when we graduated, my roommate and I wrote a letter to the local telephone company and asked if they wanted their money back.

"The president of the company wrote us a letter of congratulations and told us that he'd never felt the company's money was better spent."

"Do you think this was a fluke or meant to be?"

"I've thought about it often over the years. I wondered if the operator might have heard the fear in my voice; perhaps she prevented the machine from accepting the coins. Or maybe... it was an act of God."

"You'll never know for sure, will you?"

He shook his head, touching the paperweight as if he drew strength from it. "No, but I'll always remember that moment and that dime. I have repaid that debt many times over the years. I hope that I have helped someone else as much as a dime helped me."

~Patricia S. Laye
*Chicken Soup for the Christian Family Soul*

# Desperate Hope

*A bend in the road is not the end of the road...*
*unless you fail to make the turn.*
*~Author Unknown*

As the train rumbled past the East Coast countryside, taking my daughter and me to New York City for a mother/daughter vacation, my thoughts were as piercing as the screeching wheels of the train. Why did he do it? Why did Greg take his own life? He was a distant relative whom I rarely saw, yet the news that Greg had committed suicide made tears spring into my eyes and a deep sadness fill my heart. Relatives asked, "How could anyone be that hopeless and helpless?"

But I knew.

As I glanced over at my twenty-eight-year-old daughter napping next to me on the double seat, I realized with a force I hadn't felt for a long time that if I'd taken my life, I would not have the fabulous mother-daughter relationship I now enjoyed with my daughter.

Twenty-six years ago, I couldn't imagine that would ever happen. The hopelessness and helplessness had been building for months. Larry and I had celebrated our seventh anniversary, but it wasn't a happy occasion. Unwisely, I'd asked again, "Larry, why do you work so many hours? Having a two-year-old and a newborn is such hard work; I need you to help me."

He frowned. "Kathy, I've tried to help you see that I'm working all these hours to secure our financial future. That's not easy on a cop's wages." Silence surrounded us like a dense fog.

The next day, tensions escalated. Would we get a divorce? Why couldn't we talk? We used to be so in love. Just as quickly, I prayed, "Lord, what's wrong?"

That question was a prayer I repeated many times, both about my marriage and my reactions to our two-year-old daughter, Darcy. My anger toward her seemed to explode more often when I felt rejected by Larry. Her strong-willed nature, which resisted my toilet training plan and resulted in constant temper tantrums, wore me down. My reactions had deteriorated into angry spankings.

One desperate day my rage was out of control. I ran into my bedroom and slammed the door behind me. I'm no kind of mother! I can't believe I did that!

Then I suddenly remembered where Larry stored his off-duty service revolver.

The gun! That's the answer! The gun! A tiny, sinister voice in my head whispered, "Take your life. It's hopeless. Nothing has changed for months even though I've prayed over and over again; it's only gotten worse. God doesn't care. Otherwise He would instantaneously deliver me from my anger and heal our marriage. Larry hates me. I hate him and my life."

With trembling hands, I opened the locked drawer and almost gasped when the gleam from the shiny barrel of the gun glinted at me so invitingly. Darcy is better off without a mother like me. I'm ruining her for life.

Seconds clicked off and then I reached for the cold revolver. But then a new thought suddenly popped into my mind. What will people think of Jesus if they hear that Kathy Miller took her life?

My hand stopped. The faces of the women in the neighborhood Bible study I led flitted before me. My family members who didn't know Christ came to mind. I thought of my neighbors I had witnessed to. Oh, Lord, I don't care about my reputation, but I do care about Yours!

I slammed the drawer shut and fell to my knees.

The concern about Jesus' reputation saved my life that day, and I knew it was prompted by the Holy Spirit.

I didn't have any hope at that point, but in the following months God proved Himself faithful by revealing the underlying causes of my anger, giving me patience to be a loving mom and then healing my relationship with Larry. I read in Ephesians 4:26, "Be angry, and yet do not sin...." I realized that it wasn't sinful to feel angry, but it was sinful to respond in a rage or in bitterness. So I stopped trying to bury my anger and learned to express it constructively. I quit using it as a disciplinary tool and began consistently giving consequences for Darcy's misbehavior. I released Larry from holding the key to my joy and contentment and counted on God for that. As a result, Larry wanted to spend more time with me.

My reverie snapped back to the present as the train began slowing for the next stop. I looked over at my daughter, who had awakened and was gazing out the window. I smiled as I thought of her beautiful wedding we'd all enjoyed four years earlier. I wouldn't have been there if I'd committed suicide! The thought struck me so forcefully, like never before. Then I recalled all the happy family events I would have missed if I'd taken my life, including our son's graduation from college—despite his learning disabilities. I thought of the opportunities I'd had to speak in thirty states and five foreign countries and the forty-eight books I'd authored. I smiled thinking of Larry, my best friend, and our glorious love affair; we'd recently celebrated our thirty-second anniversary. The list went on and on. If I'd used that gun that day, I wouldn't have been at all those family events, but Larry's second wife may have been. And how my daughter and son would have grieved over a missing mother who seemed to be more absorbed in her own pain than them.

Yes, I understood how Greg could have felt so little hope—in fact, no hope at all. How I wish I could have shared with him that there is always hope, and God is faithful if we will hold on to His promises.

My daughter faced me on the train. "Mom, I'm so excited we're going to New York City together. I wouldn't have missed this for anything."

"Me neither, honey. Me neither."

~Kathy Collard Miller
*Chicken Soup for the Christian Soul 2*

# By Accident

*Once you choose hope, anything's possible.*
*~Christopher Reeve*

The instant my horse bucked, I knew I was going to die. As the reins were wrenched from my fingers, I felt myself thrown violently over his head and onto the ground. With sickening clarity, I heard my bones break. I thought of Christopher Reeve.

"Help me," I cried. "Please, someone help me." Searing pain in my chest and back strangled my words into a whisper. I'm alone, I thought. No one heard me. I raised my head, and the movement sent an electric shock coursing down my right arm. And then the arm went numb.

In a daze, I struggled to my feet and crawled through the arena fence. You are strong, I told myself, and you can do this. Pain contorted my posture, but I forced myself to walk the distance back to the ranch house. Doctors told me later that I'd done all of this with seven broken ribs, a fractured spine, a bleeding lung and a broken neck.

"Mary, I fell off 'Nate,'" I groaned into the phone. "I think it's bad. I can't feel my right arm anymore." I'd called my coworkers at the hospital, knowing they would be my lifelines.

An hour later, I lay strapped in the CT scanner with a stiff foam collar around my neck and oxygen tubing in my nostrils. I was no longer a nurse; I was a patient in my own emergency department. An unexpected wave of fear washed over me. Confusion compounded the pain—fear? Hadn't I conquered fear? Buoyed by morphine, I let my memory drift back some four weeks.

"Okay, just roll out," Duke commanded. As I crouched in the doorway of the plane, the wind whipped against my face. I squinted down at the ground, thirteen thousand feet below. Today I would prove how strong I was. Today I would be a skydiver, not a cast-off wife and an empty-nest mother.

"Let's do it!" I shouted back from the plane's open doorway. I gave my instructor the "thumbs up" and I jumped.

The jolting stop of the CT scanner table interrupted my memory. I let the medical team, my friends, do their jobs while I was forced to do my own personal evaluation: Why did this have to happen to me? In the past eighteen months, I'd survived the loss of a twenty-four-year marriage to infidelity, and the ravages of a flood that had threatened to take my home. Was this some sort of cosmic triple play to make me prove how strong I could be? Or three strikes and I'm out? Again, that shadowy fear surrounded my heart. What was I afraid of?

I took inventory: I was a single mother, a veteran emergency-room nurse, and a sturdy ranch woman who could haul a horse trailer, stack hay and deliver a foal. The misfortunes of the past two years had required me to stand taller, to be more assertive and, when necessary, to take it on the chin.

And now that chin was tucked into a foam collar, and there were whispers of "spinal cord injury, permanent weakness." I began to realize what that icy, nameless fear was—I was losing control. A strong woman stays in control and doesn't have to fully trust anyone. After all, I'd trusted my husband, and he left; I'd trusted the security of my home, and the floodwaters came. I had to ask myself the big question now: Did I trust God? I prayed to him, I worshipped him, but did I really allow myself to depend on him? A little card on my dresser mirror read, "Let Go and Let God," yet how desperately I'd fought to keep life's reins in my own hands. Now those reins had been yanked from me.

In the following months, as I worked in physical therapy to

regain the full use of my arms, I had time to ponder and to pray. I wondered about my need to feel strong. Was it simply armor to ward off other unimaginable hurts? My cavalier leap from the skydiving plane certainly hadn't left fear far enough behind. I began to set new priorities, to evaluate success and survival in different ways. With great relief, I let God take the burdens from my sore shoulders; I began to trust again.

I hadn't been alone that day in my riding arena, and someone had heard me when I cried out. The accident stopped me from being strong, long enough to find my strength.

Months later, I returned to work at the hospital to find I'd become a local legend. The story was told and retold. "She walked into the hospital with a broken neck," they'd say. One day a new employee heard the story—heard that I'd been alone in the riding arena—and he asked me, incredulously, "Who picked you up off the ground out there, after you fell?"

I felt myself take a deep breath—it was warm and alive in my chest. "Who picked me up?" A knowing smile spread across my face. "Think big," I told him, "really big."

~Candace L. Calvert
*Chicken Soup for the Nurse's Soul*

# Seed Faith Money

My friend Rosemary was newly divorced and overwhelmed by the awesome responsibility of raising two daughters alone. There were many weeks when she had less than fifty dollars to her name.

At Easter time, Rosemary's daughter Theresa discovered a pea-sized lump on her collarbone. Tests showed Hodgkin's disease and a tumor that filled forty percent of her chest cavity.

In addition to the terror of watching Theresa suffer, Rosemary was also distraught over the enormous medical bills piling up. The hospital was demanding a fifteen-hundred-dollar payment.

A few weeks later, quite unexpectedly, Rosemary was named "Employee of the Year" at work and received a prize of fifteen hundred dollars: exactly the amount she needed. What a stroke of luck!

At church that Sunday, an overpowering inner voice was so loud and clear she shook her head to make sure she wasn't dreaming. The voice said, "Give Maggie a hundred dollars."

"What?" Rosemary demanded.

"Give Maggie a hundred dollars."

Maggie? The Maggie whose job I took over when she quit at work? She was the only Maggie that Rosemary knew. Why does this woman need me to give her a hundred dollars? Rosemary asked the inner voice. I'm the one struggling financially! At least Maggie has a husband to help her.

Rosemary thought about her recent windfall. After tithing and paying taxes on it, the amount she actually cleared from that prize was less than a thousand dollars—not even enough to cover the hospital payment. Now someone—was it God?—was asking her to give one hundred dollars to a woman she hardly knew.

"This is ridiculous," she said to herself. "Why, it's total fiscal irresponsibility!"

At home that afternoon, Rosemary kept hearing the voice: "Give Maggie a hundred dollars."

She dug deep into her faith reserve and remembered the verse from Matthew 28:20 that says, "And surely I am with you always, to the very end of the age."

Rosemary thought back to the last few months of Theresa's struggle with Hodgkin's disease. By now, she was well on the road to recovery. She hadn't even gotten sick from the chemotherapy. Yes, God had been with them throughout the whole ordeal, but Rosemary also knew that God didn't ask for paybacks.

It didn't make sense, but Rosemary reached for her checkbook. Shaking and sweating, she wrote the check and mailed it to Maggie. A week later Maggie stood on Rosemary's doorstep. Smiling, Maggie handed the check back. "I can't accept this, Rosemary, but I want you to know that you certainly did God's work when you sent it. My husband was getting so bitter about God and religion. He was so touched by your generosity, he's acting like a whole new person. Thank you so much," she beamed as she pressed the hundred-dollar check back into Rosemary's hand.

The next Sunday, Rosemary tithed an extra ten dollars for the hundred dollars Maggie had given back to her. On Monday, Rosemary received a check in the mail from her Aunt Joey for a hundred dollars for no particular reason—something her aunt had never done before.

On Tuesday, Rosemary tithed ten dollars of that money to the church.

On Friday, she received a hundred-dollar check in the mail from her good friend, Sharon, who enclosed a note that said simply, "I'm sure you can use this." Sharon had never done such a thing before.

That's when it hit Rosemary square in the eye. She thought to herself, "When God asked me to give Maggie a hundred dollars for no apparent reason, I listened—a bit grudgingly, I'll admit. Was it a test, like when God instructed Abraham to sacrifice Isaac, his beloved son? And just as God spared Isaac at the last minute, did He 'spare me' by bringing back that one hundred dollars three times in six days?"

Several years later, Rosemary's finances were again extremely grim. Her older daughter, Claire, was getting ready to go back to college, and Rosemary was frantic over how she would come up with the money for her tuition. In faith, she reluctantly sold some antique jewelry that had been given to her years earlier.

The next Sunday, Rosemary slipped into the pew next to Margaret, a struggling single parent. The familiar inner voice said, "Give a hundred dollars to Margaret."

Rosemary almost wailed out loud. "Now just a minute!" she said to that inner voice. "I took a loss on the jewelry when I sold it, because I have faith in You! And You're still asking me to give Margaret a hundred dollars?"

Rosemary knew it was useless to argue. The world says "Hang onto your money." But sometimes, God says "Give it away." She gave Margaret a hundred dollars.

Within five days, the bank suddenly approved an "iffy" college loan toward Claire's tuition. In addition, the following week Rosemary received a generous and quite unexpected raise at work.

The next week in church, she quieted herself and prepared to "listen" to what God had in mind for her now—more out of curiosity at the absurdity of it all than with real eagerness. Within a few minutes, she was directed to give another struggling single parent, whom she barely knew, one hundred and fifty dollars. This time there was no, "Aw, come on, God, You've got to be kidding!" By this time, she was a believer. She'd been taught more than once that if she just put out a seedling effort, God would return His bounty in bushels.

~Patricia Lorenz

*Chicken Soup for the Christian Woman's Soul*

# Reply to Box 222B

Was it loneliness, the call of adventure or just plain insanity that made me answer that newspaper ad? I paced back and forth through my house, telling myself it was a really stupid thing to do. But like a jeweler crafting a priceless, one-of-a-kind brooch, I composed my reply to the tantalizing ad.

I actually answered a lonely hearts ad. Am I really that desperate for a man?

I'd always believed that only born losers advertised for a companion or answered the ads of those who did. Surely you had to be dying of loneliness, ugly or really dumb!

That's what I am, I thought, really dumb!

What would my children think? Would they understand that the bold, black letters just leaped out at my unsuspecting eye? "Christian Rancher. 6' tall, 180 pounds, 50+. Hardworking, clean-cut, healthy, good physical condition. Enjoys fishing, camping, cross-country skiing, animals, dining out. Wants to meet sensible and sincere lady, 40-50, attractive, neat, loving, honest, for meaningful relationship. Box 222B."

Mama mia! What loving, sensible, honest and lonely woman could resist? Well, maybe not sensible.

"Fifty-plus what?" my letter began. "I'm a healthy, hardworking woman who loves to cook, sew, travel, pray, and walk in a desert sunset or barefoot on the beach."

I didn't say I could meet all the requirements in his ad, but I didn't give him any reason to think that I couldn't. But could I?

I was already past fifty, questionably attractive, not always neat and very uncertain about pursuing a meaningful relationship. What I really wanted was a friend. Had I been dishonest not to tell him so?

Holding the letter heavenward, I asked God, "If you want me to meet this man, will you bring him to me?" Then I set the stamped envelope on the desk for the following day's mail.

During the next few weeks, I found my hands getting sweaty every time the phone rang. Could it be him? What if he didn't like me? What if he showed disappointment as soon as he set eyes on me? Could I handle that?

Contriving excuses to be away from the telephone became a game I played with myself. At the car wash one afternoon, towel-drying the finish and shining the windows, I found myself fantasizing about every man who came in to wash his car. Look at him; I bet he's 50+. He's almost bald, has floppy jowls and a big stomach. Oh, dear, he's wearing a cowboy shirt and boots. I'll just die if that's my Christian rancher!

I didn't see even one man there who I hoped might be Box 222B. Damp and discouraged, I went home to shower, questioning my motives, suppressing my loneliness. Dressing before the mirror, I turned from side to side, surveying the ravages of fifty-plus years on this Earth.

I studied my face, hollow and gaunt, perched atop muscular shoulders and arms. Large, sturdy hands that never knew what to do with themselves. Twenty extra pounds, a thick waist, stalwart thighs above husky calves and large, scrawny feet. I remembered the boy in the fifth grade who told me I was built like a brick outhouse: strong and useful but not much class.

Tears began to flow freely as I slumped to my knees beside my bed. "Oh, God, look at me, I'm a mess. Why did I send that letter? Please forgive me for misleading that man, for communicating the woman I want to be, not the woman I am."

It was a Sunday evening a few weeks later when I invited my

friend, Jeanette, for waffles after church. As we were leaving the service, she introduced me to a friend from the singles group she sometimes attended. Impulsively, I asked him if he'd like to join us for waffles and he said yes.

We spent the next three hours stuffing ourselves, laughing and talking. Jim was divorced, had several grown children and raised alfalfa for cattle feed. He was a likable man, tall and handsome, considerate, and seemingly ambitious. I felt sad for him as he talked about his loneliness.

Shutting the door behind them after a delightful evening, I began to clear up the clutter. I'd dumped my past few days' mail on the big maple desk in the dining room, and it seemed like a good time to sort it out. I tossed the junk mail in the trash and filed some bills for payment. Then I stared in astonishment. There was the letter! My reply to "Christian Rancher" had never been mailed. All that emotion and self-doubt for nothing.

Then a suspicion crept into my thoughts. Pieces started to fall into place. Jim wore cowboy boots and a western shirt; he was a rancher; he was lonely. Could he and the Christian rancher possibly be one and the same?

I rushed to the phone to call Jeanette. "Do you think he ever put an ad in the newspaper for a woman? Do you suppose he'd call himself a Christian rancher?"

Jeanette roared with laughter. "Yes, everybody at the singles group knows he did that. I guess he's gotten some seventy or eighty answers by now. Some real lu-lu's, too."

I hung up the telephone feeling a trace of excitement, a bit of foolishness and a lot of awe at a God who would arrange for a letter that I never mailed to receive an answer. And God and I were the only ones who knew about it.

Several days passed before I picked up the telephone to hear Jim's voice suggesting that we go to the state fair for the day. "I'd love to," I said. Wow! A real live date with a guy who had seventy or eighty women to choose from!

A warm toastiness cradled me as I hung up the telephone. Then

I raced to the bedroom, my heart pounding with excitement. What would I wear? In front of the mirror once more, I observed a middle-aged woman, still awkward and overweight, with a skinny face and bony feet, but she wasn't afraid anymore. "What you see is what you get," I chuckled.

The next day I stepped out into the sunshine to begin a new friendship with a Christian rancher.

What happened that day at the fair? We had fun together. Did we see each other again? Yes. Did we marry? No. But that didn't matter. My self-confidence soared, and I learned something else too: If you're destined to meet a particular person, whether future friend or spouse, it will happen, as surely as the sun rises every morning. And it'll happen even if your perfectly crafted letter sits gathering dust on an old maple desk.

~Barbara Baumgardner
*Chicken Soup for the Single's Soul*

# Pennies from Heaven

*I met a man who picks up pennies he finds on the ground because he says they're government property.*
*I pick them up because I see them as signs from angels to let us know they're around.*
*~Carmen Rutlen*

Years ago, when our finances were less than ideal, I took a job vacuuming the halls and carpeted stairwells of our run-down condominium building. Work is work, and I told myself it was honest work. But it wasn't what I'd imagined myself doing for employment and it dented my pride.

It was certainly difficult work; the portable vacuum weighed twenty pounds and the condominium hallways were mostly stairs, twelve staircases in all, three flights up each. Six staircases a day was all I could manage. Stirred up dirt and dust clung to my skin, sweaty from hauling the vacuum up and down the airless staircases, and there were days when self-pity and wounded pride made the vacuum weigh even more.

On a day that had been particularly hard, when my pride tweaked with every cigarette butt and piece of trash I picked up, I hauled my portable vacuum up the stairs and asked God, in a tone more rueful than meditative, to give me something, anything, to perk up my sagging spirit.

On the third floor, nearly hidden in the crevice where the frayed carpet met the wall, glinted a shiny penny. "This?" I asked God. "This is what you give me?" I sighed, but I pocketed the penny and didn't give it much thought beyond that.

Curiously, pennies began to turn up each time I vacuumed the halls. They hadn't been there in the months before as I'd vacuumed up dried-up leaves and crumpled gum wrappers. But now, each time, there was a penny. One penny only. It became a game to me, wondering where and when the lone penny would turn up. Always, before the job was completed, there would be that one coin, as if it were waiting for me. I started to say a thank you to God each time I retrieved the penny and pocketed it, and began to think of these small, found treasures as my pennies from heaven.

I didn't tell anyone. There are pennies everywhere, right? Considered outdated, what is a penny but a useless coin that doesn't buy anything in this expensive age? The condo-cleaning job was the least of the hardships visited upon me in the last few years, and pennies weighed against family misfortunes and ill luck seemed small change, indeed.

Still, it gave me a jolt of renewed hope each time I spotted one—and more often than not, that hope alone was enough for me.

Finances improved and we moved, and my two children blossomed in their new neighborhood. Life uninterrupted by adversity was welcome, if surprising. Occasionally I picked up a penny when I found it, thanking God in what had now become a knee-jerk response.

When I found myself pregnant with twins, I viewed it as the mother lode of rewards for having survived the previous years so well. When the ultrasound revealed them to be healthy baby girls, I named them Anne and Grace. I grew so huge over the next eight months, there was no more bending down to pick up anything, much less a mere penny.

When I was in early labor, the final ultrasound revealed their perfect feet, the sweet curve of their rumps, and the delicate rope of their spines. And then the flat silent discs that proved to be their unbeating hearts. They had died the night before. In the following hours before they were delivered I knew that my thinking of them as a reward had been only a cosmic joke of some sort, or more likely the imagination of a childish heart.

For months afterwards, the only prayers I offered up were enraged shouts at the kitchen ceiling, and finally even those ceased. What good is yelling at a God who doesn't care, doesn't hear, or more likely, doesn't exist.

The numbness that replaced the anger made it nearly impossible to navigate my daily life. I forgot whatever it was I had once cared for and even tried to make lists of what I loved. I'd loved my other children, hadn't I? Only now their demands and need for comfort seemed overwhelmingly large. I tried smaller lists. Hadn't I liked old books, flea markets, stolen moments with my husband? Didn't I once enjoy lunches out with friends? My funny little dog? It didn't help, and I forgot the lists, forgot my own name once when it was asked, and forgot as well any reason to continue living.

One day, while waiting for my son's karate class to end, I heard a mother call to her daughter. "Annie," she said, and a chubby blond toddler came tumbling into her arms. I fled for the hallway, and as I tried to gain control of myself, I happened to glance down. There on the carpet was a penny. I just stared at it. A penny?

I picked it up.

After that, pennies began to turn up everywhere. Almost every day but always just one. In odd places. In the rooms of my house where I had just walked before, a penny would suddenly be shining up from the middle of the room. In the waiting room of a doctor's office, outside my mailbox, in the school parking lot as I stepped out of my car. I began to pocket them again, slowly, numbly, and I began again to thank God each time.

My small frequent thanks to God made me question what I was thanking him for—my nine-year-old son slipping his hand into mine, a funny note from my daughter, evening walks with my husband, soup from a friend, even a kind smile from a grocery clerk. I looked up one morning and noticed the blue of the springtime sky. I noticed the rich taste of my morning cup of coffee. I began to be grateful just to be alive.

It occurred to me that maybe God doesn't always choose to speak in dramatic ways; maybe a burning bush isn't his calling card to everyone.

Just maybe, for some, a single penny gleaming in an unexpected place is his touch of grace, his gift of hope. And sometimes that hope is just enough.

~Susan Clarkson Moorhead
*Chicken Soup for Every Mom's Soul*

# The Tablecloth

*Let God's promises shine on your problems.*
*~Corrie Ten Boom*

A young minister had been called to serve at an old church that at one time had been a magnificent edifice in a wealthy part of town. Now the area was in a state of decline and the church was in bad shape. Nevertheless, the pastor and his wife were thrilled with the church and believed they could restore it to its former magnificence.

When the minister took charge of the church early in October 1948, he and his wife immediately went to work painting, repairing and attempting to restore it. Their goal was to have the old edifice looking its best for Christmas Eve services.

Just two days before Christmas, however, a storm swept through the area, dumping more than an inch of rain. The roof of the old church sprung a leak just behind the altar. The plaster soaked up the water as if it were a sponge and then crumbled, leaving a gaping hole in the wall.

Dejected, the pastor and his wife looked at the defaced wall. There was obviously no chance to repair the damage before Christmas. Nearly three months of hard work had been washed away. Yet the young couple accepted the damage as God's will and set about cleaning up the damp debris.

It was a depressed minister and his wife who attended a benefit auction for the church youth group that afternoon. One of the items put up for bid was an old gold-and-ivory-colored lace tablecloth, nearly fifteen feet long.

Seized with an inspiration, the pastor was the high bidder at $6.50. His idea was to hang the ornate cloth behind the altar to cover the ragged hole in the wall.

On the day before Christmas, snowflakes mingled with the howling wind. As the pastor unlocked the church doors, he noticed an older woman standing at the nearby bus stop. He knew the bus wouldn't be there for at least half an hour, so he invited her inside to keep warm.

She wasn't from the neighborhood, she explained. She had been in the area to be interviewed for a job as a governess to the children of a well-known wealthy family. She had been a war refugee, her English was poor and she didn't get the job.

Head bowed in prayer, she sat in a pew near the back of the church. She paid no attention to the pastor, who was hanging the tablecloth across the unsightly hole. When the woman looked up and saw the cloth, she rushed to the altar.

"It's mine!" she exclaimed. "It's my banquet cloth!"

Excitedly she told the surprised minister its history and even showed him her initials embroidered in one corner.

She and her husband had lived in Vienna, Austria, and had opposed the Nazis before the Second World War. They decided to flee to Switzerland, but her husband said they must go separately. She left first. Later she heard that he had died in a concentration camp.

Touched by her story, the minister insisted she take the cloth. She thought about it for a moment but said no, she didn't need it any longer, and it did look pretty hanging behind the altar. Then she said goodbye and left.

In the candlelight of the Christmas Eve services, the tablecloth looked even more magnificent. The white lace seemed dazzling in the flickering light of the candles, and the golden threads woven through it were like the brilliant rays of a new dawn.

As members of the congregation left the church, they

complimented the pastor on the services and on how beautiful the church looked.

One older gentleman lingered, admiring the tablecloth, and as he was leaving he said to the minister:

"It's strange. Many years ago my wife—God rest her—and I owned such a tablecloth. She used it only on very special occasions. But we lived in Vienna then."

The night air was freezing, but the goosebumps on the pastor's skin weren't caused by the weather. As calmly as he could, he told the man about the woman who had been to the church that very afternoon.

"Can it be," gasped the old man, tears streaming down his cheeks, "that she is alive? How can I find her?"

The pastor remembered the name of the family who had interviewed the woman. With the trembling old man at his side, he telephoned the family and learned her name and address.

In the pastor's old car they drove to her home on the other side of town. Together they knocked on her apartment door. When she opened it, the pastor witnessed the tearful, joyful and thrilling reunion of husband and wife.

Some people would call it an extremely lucky chance happening, the result of a hole in the church wall, an old tablecloth, a pastor's ingenuity in solving a problem and so on. But the combination of events was far too complex for it to have been merely "coincidence."

If one link in the fragile chain of events had been broken, the husband and wife might never have found each other. If the rain hadn't come, if the church roof hadn't leaked, if the pastor had decided not to go to the auction, if the woman hadn't been looking for a job or standing on that corner at just the right time.... The list of ifs is virtually endless.

It was simply God's will. And, as it has been said many times, He works in mysterious ways.

~Richard Bauman
*Chicken Soup for the Christian Family Soul*

# All That We Can Give

On Thanksgiving Day I awoke on the mattress that I shared with my two young children and tumbled into despair. At the time I was twenty-five and recently divorced. It was three days to payday and there was no money left. I had a job, but was only making $300 a month, and that month's entire paycheck had already gone to pay for the apartment and food for my little boys. I had swallowed my pride and applied for food stamps, but had been turned down—because I made two dollars over the monthly limit.

On that Thanksgiving Day, there was nothing left to eat in the house but three hot dogs.

Perhaps hardest of all was my feeling of isolation. There were no friends to help. No one had invited us to share the holiday dinner. The loneliness was worse than the ever-present hunger.

But it was Thanksgiving, and for the sake of the children, I knew I had to make the best of the day.

"Come on, boys," I said. "Today's a special day. We're having a picnic!"

Together the three of us went to the park and cooked the hot dogs on the grill. We played happily together until late in the afternoon.

But on the way home, the boys asked for more food. The single hot dog they had eaten did not come close to being a decent meal. I knew they were hungrier even than they let on.

I tried to joke about it with them, but inside I was very, very scared. I didn't know where our next meal was going to come from. I'd reached the end of my rope.

As we entered our apartment building, an old woman I'd never seen before stepped directly into our path. She was a tiny thing wearing a simple print dress, her wispy white hair pulled up in a bun. With her smile of greeting, she looked like a kindhearted tutu, an island grandmother.

"Oh, Honey," the old lady said as the boys and I started to walk past. "I've been waiting for you. You left this morning before I could catch you. I've got Thanksgiving dinner ready for your family."

Caught by surprise, I thought that I shouldn't accept such an offer from a complete stranger. With a word of thanks, I started to brush past.

"Oh," said the old lady, "but it's Thanksgiving. You have to come."

I looked at my boys. Their hunger tore at me. Even though it was against my better judgment, I accepted.

The old lady's apartment was on the ground floor. When she opened the door, we saw a beautiful table set for four. It was the perfect Thanksgiving meal with all the traditional trimmings. The candles were lit and it was obvious that guests were expected. We were expected.

Gradually I began to relax. We all sat down together to enjoy the meal. Somehow, I found myself talking freely of my loneliness, the difficulty of raising two small boys by myself and of the challenges I was facing. The grandmotherly woman listened with compassion and understanding. I remember I felt that for that time, at least, we were home.

As the evening ended, I wondered how I could possibly express my thanks for such incredible kindness. Eyes brimming, I simply said, "Thank you. I know that now I can go on." A complete stranger had reached out and given our little family such an important gift. The boys were grinning from ear to ear as the elderly lady loaded them down with Tupperware bowls full of leftovers.

We left her apartment that evening bubbling with joy, the boys joking and laughing. For the first time in a long time, I felt certain that I could face what had to be faced. I was a different person from the scared girl I had been that morning. I'd somehow been transformed. We all had.

Early the next day, in a happy mood, I went back to visit my new friend and to return the borrowed bowls. I knocked, but there was no answer. I looked through an open window.

What I saw shocked me. The apartment was completely empty. There wasn't a stick of furniture. There wasn't anything.

I hurried down to the manager's apartment. "What happened to the elderly lady in apartment three?" I asked.

He gave me a look and said, "What lady? That apartment's been vacant for the past ten or twelve weeks. Nobody lives there."

"But I had Thanksgiving dinner last night with the lady who lives there," I told the manager. "Here are her bowls."

The manager gave me a strange look and turned away.

For many years, I didn't tell anyone the story of that special Thanksgiving. Finally, in 1989, I felt compelled to speak out.

By then, I had become the wife of the Kahu Doug Olson, Pastor of Calvary by the Sea Church on O'ahu.

I went before the congregation and told them of my dream: to establish a program to help women in Hawai'i who find themselves in a situation similar to the one I had faced so many years ago.

Now, over a decade later, the Network has helped over 1,400 homeless, single mothers and their children to get back on their feet. After "graduation," a remarkable 93 percent of the families continue to support themselves. Last year's budget, which is funded by state, church and private monies, was $700,000.

I really surprised myself by telling the congregation my entire story that day, but I think it was meant to be. In the end, helping the homeless with money and food is only secondary.

What I learned on that Thanksgiving Day is that an hour of being loved unconditionally can truly change a life. In the end, it is all that we can give.

And the name of the organization?
Angel Network Charities, of course.

~Ivy Olson
*Chicken Soup from the Soul of Hawai'i*

# Stories of Faith

## Comfort from Heaven

*Angels descending, bring from above,*
*Echoes of mercy, whispers of love.*
*~Fanny J. Crosby*

# Lori's Wish

Lori came to the hospital with a great attitude. She was such a spunky twelve-year-old you almost forgot to notice her frail little body and blue lips and nail beds. Lori saw this heart surgery as just one more hoop to jump through on her way to becoming a grown-up. In her bag, she had packed all the essentials of a preteen girl and an afghan she was crocheting. It really looked quite nice but had a long way to go.

Lori went to surgery with an abnormal but incredibly brave heart. Late in the afternoon, she arrived in the pediatric intensive care unit with all the typical supportive medication and equipment. We knew that her many previous surgeries and time on the heart-lung machine had put her at risk for bleeding, and before long we noted an abnormal amount of blood coming from her chest tubes. This continued over the next hour until the surgeon had no choice but to take her back to the operating room. We got her parents to her bedside for a visit before Lori was quickly returned to surgery. A couple of hours later, she was back in ICU and the bleeding stopped. The relief in her parents' faces sent me home, tired but reassured.

The next day, Lori's heart was doing reasonably well, and her lips and fingernails were pink. But she had a lot of recovering to do. Her family was at her bedside as much as they could be, considering the restricted visiting hours so prevalent back then. Lori's condition rapidly declined, however, and her kidneys began to fail. She needed a ventilator. This tube, through her nose and airway, prevented her from talking, but it definitely didn't prevent her from communicating. She still had that spunky attitude. She was very thirsty but, of course, she couldn't have anything to drink. When I dipped a cloth into a little fruit punch just to wet her mouth, her eyes said thank you in no uncertain terms.

When the charge nurse came to the bedside to ask if I could stay into the evening shift, Lori overheard. I looked back at her and she mouthed, "Please stay." I did. Her urine output declined even further, and when I went home that night, I felt tired and uneasy.

By the next morning, Lori was on dialysis. We all continued to hope her kidneys would begin to recover, but each hour of no urine output was devastating. Lori became puffy as the fluid accumulated in her body and stressed her heart and lungs. She slept more. Her spunkiness faded.

Over the next couple of days, her condition continued to decline. How unfair it seemed that now, with a repaired heart, Lori had the pinkest lips ever, but the rest of her organs suffered in the process.

Her unfinished afghan stood out as a reminder of her unfinished life.

Still, her parents stood faithfully by. Her mother was five months pregnant, very tired and so devoted. She told us of Lori's biggest wish—to hold her baby sister. She was so sure it was going to be a girl, Lori had named this Christmastime baby Mary Christine.

But Lori continued to fade. The helplessness we felt was overwhelming. On a beautiful sunny August day, we all said our goodbyes and Lori died. As her parents left the hospital, I tearfully handed them Lori's belongings and the unfinished afghan.

The next spring, as I walked down the hall, I saw Lori's mom. Joyfully I blurted, "How is the new baby?" I was heartbroken to learn four-month-old Mary Christine also had congenital heart disease. On Friday of that week, Good Friday, Mary had surgery on her weak and poorly formed heart. Sadly, she followed a course so like Lori's—persistent postoperative bleeding, failure of her kidneys and so on. On Easter Sunday morning the outlook for Mary was bleak. I went with her parents to the chapel.

As we sat quietly there, a butterfly glided silently around us. I was mystified. This chapel had no access to the outdoors. Where could this butterfly have come from? The mother smiled through her tears and said, "Lori is here." She paused, then went on. "Last summer, at the cemetery, following Lori's funeral, a butterfly landed on my shoulder and stayed right with me and I felt Lori's presence. Then, when we brought Mary home from the hospital on a cold wintry Christmas Day in Indiana, a butterfly entered the house with us! Again, we knew Lori was there. And now, she is here for Mary!"

As they faced the death of another daughter, these parents looked through their sorrow and found peace, knowing their two girls would now be together. We returned to Mary's bedside and within minutes, she slipped away.

Lori's wish had come true. She was holding her baby sister.

~Gwen Fosse
*Chicken Soup for the Nurse's Soul*

# Madeleine's Wheelbarrow

*Behold, I send an angel before you to keep you in the way.*
*~Exodus 23:20*

I've always known Madeleine.

We were both born and raised in the same small Alaska town. But it wasn't until we both found ourselves married with small children and living in the same city that we became best friends.

Every morning, as soon as the older children were off to school, we'd call each other and talk over the day's plans. In the summer, we spent many days in our gardens together while the children played. At Madeleine's, we picked countless weeds off the bank in her backyard. We'd load them in her big green wheelbarrow—along with a child or two. Then we'd wheel the pile over to the other side of the bank and dump out the wheelbarrow load—taking the kids out first!

In 1996, we had just finished putting in our spring gardens. Suddenly, we weren't thinking about gardens anymore, but survival. I had been diagnosed with a rare form of cancer. Immediate surgery was my only option. I was only thirty-four, with two young children. My husband Pat and I were numb with shock.

It was Madeleine who stepped in and steadied us. While Pat, my mother and my sisters concentrated on me, Madeleine made sure the everyday tasks were taken care of. Efficient and organized, she handled everything from meals to play dates for the children.

She even thought of the garden. Already it was weedy and overgrown. She knew how frustrated I'd be, trying to recover from major surgery, staring out at a tangled jungle and too weak to do anything about it. Madeleine gathered a team of friends, and together they snipped and mowed, pruned and planted. I came home to a shining house, a full refrigerator and a beautiful garden.

Madeleine and I adjusted our routine of friendship around my slow recovery and a steady stream of doctor's appointments. The surgery appeared to be working. Life went on.

Then a year later, it stopped.

Madeleine was dead. On a bright, sunny summer afternoon, my best friend was killed in a tragic boating accident. She left a bewildered husband and three little boys, the youngest only three. The sudden, brutal loss shredded everyone who knew her—her family, her church, her friends. Our lives were dazed.

A month later, the doctors found my cancer again.

The double blow of Madeleine's death and the recurring cancer shook my faith in nearly everything. I felt sick in mind, in body, in heart.

In the gray days of October, my family and friends gathered to help me. They were as loving and supportive as anyone could wish, but I was painfully aware of who was missing.

"Try to relax," the nurses said. "Think of something happy." But the chemotherapy was agonizing. I spent days hunched over like an old woman, my muscles too cramped from vomiting to let me sit up.

When the chemotherapy treatments finally ended five months later, I told myself I would never be so weak again—spiritually or physically. I began working out, reviving my battered body. With the help of time and friends, I began to revive my battered faith. And I began to see Madeleine, not as the friend I no longer had, but as a friend who would be with me always. I pictured her watching us all from heaven. I pictured her wheeling her green wheelbarrow around and making a beautiful garden even more beautiful. God must really be organized now, I thought.

Gray autumn came again. The cancer was back. But this time was different. This time, I was ready. Madeleine was with me again.

Once a week for twelve weeks, I lay in the hospital, watching the chemo move through the IV tube. "Try to relax," the nurses said again. "Think of something happy."

So this time, I pictured Madeleine walking through heaven with her big green wheelbarrow. I pictured all the prayers my family and friends had for me, floating around like bits of light. Madeleine gathered up each prayer, one by one, and put them in her wheelbarrow. Then, as the chemo started dripping in, I imagined her tipping the wheelbarrow over me. The white lights of love and prayer floated down and into my body. I became filled with a white, starry light that protected me from harm and cleansed the "bad" spots.

Every time I envisioned the wheelbarrow and its load of prayers flooding my body, I knew I was not alone. I had my husband, my children, my parents and sisters and cousins. And an angel for a best friend.

It's autumn again. This year, I have no cancer.

~Jenny Gore Dwyer
*Chicken Soup for the Gardener's Soul*

# Here to Stay

*Vision is the world's most desperate need.*
*There are no hopeless situations, only people who think hopelessly.*
*~Winifred Newman*

Cancer. Even the sound of it gives me chills, and it always has. I always felt bad for those who had it or knew someone who had it, but it never seemed real to me. That is, until sixth grade. Then it became very real, and it changed my life forever.

My best friend James was diagnosed with cancer that year. I was so scared. He found out about it near the beginning of the school year, and he was only given a five percent chance of making it through Christmas. James proved them wrong, though, because he did live through Christmas. In fact, he lived through all of sixth and seventh grade.

Toward the end of seventh grade, James was still receiving some chemotherapy, but he had hair. He no longer wore a hat to hide his baldness, and he was happy. But by the end of June, we were all in tears. He had relapsed.

James fought the disease with all of his might, but it spread to his bone marrow. Three bone-marrow matches were found in the national registry, but James would have to be in remission before the transplant could happen. Unfortunately, in early September, the doctors said that James's body wasn't responding to the treatments he was receiving. They started him on a new round of chemo, and we prayed that it would work.

James's body never did respond to the treatments. That's when the doctors gave him four to six months to live. When he called me and told me, I started crying. It was the only time that I ever let him hear me cry. He was so strong, though. He told me it was going to be okay. I don't know how he could have done that, but James was always strong and never let anything get him down, not even cancer.

About a week before Thanksgiving, the doctors gave James a slim chance of making it through the week. I was nervous the whole time, but Thanksgiving came and went, and James was still here.

In mid-December, however, James had a reaction to his platelet injection. He wasn't expected to make it through the night, but as usual he beat the odds. The doctors were almost sure he would be gone by Christmas, but he stayed with us into the New Year.

After that, he progressively got worse. He was in a lot of pain, and things were not looking good. On January 7th, James passed away. It was the saddest day of my life. I couldn't sleep for two days. I kept repeating the same thoughts: I will never see him again. I will never hear his voice again. I will never see his smile again.

But I was wrong. That night I was on my bed crying when I heard something.

"Brittany," a voice said. "Brittany, look up." The voice was all too familiar. When I looked up, James was sitting on the edge of my bed. He looked the same as he always had, but he was sort of glowing.

"James?" I asked. "Is that you?"

"No," he said, sarcastically. "It's Santa Claus. Of course, it's me." I laughed, and he smiled. "That's what I like to see, Brittany. No more tears."

"But you're gone," I told him.

"No, I'm not," he said. "I'm right here."

I haven't seen James since that night, and I know some people think I'm a little nuts when I tell this story, but that's okay. James gave me the greatest gift that night. So much of what drives me is being afraid of losing—losing my parents, losing my friends and, most of all, losing the love that keeps me going. That night I learned. I experienced firsthand that no matter what, love never leaves us.

~Brittany Lynn Jones
*Chicken Soup for the Christian Teenage Soul*

# Message Received

*When you are sorrowful look again in your heart, and you shall see that in truth you are weeping for that which has been your delight.*
*~Kahlil Gibran*

I knew the answer before he even asked.

My boyfriend of two years dropped down on one knee, pulled out a velvet, heart-shaped box, and asked, "Will you marry me?"

Louis looked so adorable. Such a large, strong man suddenly turned so vulnerable. I couldn't have found a better mate, so gorgeous, caring and easygoing. He had become my best friend, and I knew in my heart that I loved him.

"Yes," I answered.

A wave of relief washed over his face, then a huge, boyish smile that preceded a passionate kiss. "Thank you for making me the happiest man in the world!"

That week, we set the date for August 8th of the following year, and I started to pick out cards for our engagement announcement—and the memories immediately flooded back.

This wasn't the first time I had planned a wedding. Five years ago, Jono, my first fiancé, had died unexpectedly only six months prior to our wedding date. Pain paralyzed my heart as unfinished grief and longing reared up. I realized that planning another wedding brought all my feelings to the surface. I wondered if I'd ever heal from that loss.

I thought I had gotten over losing him. Because I was so young—only twenty-three years old—when Jono died, family and friends expected I would move on and date others, which I had... but marriage? As the months passed, I began to ponder whether Jono, the angel, felt anger toward me for wanting to marry someone else. After all, I had once promised to be his one and only.

The next morning, I found myself praying. Dear God, tell Jono that I know I said I would be his wife. But since you needed him, I've fallen in love with a beautiful man who treats me wonderfully. I'm very happy, yet afraid that Jono might be mad that I am going to have to break my word. Please have him forgive me. Tell him I'm sorry, and that I hope he will send me a sign so I know he approves.

Just then, a knock on the door startled me. I jumped, almost expecting Jono to be there.

Louis came in. "Are you ready?"

"For?" I wondered.

"We've got premarital counseling today. Remember the pastor changed it to this morning."

"Oh, that's right!" Quickly I got ready, and we decided to take my car since it was faster than his.

"Are you okay?" Louis asked as he started the engine.

"Uh-huh," I nodded halfheartedly.

"You still want to marry me, don't you?"

I turned to him knowing I couldn't let this man out of my life. If only Louis knew how much I really did love him. In that moment, I knew without a doubt that I was willing and ready to break a solemn vow I'd once made to someone else, to move forward and marry Louis.

"Yes," I replied.

Louis stopped the car in the church's parking lot, stepped out and came around to my side to let me out. "Did you see my wallet anywhere?" He suddenly began patting his pockets.

"Maybe it's underneath the seat."

Louis went back to the driver's side as I walked around the car to help him search.

He found his wallet under the seat, but something else caught his eye. He reached farther back and pulled out a shiny gold object. "What's this?"

My hands flew to my face. I had lost that "Xs and Os" gold bracelet six years ago. It was my birthday present from Jono, given to me the last day he told me how much he loved me. I had searched my car many times looking for this special bracelet and had given up hope of ever finding it.

"Wow, this is beautiful," Louis said, impressed.

With some hesitation, I explained who had given me the bracelet so many years before.

For a moment, Louis just stared at the piece shimmering in the sun. Then he took my hand and tenderly fastened Jono's bracelet on my wrist.

"You don't mind my wearing it?" I asked.

"No," he replied. "Now you can think of it as a present from both of us."

Years ago, I had searched this car for days trying to find that bracelet with its message of "hugs and kisses" from my first love. As I watched it shine on my wrist, I knew my prayer to hear from Jono had been answered. I soaked in this divine moment and the symbolism attached to it now that the bracelet, Jono, Louis and I were all brought together at our church.

Louis took my hand and we began to walk into the church. Next to the brass door handle was a plaque that had the complete Bible scripture "Love bears all things" engraved. Louis opened the door for me, and I took one last look at the plaque. As we walked through the archway, my eyes focused on the next words, "Love is not jealous."

~Michele Wallace Campanelli
*Chicken Soup for the Romantic Soul*

# Traveling with Visitors

*He that gives all, though but little, gives much;*
*because God looks not to the quantity of the gift,*
*but the quality of the givers.*
*~Francis Quarles*

My mother's face was illuminated, free of signs of anxiety or pain. Her eyes were wide open and brilliantly clear, their lids no longer shuttering from acute spasms of pain. A wonderful, bubbling laughter spilled forth from her lips while she conversed with her visitor.

Standing unseen in the doorway of her bedroom, I peered silently at the miraculous transformation in my terminally ill mother, watching her wait patiently for a reply from her visitor then continue with her animated words and laughter. My mother was quite lucid, and her aphasia (difficult speech) improved when she spoke with her visitor.

This wasn't the first time I'd noticed this strange, baffling phenomenon. Physically, her body lay in a hospital bed in my home, ravaged by breast cancer, which spread to her bones, brain and other organs. She required complete care for every daily need, which I provided with the help of hospice. But I knew she was slowly traveling away from this physical earth, preparing to take her final journey. It had started the day she called me into her room with a voice that was coherent and clear as a bell. "Claire, tell that man to move away from the television. I can't see my soaps."

I, of course, saw no one, but my mother's head was tilted, trying to watch her shows. I yelled out anyway, "Hey, move it! My mom can't see around you!"

"He's not moving," Mother chuckled. She waved her hand at me and just continued to watch her show, peering around her visitor. I asked her who he was, and she gave me a look that intimated I was the one who was utterly confused. "You know who. Now be quiet, I'm watching my show." She wrinkled her face at me then ignored me, keeping her head tilted at that strange angle.

During the past weeks, a man came to play cards in a chair in her room. Her deceased mother stood there shaking her finger at her. Her deceased aunt sat on her bed, talking about past days when they were young. And there were others who she wouldn't introduce me to. Sometimes I interrupted their talks, questioning Mother about her visitors. She tried to include me in their conversations, but soon I got an exasperated look thrown my way before she turned and explained to her visitor that I was her strange daughter.

But I knew my mother was leaving me and starting to travel closer to her new home. Were her visitors guides, helping her begin her journey to her new home as she leaves her tired worn-out body behind? Some days I asked her if she wanted to go with them. Her reply was, "They're visiting me, Claire. I'll go visit them soon. Now I'd like something to drink."

The past days, her visitors have been coming more frequently, spending more time in her room. Between visits she sleeps, restless, moving her hands and legs. I even whisper in her ear, "Go to the light, Mother." How can I be selfish and try to keep her here when there is a better place for her where she won't suffer any longer?

Today, my mother was staring up at one corner of the ceiling as I encouraged her to eat at least three spoonfuls of food. I inquired what she was staring at. Very calmly, she answered, "I'm just watching those three angels fly around. Each time they come, I know I'm going to have another visitor."

My mouth dropped open in shock. Angels. I watched her glazed eyes clear up once again, her facial features smooth out and a warm smile appear on her lips.

Her death quickly approaches, but my mother, her angels and her visitors have shown me not to be fearful or upset about her next step of leaving this earth. I know now she won't be alone.

~Claire Luna-Pinsker
*Chicken Soup for the Caregiver's Soul*

# An Unexpected Gift of Peace

*Nothing ever succeeds which exuberant spirits have not helped to produce.*
*~Friedrich Nietzsche*

September 11th will be remembered by all Americans as the date of a terrible national tragedy. Thousands of us who were airborne at the time will also have personal memories of becoming grounded and stranded. The most memorable event in my own life occurred the following day, September 12th.

"Your dad just called," my husband, Dick, said solemnly, as I walked back into our house from visiting our neighbor. "Your mother suffered a stroke and has slipped into a coma." It was Sunday afternoon, September 9th. I immediately called my father back and heard him repeat that my mother's condition was critical.

The following morning, my father called again. "I think you should come as soon as possible," he said. "It does not look like your mother will live much longer." I told him that I would be on an airplane by that evening.

As with a lot of families today, many miles separate us from one another. But thanks to the world of aviation, getting on an airplane to go anywhere in the world has not only become a convenience but also an expected part of our lives. I was attempting to get to Oak Ridge, Tennessee, from where I lived in Carlsbad, New Mexico.

Whether it was fate or Murphy's Law, something definitely

seemed to be putting my trip to Tennessee in slow motion. The commuter plane that I was taking to reach a major airport was late leaving. I could not make a connection by the time I finally reached the Albuquerque airport. Consequently, I spent the night at a hotel there. Early the next morning, I was on a flight to Phoenix, where I would connect with another flight to Nashville. It was while I was on the Phoenix-bound flight that the horrific plane crashes occurred. The plane I was on landed, but those passengers who had connecting flights became stranded. An announcement in the terminal simply told us to go to baggage claim for our luggage.

Being informed by others in the terminal of what had occurred within the past hour, their faces aghast as they focused on a television showing scenes of the plane crashes in New York, Washington, D.C., and Pennsylvania, I went to get my luggage. Passengers were lined up in the baggage-claim area to make calls on the hotel shuttle phones, in hope of finding a hotel that still had vacancies.

Upon checking into a hotel and settling in, I called my husband to let him know where I was. As the whole country seemed glued to the television that day, I, too, watched in horror and wondered how long I would be stranded in Phoenix. During the night, I was awakened by a phone call. My mother had died.

Early Wednesday morning, September 12th, I was informed that no planes were yet allowed in the air. Needing to purchase some items, I walked a quarter of a mile from the hotel to a shopping center. Walking slowly back to the hotel, I started to feel very distraught. All I could think about was how our country had been attacked by an evil force, my mother had died a few hours earlier, I couldn't get there before she passed away and didn't know how long I might be stranded. Grief began to overwhelm me.

Out of the blue, a beautiful white dove flew down and began walking with me. The dove continued to turn its head and look at me as we walked. I smiled through my tears and became increasingly aware that something very unusual was happening. "Are you from Heaven?" I asked the dove, as we walked, and instantly thought,

"Gosh, I'm talking to a bird!" The dove just continued to walk with me and look at me.

I unexpectedly began feeling that my mother's spirit was with me. When I reached the hotel, the dove and I looked at each other once more. A peace and warmth came over my entire being, and I felt God had just given me a special gift. Tranquility had replaced my feelings of fear, loneliness and desperation. I knew that God was still in control of this world.

I went back into my hotel room and called my husband. He had driven that morning to El Paso, Texas, attempting to get on a flight to Nashville. Being told that there would be no flights that day, he was booked on a flight for the next morning out of Midland, Texas. As a result, he drove the three-hour trip back home to Carlsbad. Later in the evening, he started driving to Midland to stay at a motel near the airport in order to be on an early flight the next morning. Hearing the news that flights were cancelled for the next day also, Dick turned around and drove all night to reach Phoenix the next morning. He later told me how very aware he was of God being with him in the car as he drove the 1,000 miles to reach me.

We both felt God's presence as we drove all day, all night, all the next day (another 1,900 miles in thirty-one hours), arriving one hour before the family was to receive friends at the funeral home. The funeral service immediately followed, and we were able to share with others my unexpected gift of peace.

~Linda Lipinski
*Chicken Soup to Inspire a Woman's Soul*

# The Message

My mother had battled breast cancer and won. She had been cancer-free for five years when she went into the hospital to have exploratory surgery. After the operation, her doctor took me aside and told me that not only had the cancer returned, but there was nothing he could do. "Three months," the doctor told me sadly.

I wondered how my mother would take the news, but as each day passed, I realized the doctors hadn't let her in on the miserable secret. Did they really expect me, her son, to have to break it to her? I didn't see how I could.

Three days passed with no word spoken. I watched as she packed up her things, ready to leave the hospital after recovering from her surgery. She was cheerful, telling me her plans for the next week, when something she saw in my face stopped her.

"Mom," I managed to say, "haven't they... haven't they told you?"

"Told me what?" she said.

I couldn't answer, but I didn't have to. The tears coursing down my face told her everything.

We held each other as I explained what I knew.

We had always been close, but after that day, I opened up to my mother in a way I never thought possible. I returned to New York, to my job as a hairstylist and the life I'd created there, but we talked long and often on the phone—not just as mother and son, but as friends.

Not long after, I took a month off and spent it with her, talking about anything and everything—her life and mine, politics, philosophy, religion. She was disappointed that I hadn't kept to the faith in which I'd been raised. She tried to convince me of God's existence, but although I didn't argue, nothing she said persuaded me that she was right. I suppose I was an agnostic: I just didn't know.

When I left, I wasn't sure if I would ever see her again, but in a certain way it didn't matter. Although we didn't agree on everything, we were complete with one another.

The day before I left, my mother presented me with a beautiful cross, one of her most valued possessions.

My mother had always been a deeply religious person. And although she rarely mentioned it, as a young woman she had entered the convent and spent two years as a nun. When her family urgently needed her to help with the family business, she made the difficult decision to leave the convent and go home.

Eventually, she married and I, her only child, was born. The cross she gave me that day was the one she received when she became a nun. It was exquisitely made, and as I took it in my hand, I could feel the love she gave to me along with it.

Within a month, the call I'd been dreading came. My mother had slipped into a coma. The doctors felt she didn't have much time left, so I hurried to the airport to catch the next flight home. As the plane took off, I looked out my window, watching the sky color with the setting sun. All at once, I was overcome with grief.

This heaviness stayed with me for the entire flight. When I arrived at the hospital, I was informed that I was too late. My mother had died while I was on the plane—at the exact time the sadness had overwhelmed me.

After my mother's funeral, I returned to New York. I missed my mother but was grateful that nothing had been left unsaid. She was gone, leaving an empty spot in me. That's how life is, I thought wistfully. When it's over, it's over. You're dead, and that's the end.

One day, three months after my mother died, a client came into the salon for her appointment. This particular woman had been coming to me for almost a year, but she was not a client with whom I was friendly. She was a high-powered businesswoman with a reserved air of cool politeness. We didn't talk about our lives. In fact, I had been surprised when, at her last appointment, she let it slip that she had been diagnosed with breast cancer.

Today, she didn't mention her illness and neither did I. I put her under the hair dryer and turned to walk away.

"Thomas," she said, lifting the dryer hood. "I hesitate to tell you this because I know this is going to sound strange. I have this very strong feeling that I'm supposed to tell you that Anita?... Marie?... Mary?... Anita Mary is okay. She said to tell you everything is all right."

I was floored. My jaw dropped. How could she know? For although my mother's name was Joyce, the name she'd taken as a nun—the name inscribed on the cross my mother had given me—was Sister Anita Mary. Nobody knew that but the other nuns and me.

In an instant, my whole view of reality turned upside-down. Mom had chosen a woman with breast cancer to tell me, in a way that could leave no doubt, that death is not the end and that the spirit survives.

~Thomas Brown
*Chicken Soup for the Mother's Soul 2*

# A Forever Friend

*Pay attention to your dreams—*
*God's angels often speak directly to our hearts when we are asleep.*
*~Eileen Elias Freeman,* The Angels' Little Instruction Book, *1994*

I ended up sitting next to Julie by chance at a motivational seminar. We had ample opportunity to tell stories about ourselves and found that we shared a common interest: passion for the spiritual and "unseen" parts of life. I told her I was studying dreamwork. This interest was to become the glue that bound our lives together. At the end of the day, we exchanged business cards and promised to meet again soon.

When we got together for lunch, Julie casually mentioned that she'd been having random and disturbing pains in her lower legs. The next few months proved to be an emotional and pivotal time in Julie's life. She was becoming increasingly immobilized from the pain and from muscle spasms. Numerous physicians, including neurologists, attempted to diagnose the growing lack of control of her extremities. After endless agonizing tests, Julie had no conclusive answers. She began doing research of her own.

I had never really understood what Lou Gehrig's disease (amyotrophic lateral sclerosis or ALS) was until Julie's research pointed to it as the insidious illness causing her affliction. She educated me about the symptoms, treatments, side effects and, worst of all, prognosis. Unfortunately, the suspicions of her research were confirmed.

Five years after I met Julie, she knew her time was short. We had many conversations concerning her beliefs about death and dying, how she did not want to be a burden and wanted to pass from this existence with dignity. Julie's conversations with God increased in frequency. Near the end, she heard a voice tell her it was time for her to move from her home into a hospice care facility.

By that time, Julie talked often about wanting to leave this Earth, saying that she was ready to go. This was a difficult yet special time for me, as I learned to honor the present moment when visiting her. Time was running out for us. My dear friend was in the active stages of dying. During our last visit together, we made a pact. She said she would contact me, if at all possible, after her death. Due to an out-of-town commitment that could not be postponed, I was not present at Julie's memorial service. A month later, my husband and I went to our beach cabin for the weekend. There, I was able to heal and reflect on this amazingly strong and courageous woman who had taught me so much about the miracle of the human spirit.

On our second night there, I had a very real and intense dream of Julie actually standing in our bedroom. She was radiant, vibrant and smiling just as she had been when I first met her. She opened her arms to me and hugged me hard, then held me at arm's length so that I could see her eyes and her joy. Julie said clearly, "We do not die!" This was more than a dream—I knew I had experienced something very real. It made sense for Julie to contact me this way. She knew my life's work was based on art and dreams. I shook my husband awake and told him that Julie had visited me, what she said and how wonderful she looked.

On the way home, I could not stop thinking about the feeling and image of Julie. I began to cry and thought to myself: "Julie, your strength and spirit and amazing courage touched many lives and hearts. I, for one, will never be the same for having known you."

Before reaching home, we stopped by our offices to pick up the weekend mail. I found that I had been sent a program from Julie's memorial service. When I opened the envelope, there was Julie's radiant, smiling face on the cover of the leaflet. It was the exact image of her I had seen in my dream! A Native American poem that Julie had selected before her death was printed on the inside page. It began with the words: "Do not sit at my grave and weep, for I am not there. The last line read: "Do not stand at my grave and cry, for we do not die."

~Marlene King
*Chicken Soup for the Girlfriend's Soul*

# A Cherished Angel

*Angels are the guardians of hope and wonder,*
*the keepers of magic and dreams...*
*~Author Unknown*

Cherished is the word I'd use to describe Grandma Madge. Her loving generosity poured out to every friend and family member needing help. Madge was always the first person to take a home-cooked meal to someone who was sick. The treasured time she spent with them surpassed even the healing benefit of her famous German dumplings.

That's why it seemed sadly ironic that friends and family now came to sit at her bedside. When Madge had learned about her fatal illness, she'd insisted on remaining at home. "To be surrounded by my angel collection," she beamed.

Madge's colossal collection of angels—fifteen hundred, to be exact—had started with just a few Christmas tree ornaments and an occasional figurine she'd picked up at souvenir shops or garage sales. But, it didn't take long for her sons to discover that contributions to Madge's menagerie were the perfect solution to the "what to get Mom" dilemma. Soon every friend, neighbor, grandchild and in-law bought her an angel for every holiday, birthday and anniversary. It wasn't long before her tiny cottage overflowed with a host of heavenly beings. She proudly displayed many of them year-round on shelves, the coffee table, end tables and on top of the TV. Her choir of angels assembled in the teeny guest room, reserved for musical figurines only. There, hundreds more singing, twirling, dancing angels crowded antique shelves, hutches and bedside stands.

Each November first, Madge began the month-long process of bringing out the rest of her collection. Angels graced her Christmas tree and the floor beneath it, then cascaded everywhere, from the buffet, to the mantel, to the back of the toilet and top of the refrigerator! To Madge, each angel was a reminder of a person who loved her. She inscribed the name of the giver on the bottom of each, along with the date she had received it. She gave explicit directions. "When I pass through the Pearly Gates, make sure every angel goes back to the person who gave it to me."

Now, with a caring hospice nurse and Madge's two sisters staying with her, that loving task seemed imminent. Late one afternoon, her grandson Troy stopped to spend some precious time. Sitting on the edge of the bed, he tenderly caressed her hand. "You've been an angel to us all, Grandma, a true gift from God."

A few hours later, Grandma Madge ascended through those Pearly Gates.

Her sisters, Rene and Gladys, and the hospice nurse, gathered in the living room marveling at how Madge had died with the same dignity, courage and grace with which she had lived. A faint melody interrupted their testimony. Bewildered, they turned their heads, trying to discover the source of the music. Rene and Gladys followed the hospice nurse to the guest bedroom while the tune grew louder. There on a table, one lone angel played the song "Cherish" from beginning to end. Then it stopped. With trembling hands, Gladys picked it up and read, "From Troy, 1992."

Gladys held the figurine to her chest. "Thanks, Madge, for letting us know you've joined God's heavenly collection of angels."

"Your angel," whispered the hospice nurse, "has returned to the Giver."

~Margie Seyfer as told to LeAnn Thieman
*Chicken Soup for the Nurse's Soul*

# Tommy's Tangerine Tree

*Keep a green tree in your heart and perhaps the singing bird will come.*
*~Chinese Proverb*

When Tommy, our youngest son, was a little boy, he loved tangerines. At Christmas, when they came on the market, I always kept a plentiful supply especially for him. He ate them for breakfast and supper, and there were always lots of them in his lunch box. As well, he loved to snack on them while he read or watched television.

One day I caught him flipping the seeds on the carpet. I scolded him, telling him to put them in an ashtray or a flowerpot. The result was that come spring, four little orange trees sprang up in a pot of geraniums in the kitchen window. I selected the tallest and sturdiest and replanted it in its own little pot. Tommy was intrigued.

"Do you think I can have my own tangerines?" he asked. I told him that it might take a very long time.

Time passed. Tommy grew up and became a petroleum geologist on the east coast, searching for oil and gas off Newfoundland. He loved the Atlantic Ocean with a fervor which I attributed to the fact that he had seagoing ancestors on both sides of the family. He married and built a house in Nova Scotia in sight of the Atlantic.

But he always came to visit us on his birthday, which was on New Year's Eve, and each time he would ask to see his tangerine tree.

In the twenty years that had passed since the little tree sprang up, it had grown amazingly. Each year I would put it into a bigger pot and place it in a warm, sunny spot in the garden, then bring it inside for the winter. But by the fall of 1981, I had no receptacle large enough to hold it, as it was now six feet tall.

Our daughter, who lived near us, offered to look after it as she had a very large urn, which she placed in a sunny window. When Tom came that New Year's Eve, he wanted to see his tangerine tree in his sister's home.

"Do you think it will ever bear fruit?" he asked.

I told him not to hold his breath—that although it would bear both male and female flowers if it ever bloomed, it was a Japanese tree and probably our climate was too cold for the flowers to set. He decided that he would take it down to his home in Nova Scotia the following summer. The foliage was beautiful anyway, he thought.

At that time he was working as a geologist on the Ocean Ranger oil rig off the coast of Newfoundland, and he was very proud to be doing exploration on what was probably the largest and most modern oil rig in the world. It was like a huge man-made island—indeed, the crew called it "Fantasy Island." They had to go out to it by helicopter, the only time, Tom said, that he was actually nervous. "It's a long, long way down there, Mum!"

I said, "I do wish you didn't have to go out in this bitter winter weather."

"I'm safer than you are, driving out of your driveway between ten-foot snowbanks," he assured me. "Besides, the rig's unsinkable!"

"So was the Titanic!" I said.

"You're mixing apples and oranges," he replied.

So when he telephoned us after he had returned to Nova Scotia and said he would be going out on the next shift change in a few days' time, I said, as I always did, "Be careful!"

Early on the morning of February 15th, my husband turned on the radio and woke me.

"Tommy's in trouble," he said. "The Ocean Ranger is listing!" We did not know it then, but it had already gone under the waves around one o'clock that morning.

There followed grief mixed with desperate fear, until we finally realized the unthinkable had occurred. Our dear, kindhearted, life-loving son had been taken from us. Amidst the wild despair and unbearable sorrow, we were borne by the belief that a spirit such as our beloved son's could not possibly disappear completely—that he was still with us and loving us.

But I longed for some kind of assurance. And how I dreaded the coming of Easter that year! How could I join in the celebration of eternal life when I was not sure of it myself?

Then, on Good Friday, I got an answer. When our daughter telephoned, she said excitedly, "Mum, you won't believe this, but Tom's tangerine tree is full of blossoms!"

It was true. On Easter Sunday they opened fully, and their fragrance filled the house. Surely no flowers had ever been so beautiful! Someone had responded to my doubt and hopelessness with this little miracle.

Since the tree was inside, with no honeybees to pollinate it, we did not expect the blossoms to set. But again a miracle happened! Four tiny tangerines appeared. A short time later, two of them dropped off. Over the next few months, however, two more beautiful tangerines grew and eventually ripened. On the following Christmas Day we ceremoniously divided and ate Tom's tangerines. We felt that he knew it, and we were comforted.

A horticulturist has said that perhaps people had spread the pollen when they smelled the fragrant blooms. But I believe "someone" sent those blossoms to comfort us when we most needed a miracle—the miracle of Tom's tangerine tree.

Now, five years later, another little tangerine tree, a child of Tommy's tree, is growing on my windowsill. We had planted the seeds of the tangerines we ate on Christmas Day, 1982. I shall not live to see it blossom, but I shall nurture it as a symbol of life everlasting.

~Ruth Hilton Hatfield
*Chicken Soup for the Canadian Soul*

# Stories of Faith

## Answered Prayers

*Prayer does not change God, but it changes him who prays.*
*~Søren Kierkegaard*

# The Band Played

*As your faith is strengthened you will find that there is no longer the need to have a sense of control, that things will flow as they will, and that you will flow with them, to your great delight and benefit.*
*~Emmanuel*

For years I'd dreamed about pulling up to a house and knowing that's the house—the house I want to build my family in. I vowed not to be like everyone who tells house-hunting horror stories.

My newlywed husband, Ward, and I had spent many months praying for the perfect house to start our new life together in. We'd done all our research on the cities, neighborhoods and school districts, and the market was perfect.

But after three months of looking, I felt lost. I was becoming my worst nightmare. It was hard to find a house in Southern California that had the appeal of back East. I grew up in a very rural place with unique houses and large yards with no fences. But here they all looked alike—and I hated stucco! Was it too much to ask for a cute English-style home with wood trim, a garden and picket fence? That was my petition to God every night.

Our Realtor continued to patiently take us everywhere and kept a positive attitude as we declined each house. But I was losing it. Emotionally exhausted and frustrated, I thought that it was going to happen. I would have to settle for a salmon-colored stucco house with the same garage door and number of windows as everyone else.

My husband was so good. "Don't worry, Maria," he'd say. "Keep praying and have faith. God knows where we're supposed to live, and He has the perfect house for us." I was so thankful for Ward's faith and strength; he kept me going and comforted me after each stucco house we saw.

One Friday morning, our Realtor called with a new listing in Costa Mesa—a three-bedroom house with a large backyard. Since I worked in the area and our church was there, I told Ward I'd go by and look at it before work. I knew exactly where the house was. It had a good neighborhood and was located near the college I attended. As I rounded the corner, I saw a For Sale sign up the street—that must be the house. As I got nearer, I couldn't believe my eyes. A white picket fence surrounded a white, green-trimmed, English-style house with an old brick sidewalk entrance up to the front door. That was the house—the house I wanted to build my family in.

I was so excited, I called Ward even before I parked my car. "I found the house! Quick, you have to come! We have to put an offer on it today!"

The Realtor met us there, and as Ward and I entered the house, I felt him cringe. He hated the inside. As we walked around and looked at all the old windows and stained glass, I could see beyond the seventies' rust-colored shag rug, dark blue drapes and pink walls. I could see past the old bathrooms and popcorn ceiling. Then we stepped into the backyard; it was like stepping back East. The large lawn was lined with trees, and there was even an old willow, just like at Grandma's. The big yard was out of place in Southern California. I knew then this was the house.

Still unsure, Ward suggested we needed to pray about it and sleep on it. There had been no offers on the house, and, since it had been on the market for six months, they were lowering the price. So we felt pretty comfortable about sleeping on it.

After a full day of continued house shopping, Ward found another house he wanted, so we were both stressed to the max. We lay on the bed that night, talking over both homes and praying, then finally falling asleep... in our clothes. We must have slept pretty hard, because when we woke, we both laughed—we still had our shoes on!

That morning, we decided to make an offer on the house I loved. As we drove to look at it one more time, all the while I was praying, "God, please show me a sign." We exited the freeway, turned on the street and parked outside. Ward noticed a neighbor doing lawn work, so he strolled over to chat with him and find out his opinion of the neighborhood.

As I sat in the car praying, I heard a band practicing at the high school just across the field. It brought back memories of my high school days, when I was in the band. I sat reflecting, enjoying the community feel. Would Ward feel that too? Or would he say, "Do you hear that band? I don't think I could live with that next door!"

Ward walked back to the car and said, "Did you hear the band playing? Isn't that cool? It really makes this place feel like a community."

I knew right then this was my sign from God. We must have this house. Ward agreed. We called the Realtor and went straight to her office to sign an offer. We eagerly told her about the band playing, about how much the neighborhood felt like our community and how we'd love to live there.

She told us there were three offers pending on the house. Just that morning, three offers had come in. The homeowners would look at them and accept the one they wanted.

My heart sank. There weren't any offers yesterday! As I began the woulda, coulda, shoulda game in my head and out loud, Ward put me in my place. "God knows the house for us. Don't worry."

But worry—and pray—I did all day long.

Early that evening we finished up dinner and talked, coming to peace with the house deal, be it ours or not. The phone rang; it was our Realtor. The house was ours! The owners accepted us above the others because of something our agent had written in a letter to them.

A letter? What letter? I asked her. She admitted writing about Ward and me, how our church and work were in that neighborhood, how we had just gotten married and how, when we heard the band practicing at the high school, we knew that was the house for us. The owners said they chose us because we liked the band playing.

My sign. God's sign. Music to my ears.

~Maria Nickless
*Chicken Soup for the Christian Soul 2*

# God Listens

*Let the morning bring me word of your unfailing love, for I have put my trust in you. Show me the way I should go, for to you I lift up my soul.*
*~Psalm 143:8*

"God, if you ever want a man in my life, you will have to put him there. In fact, he will have to be standing at my front door wearing a T-shirt that says you sent him." Those words, spoken from bitterness and disappointment for the crushed relationships in my life, stated exactly how I felt about men, as a single mother.

Years passed, and my busy life centered around church, my four sons and my job. My parents lived out of state, so our church became our family.

Slowly, I turned all my joys, heartaches and triumphs over to God.

During those healing years, my youngest son established a friendship with a man who assisted our youth music minister. Dean was a quiet, somber man, but one who lived a life modeled after our Lord. He urged youth to find their identity through God's unfailing love. I admired Dean's patience, understanding and giving ways. More so, I appreciated his friendship with my sons.

At first, I felt suspicious of him spending time and effort on them, and I researched his background to ensure my sons' safety and well-being. He received glowing reports for his integrity and devotion to God. I decided he had been sent to fill the void in my sons' lives and to be the role model they so desperately needed.

Over the next year and a half, Dean spent more and more time with them. He took the youngest to Cancún during Christmas break and took two of them to Branson, Missouri, shortly afterwards. He purchased one of the boys a car so he could take a part-time job. Dean showed him how to pay for gas and insurance and still have spending money. He listened to my sons' escapades and problems, and he never judged or condemned their behavior. He and I were great friends. I felt no threat, because Dean was twelve years younger than I.

One summer day, the doorbell rang. Dean stood in the doorway wearing a T-shirt with the logo "God Listens." At that moment I remembered the words I had uttered years before. I felt the color rise to my cheeks, and my stomach knotted. Dean handed me five additional shirts with the same "God Listens" logo printed on the front.

"I got these at the Christian bookstore, and there's one for each of you," he said.

All I could think was, "Oh no, Lord, not Dean. He's not the right one. He's too young, and he's—well, he's my friend." Naturally, I said nothing, but thereafter the "God Listens" logo haunted me. I attempted to rationalize the entire incident, and I asked God to handle the matter for me. He did.

Two months later, Dean proposed. The boys were excited, and I realized how happy our lives had become since he first began a relationship with us. Still, I felt nervous and fearful of being hurt again.

Dean and I talked a great deal about a Christian marriage and the value of open communication. We made a budget, attended premarital classes, prayed together and talked about our future.

Neither of us had family nearby, so my sons and a few close friends were all we wanted to attend the ceremony. We scheduled the wedding for ten o'clock on a November morning. Shortly before 9:30, the boys and I drove to the church where one of Dean's friends waited outside to video the whole thing. I'm not very comfortable in front of a camera, but I tried to relax and act normal—whatever that is.

Once inside, I stared amazed at the number of friends who had come to share in our vows. My best friend, my sons and I stood in an empty office while a photographer snapped various poses of us. Of course, the video rolled on.

Promptly at ten, the pastor stepped in and announced it was time for the wedding. We walked down the hallway to find even more friends waiting.

But Dean did not stand among them.

The pastor reached inside his suit pocket and produced a folded piece of paper. "Dean could not be with us this morning, but he did leave a letter for DiAnn."

A hush fell over the room, and I teetered between hysterics and sheer bewilderment. Why couldn't the pastor have pulled me aside to break the news? My heart pounded furiously as I stood there in total humiliation and disappointment. Too stunned to even utter a protest, I watched in horror while the pastor unfolded the letter. Suddenly, the thought of fainting held merit. If only I could stop him—but it was too late.

With heartfelt words, Dean began his letter explaining how he had gradually fallen in love with each member of my family. He stated how his friendship with me had grown from admiration to a deep love. His first love was Jesus, and he knew I shared the same feelings. Together we would establish a loving, Christian marriage and realize the blessings of our Lord. His love and commitment extended to my sons as well.

The letter concluded that he waited for us at a secret destination. There, he awaited me at the altar.

The pastor tucked the letter back inside his suit coat and escorted me to a church bus. I didn't know what to say for fear the lump in my throat would explode into a pool of tears. Where could Dean be?

We boarded a church bus, with the video still filming my every emotion, while I searched futilely for a possible wedding location. Each time I thought I knew where Dean intended to meet me, the bus drove right on by. We continued driving, and my mind raced with the possibilities. Then the bus turned into a lovely subdivision.

There stood my husband-to-be in front of a beautiful and spacious new home. In the front yard, a sign leaned against a huge pine tree. It read: The Mills Residence, established November 24, 1993.

Inside, in the dining room, I found a wedding cake and food for all our friends. Candles and baskets of pink flowers surrounded a kneeling bench in front of a marble fireplace. Dean stood there, arms outstretched. A black grand piano filled the room with the music of love.

Dean's T-shirt had been right—God does listen.

~DiAnn G. Mills
*Chicken Soup for the Christian Woman's Soul*

# In Good Hands

*How sweet the name of Jesus sounds*
*In a believer's ear;*
*It soothes his sorrows, heals his wounds,*
*And drives away his fear.*
*~John Newton*

The phone rang early. Hal, my husband, answered it before it rang again.

"Yes?" he said. "Oh... I see." By the tone of his voice I knew it was the phone call we'd expected and dreaded.

We'd watched Hal's father, Harold, grow weaker since his heart attack in January. Dad's bypass surgery eight years earlier had given us far more than the five years doctors had promised. Then Dad experienced several smaller heart attacks. His lungs began filling with fluid. Doctors had reached the end of what they could do for him in the hospital and transferred him to an extended care facility.

With his needs beyond what care we could give and because he lived an hour and a half away, the most we could do was visit him as often as possible. Since we couldn't help him physically, the best care we could give was to care for his soul.

Hal and I had become Christians fifteen years earlier, and we wanted to share our faith with his family. His mother, Grace, had taken Hal and his brothers to church when they were young, but his father never went. Grace quit attending after Dad's first heart attack.

Did she stay home to make sure Dad was okay after his quadruple bypass? Or had his heart attack shaken her faith? I didn't know.

"Give us an opportunity to tell Dad about you," I prayed to Jesus. "He must decide whether he will take you as his Savior, but please don't let him die without a clear opportunity to respond to you." I had prayed similar prayers for years, but when Dad became sick my urgency increased.

Hal hung up the phone. "Dad died at 3:30 this morning."

"Lord," I prayed silently, "did he have the opportunity I asked for?"

Hal and I had both looked for that opportunity to tell Dad about Jesus, but we saw none. With each visit, Dad seemed less willing to talk to us at all. He just stared at the television. When we tried to start a conversation, he pressed the "up" button on the volume control. The more we tried, the more he increased the volume. The urgency I felt inside increased as well.

We asked a hospital chaplain to visit Dad. He did. We asked our own pastor to visit. He made the trip. A pastor from Mom's church visited too, but the result was always the same. Up, up went the volume on the TV. I didn't know what else to do but pray.

And now Dad was gone.

According to my faith, those who accept Jesus Christ as Savior are ensured an eternity in heaven with Him. However, those who refuse this gift of salvation spend eternity separated from God. I still hoped somehow God had answered my prayer and had helped Dad understand, but had He? I didn't know.

We buried Dad in the veterans' portion of the cemetery. Mom, a veteran of World War II herself, made her own final arrangements at the same time. But none of us knew how soon she would need them.

The week after Dad's funeral, she started showing signs of illness. One day, a neighbor found her on the floor, incoherent. Doctors diagnosed Mom with a cancerous tumor in her stomach plus lymphoma. She was hospitalized and we resumed the endless trips to visit.

Mom was too weak to live alone, and her sons discussed their options, each offering to care for her. But it became clear her needs exceeded what any of us could give. The best we could do as her caregivers was to let professionals help. She moved into an extended care facility. The chemo weakened her so that she didn't speak anymore. She began having small strokes, then a major stroke. And there we were, the week of Christmas, laying Grace to rest beside her husband.

We invited everyone to gather at our home that Christmas. As we quietly celebrated the birth of Jesus, I not only wondered about Harold, I also wondered if Grace had a true understanding of Jesus Christ. How I wished I knew.

The new year dawned, and we all felt emotionally and physically drained. Nevertheless, the work of dealing with Harold and Grace's estate lay before us. Each of us sorted, separated, donated, gave away or sold their belongings. We fixed up their home for sale, painting inside and out. Finally, six months later, Hal and I set the few remaining items in the driveway for one last garage sale.

Neighbors, Christine and Alfonso, stopped by. "You know, we visited your dad in the nursing home," Alfonso told us.

"No, we didn't know that," Hal said.

"One afternoon I told Christine, 'We need to go see Harold.' We went right then. When I walked into his room," Alfonso said, "his face lit up! He was so happy to see us. So I just started telling him about Jesus."

"Really?" Hal asked, glancing at me.

"Your Dad said he wasn't ready to go," Alfonso said. "I told him, 'I'm not saying you're going to die, but we all need to be ready.' I explained to him about Jesus and then asked if he'd like to ask Jesus to be his Savior. He began to weep and said yes, so I led him in a prayer."

"We had no idea! When did this happen?" I asked, incredulously.

"Well," Alfonso thought for a moment, "he died early the next morning."

"I prayed with your mother, too," Christine added. "When the ambulance came for your dad, I stayed with her. I asked her if she was sure she'd go to heaven when she died and she said no, so I prayed with her so she could be sure."

"Your parents are in heaven," Alfonso declared.

I know.

~Dianne E. Butts
*Chicken Soup for the Christian Soul 2*

# How Prayer Made Me a Father Again

*Our greatest glory is not in never falling, but in rising every time we fall.*
*~Confucius*

I can't begin to count the number of times that prayer has played an important part in my life. As often as God has answered my prayers, I realize it's important to pray for others, too. So when our church started a Tuesday night prayer service, I became a regular participant. The pastor sometimes would begin with a short devotion, and then we'd sing a couple of praise choruses before getting down to serious conversations with God. From the beginning we knew we were there to pray.

During the first few months, attendance was sparse. Those who came gave their prayer requests and there'd still be plenty of time to bring them to the Lord. However, as prayers were answered, more people joined and the number of requests multiplied. It took most of the service to hear all the requests.

The pastor solved the problem. Now when we arrive for the service, we write down our prayer requests on a sign-in sheet in the foyer. During our praise time, the pastor makes a copy of these requests for each person. With list in hand, we find a quiet place to pray individually.

One Tuesday evening our prayer list was short. I prayed for each need listed. I prayed for the church, our community, our state and our country. Then I prayed over the list again.

I looked at my watch thinking the hour ought to be up. I still had fifteen minutes left! There had to be something more I could pray about.

Then my son came to mind. I had not seen Teddy in twenty-seven years. When he was less than a year old, his mother and I divorced, and she moved with Teddy out of state. I smiled to myself as I thought back to those months with my firstborn son. I would get off the bus from work and could hear him crying half a block away. As soon as I walked into his room, his cries turned into laughter.

After the divorce, I made an effort to keep in touch, but my first letters were returned unopened. Later they were marked, "Addressee moved, left no forwarding address." I had no idea where either Teddy or his mother lived.

When Teddy was about five, I learned through an attorney that my ex-wife had remarried and her new husband wanted to adopt my son. I agonized over my decision.

The attorney wouldn't disclose Teddy's whereabouts unless I chose to seek custodial rights. But a custody battle might forfeit any chance for Teddy to enjoy a stable life. I reasoned: Teddy doesn't know me. Would it really be fair to deny him a father to satisfy my own need to see him? Would my selfishness cause more emotional damage?

I loved Teddy and missed him terribly, but I decided I couldn't interfere with a chance for happiness in his life. I waived my rights, hoping it was the best thing to do for my son.

Now years later, I simply asked prayerfully, "Lord, my son is a grown man now. I love him and miss him. Please just let me know what kind of a man Teddy has turned out to be. Anything more than that I leave in your hands. In fact, Lord, I don't even know where to start looking for him, so I am truly leaving it all up to you. Please, let me know my son. Amen."

As I left that prayer service, the Lord gave me peace from the words of Malachi 4:6—"He will turn the hearts of fathers to their children, and the hearts of the children to their fathers."

The rest of the week I went about my normal routine and forgot about my prayer. But God hadn't forgotten.

The Saturday after the prayer meeting, I ran into our pastor at the post office. After I collected the mail from my box, we started to chat. As I scanned through my mail, a letter caught my eye.

I couldn't place the name or the return address. As the pastor commented on Sunday's church activities, I started reading the mysterious letter.

"Are you okay?" he asked me. Tears were rolling down my face. I couldn't speak; I handed him the letter I had just read—from Teddy.

Teddy explained that he had decided to search the Internet for me. This letter was one of forty-seven letters that my son had written to Richard Whetstones all over the country. Then I noticed the postmark: It was dated Wednesday, the day after my Tuesday night prayer. This wasn't a coincidence. This was a direct answer to my prayer.

When I told my wife, Rose, she was excited because she had encouraged me to try to find Teddy. Since I hadn't mentioned my Tuesday night prayer to her, she was even more thrilled when she learned the whole story.

I decided to call Teddy that day, but I was nervous as I dialed the phone number in Amarillo, Texas. When he answered the phone, I said I had received the letter and I was his father. We agreed to pursue the relationship further.

So I sat down and wrote him back, enclosing a photo I had of him—a color snapshot taken by a family friend at Teddy's christening. In the photo, Teddy was in his mother's arms while my dad and I stood proudly beside him.

In Teddy's return letter, he enclosed the exact same photo—the only family photo he had! That was the confirmation we both needed. I had found my son—or rather, he had found me.

When I told my sister Donna about Teddy, she began corresponding with him, secretly arranging a person-to-person reunion for the two of us at her wedding in May. Teddy and I had time to slip away for breakfast, then walked on the Clearwater beach, talking the whole time.

Teddy had a lot of questions. He had had suspicions about being adopted early on, but didn't learn the truth until he was fifteen years old. His mother hadn't mentioned me at all; I was thankful she hadn't painted me as a terrible person. Having heard all kinds of horror stories about reunions that turned bad, I was reminded once again that God remained faithful.

In October 1997, Teddy and his family—wife Dana, and their children Hayden and Jorden—visited Rose and me in Florida. Teddy's wife couldn't get over how similar Teddy and I were—in looks, mannerisms, speech and ideals—even though we lived completely separate lives.

My Tuesday night prayer wasn't the first or the last prayer that God has answered in my life. But it is one of the most wonderful and satisfying blessings He has ever given me. All I did was simply ask, trusting for His answer.

~Richard Whetstone
*Chicken Soup for the Christian Family Soul*

# I Can't Do a Thing

Wilma poured the puréed mixture of chicken and vegetables into a bowl, then touched a spoonful to her lips, testing the temperature for her sister, Adah.

Adah had lived with Wilma and her husband for several years before her paralysis began. It first appeared as only a slight slowing of Adah's movements when she lifted a fork to her mouth. Then the day came when she couldn't push herself up from the table. The next morning she fell as she got out of bed.

Wilma made a doctor's appointment immediately, and a wearying round to specialists began. Finally, they received the dreaded diagnosis. Adah had super-progressive nuclear palsy—a mean cousin to Parkinson's disease that would gradually stiffen her muscles and paralyze her.

The next couple of years passed far too quickly, each month bringing more debilitation, until Adah's condition forced her to a walker, then a wheelchair and finally to bed. Adah's nieces and nephews remembered how they used to have trouble keeping up with this active woman when she escorted them to town. They missed her lessons in family history given as she mended their blue jeans or embroidered pillowcases for their weddings. Now her hands lay twisted and still upon the quilt covering her frail body. The change was so painful for many of the relatives, they stopped coming by, choosing instead to send another card that Wilma taped to the wall above Adah's railed bed.

Wilma, only two years younger and not in the best of health herself, took care of Adah—bathing her, turning her, feeding her, and trying to rub the achy pain out of a tired body that only vaguely resembled the woman her sister had once been.

One day had been particularly difficult when Adah managed to whisper apologetically, "I can't do a thing." Wilma patted her arm, fighting back tears as she said a silent prayer: "Lord, give me something encouraging to say."

The answer came in a sudden brainstorm. "Adah, you can still pray," Wilma said. "Goodness knows the family needs plenty of that. Thea and the children left this morning for a long drive. Will you pray for them?"

Adah smiled and whispered, "I will."

During the next several weeks, each time Wilma received word of a particular need, she passed it along to her sister. When a neighbor mentioned his brother was facing a series of complicated medical tests, Wilma assured him of her prayers. Then she added, "And I'll tell Adah, too. She'll pray the whole time he's in the hospital."

A few days later the elated neighbor called. The doctors had decided his brother's problem could be controlled with medication. Surgery wouldn't be necessary after all.

When one of the men at church lost his job because the small company where he'd worked for twelve years closed, Wilma told Adah. The man found work the next month.

Gradually, folks began to hear about Adah's constant prayers and started calling with requests. Sometimes a worried mother called about an ill child; sometimes a child called about an ailing pet. Once a gruff husband called, clearing his throat several times before finally saying that well, yes, he, uh, had heard that Adah was a praying woman. Would she, uh, pray for his marriage?

Sometimes Adah's family wondered aloud how those prayers affected Adah herself. They couldn't help but notice that even in the midst of her pain, she possessed a graciousness and peace not expected from one so bound to a disease-captured body. Perhaps her concentration on others pulled her thoughts away from her own situation. Perhaps her constant prayerfulness wrapped her in God's grace.

Day after day the requests came, and day after day Adah whispered her prayers. The time came, though, when her voice faded totally. When she didn't whisper her usual morning greeting, Wilma pulled the bed rail down to comfort her sister with a hug. Then she said, "Adah, even if you pray only in your mind, the Lord hears you." Adah nodded.

Then one morning as Wilma relayed yet another prayer request, Adah only stared at her, unable to nod her acknowledgment. Wilma silently prayed for her sister's suffering, then patted her on the arm. "That's okay, Adah, honey. You just blink your eyes to answer me; one blink will mean yes, two blinks will mean no. Now, do you understand that Josie called to ask you to pray about moving her widowed mother?"

Adah blinked once. Yes, she understood.

That was the beginning of Adah's third and final year, still praying for others, until God released her.

Today, relatives are grateful that she is free after years of painful paralysis, yet they miss her still. They know Adah's prayers lifted their pain—and Adah straight to heaven.

~Sandra Picklesimer Aldrich
*Chicken Soup for the Caregiver's Soul*

# Bringing It to Pass, Football and All

It was a crisp fall day in Madison, Wisconsin, when our University of Wisconsin football team defeated the University of Illinois in the final Big Ten Conference home game of the season. Now Wisconsin was headed to the Hall of Fame Bowl in Tampa, Florida, over the Christmas holidays. My twenty-two-year-old son, Michael, a senior at University of Wisconsin at Madison, was a four-year member of their marching band, famous for their wildly entertaining high-stepping antics that dazzled crowds.

I'd desperately wanted to go to the Rose Bowl game the year before to watch him perform, but the trip was too expensive. I didn't know anyone in Pasadena to stay with, and airfare was out of the question. On New Year's Day 1994, my house was full of relatives as we all watched Michael on TV. He played his drums with such precision during the Rose Bowl parade and game that my heart nearly burst with excitement and pride.

When the Wisconsin Badgers won the right to play in the Hall of Fame Bowl the very next season, I realized that that game would be Michael's last time ever to march with the band before he graduated. I had to be there. Right!—a single parent with a small income and bigger-than-life dreams; that's me.

In late November, I mentioned my dream to my airline pilot friends who use the extra bedrooms in our home as their Milwaukee-area home away from home. One said he had a couple of low-cost "friend" passes that my fifteen-year-old son Andrew and I could use to get to Tampa and back.

"The passes are only about ninety dollars each, round-trip," he said. "But you'll have to fly standby."

I jumped at the chance as he set things in motion. Next, I had to find housing. I looked on the map and saw that our retired friends, Wally and Shirley, lived just forty-five minutes from Tampa. I was sure they'd put us up for the week in their Florida condo.

Everything seemed to be working smoothly until I called my dad in Illinois to tell him the good news. Dad planted my feet back on the ground when he said, "You're going to Florida between Christmas and New Year's? That's the busiest tourist week of the year down there! And you're flying standby? What do you think your chances are of getting on a plane that week?"

My bubble of optimism burst again when I heard on the radio that nearly thirty thousand Wisconsinites had already bought tickets to the Hall of Fame Bowl. Our chances of getting down there flying standby certainly didn't look good. In fact, they looked impossible.

Besides, there was another glitch in the plans. The airline we'd be flying on had only one flight a day to Tampa. How could I even think there'd be empty seats on that plane during the week between Christmas and New Year's?

I told myself disgustedly, "How could you be so stupid? This will never work!"

In addition to decorating for Christmas, buying gifts, cleaning house and planning meals for the holidays, I now had an additional stressor in my life.

I commiserated with my friend Heather, who told me, "Pat, stop worrying. Do something for me. Look through the book of Psalms. Read it until you find a verse that seems to be speaking to you."

"Psalms? What am I going to find in there?" I asked Heather.

"Just do it. You'll find what you're looking for."

That afternoon I opened my Bible and read the first two psalms. Nothing hit me. The third verse said something about a tree yielding "its fruit in season," which only depressed me more. It made me think of ruby-red grapefruit and large, juicy oranges hanging on trees all over Florida—fruit that I certainly wouldn't be enjoying.

This can't be the verse that's supposed to make me feel better, I thought. I closed the book and opened it again at random. This time, my eyes went directly to Psalms 37:5: "Commit thy way unto the Lord; trust also in Him; and He shall bring it to pass."

Two things about that verse threw me for a loop. The part about committing my way to the Lord—my way to see my son perform in his last game, perhaps? The other was the notion that the Lord would "do this." If I did my part, then God would do His. In other words, if I really, truly trusted in the Lord, then He would bring all things to pass. That was the clincher, since Andrew and I would be flying standby on a "pass."

I thought, "Okay, Patricia, this is it. If Heather can be so dead-bolt certain of her faith, why can't you? You have to put it on the line. Do you truly believe that this is in the hands of the Lord and that He will bring it to pass?"

I only had to ask myself that question once. I sat down that moment and memorized verse 37:5. It was the first Bible verse I'd ever memorized in my life. I've been a longtime Bible reader and student, but memorizing is very difficult for me. I chanted the verse at least a hundred times a day during those weeks before Christmas: "Commit thy way unto the Lord; trust also in Him; and He shall bring it to pass."

The minute I turned the problem over to the Lord, I relaxed completely and virtually sailed through the preparations for Christmas.

Never again did I worry about whether or not we'd get on the plane, not even when I learned every flight had been greatly oversold with the exception of Christmas morning. And even for that flight, eighty of the eighty-four seats had been sold, with three weeks still to go before Christmas.

For the next three weeks, I repeated my newly memorized verse a thousand times: before I got out of bed in the morning, before each meal, during the day, in the car, in my home office, walking down the hall, in bed at night. I repeated it to all my friends and family and assured them that Andrew and I would be in Tampa for the Hall of Fame Bowl on January 2nd, and that we'd be flying down there on Christmas morning.

Christmas Eve day dawned holy and cold in Milwaukee. Andrew, my grown children, son-in-law, granddaughter, and friends Rusty and Heather and their two little daughters, all celebrated Christ's birth amidst my giggling excitement as I packed our bags for Florida. I shared my memorized Bible verse from Psalms with them as part of the grace before our Christmas Eve dinner.

"So Mom, are you just going to keep going back to the airport every day all week until you get on a plane?" my daughter Julia asked during dessert.

"No, honey, we'll be getting on the plane tomorrow morning. I'll send you postcards and bring you seashells!"

Never before in my life had I been so sure of something—something that to all the sensible people around me seemed to be the folly of the century.

Bags packed, car loaded, Michael drove us to the airport at 7:30 A.M. Christmas Day. The gate agent said there'd been four people with emergencies in Florida, and they'd been given priority standby status.

It didn't matter. I knew that when that gate closed we'd be on the plane.

That afternoon, Andrew and I picked grapefruit from the tree next to the hot tub in the backyard of our friends' house in Florida. Nine days later, after sunning ourselves on Gulf beaches, exploring exotic wonders and following the Wisconsin marching band as they performed all over Tampa, we watched as the University of Wisconsin defeated Duke in the Hall of Fame Bowl on a beautiful, sunny, eighty-degree day.

Michael's last performance with the band was stellar.

But not quite as stellar as my faith in the Lord—who brings all things to pass.

~Patricia Lorenz
*Chicken Soup for the Christian Woman's Soul*

# Winter Morning Guest

*The heart of the giver makes the gift dear and precious.*
*~Martin Luther*

One winter morning in 1931, I came down to breakfast—and found the table empty.

It was cold outside. The worst blizzard on record had paralyzed the city. No cars were out. The snow had drifted up two stories high against our house, blackening the windows.

"Daddy, what's happening?" I asked.

I was six years old. Gently Dad told me our fuel and food supplies were exhausted. He'd just put the last piece of coal on the fire. Mother had eight ounces of milk left for my baby brother, Tom. After that—nothing.

"So what are we going to eat?" I asked.

"We'll have our devotions first, John Edmund," he said, in a voice that told me I should not ask questions.

My father was a pastor. As a Christian, he'd been chased out of his Syrian homeland. He arrived as a teenager in the United States with no money and barely a word of English—nothing but his vocation to preach. He knew hardship of a kind few see today. Yet my parents consistently gave away at least ten percent of their income, and no one but God ever knew when we were in financial need.

That morning, Dad read the scriptures as usual, and afterwards we knelt for prayer. He prayed earnestly for the family, for our relatives and friends, for those he called the "missionaries of the cross" and those in the city who'd endured the blizzard without adequate shelter.

Then he prayed something like this: "Lord, Thou knowest we have no more coal to burn. If it can please Thee, send us some fuel. If not, Thy will be done—we thank Thee for warm clothes and bed covers, which will keep us comfortable, even without the fire. Also, Thou knowest we have no food except milk for Baby Thomas. If it can please Thee...."

For someone facing bitter cold and hunger, he was remarkably calm. Nothing deflected him from completing the family devotions—not even the clamor we now heard beyond the muffling wall of snow.

Finally someone pounded on the door. The visitor had cleared the snow off the windowpane, and we saw his face peering in.

"Your door's iced up," he yelled. "I can't open it."

The devotions over, Dad jumped up. He pulled; the man pushed. When the door suddenly gave, an avalanche of snow fell into the entrance hall. I didn't recognize the man, and I don't think Dad did either because he said politely, "Can I help you?"

The man explained he was a farmer who'd heard Dad preach in Allegan three years earlier.

"I awakened at four o'clock this morning," he said, "and I couldn't get you out of my mind. The truck was stuck in the garage, so I harnessed the horses to the sleigh and came over."

"Well, please come in," my father said. On any other occasion, he'd have added, "And have some breakfast with us." But, of course, today there was no breakfast.

The man thanked him. And then—to our astonishment—he plucked a large box off the sleigh. More than sixty years later, I can see that box as clear as yesterday. It contained milk, eggs, butter, pork chops, grain, homemade bread and a host of other things. When the farmer had delivered the box, he went back out and got a cord of wood. Finally, after a very hearty breakfast, he insisted Dad take a ten-dollar bill.

Almost every day Dad reminded us that "God is the Provider."

And my experience throughout adult life has confirmed it. "I have never seen the righteous forsaken nor their children begging bread." (Psalm 37:25) The Bible said it. But Dad and Mom showed me it was true.

~John Edmund Haggai
*Chicken Soup for the Christian Family Soul*

# The Piano

*Coins are round: Sometimes they roll to you, sometimes to others.*
*~Folk Saying*

During the early 1990s, being a Christian recording artist sometimes felt like one big struggle in a world of extremes. I would stand on stage in front of spotlights and thousands of people, only to go back to the hotel room with my family, wondering if anyone really cared about what I did at all. I would fall into bed in a small room shared by six, with one bathroom and suitcases piled everywhere.

We put on large contemporary Christian concerts in churches all over the country. I stepped into some of the most beautiful buildings equipped with state of the art furnishings and accoutrements, only to feel like I was on the outside looking in. For two hours I was the center of attention—lights dimmed, music played and God's presence filled all of our lives. Then moments after the concert ended, we packed it all up, rolled it out the back door into our trailer and disappeared down a lonely highway into the silence of the night.

I used to walk around those big, empty, church auditoriums as everyone scurried to get set up, wondering how they did it. How did these churches acquire all the wonderful facilities and resources they needed to make a difference in people's lives? What was the secret? I was doing the same thing they were, only I did it on the road and my "congregation" changed every night. I wondered how anyone ever acquired the unabashed boldness to just stretch their hands open, stand before God and simply receive from his overflowing abundance. It was easier to just believe that everyone else must be doing something right, and I must be somehow flawed. Maybe if I tried harder, worked longer and suffered a little bit more, I would finally be "worthy" of receiving what I needed.

One afternoon between concerts, my husband and I walked into a huge music store filled with the most impressive collection of grand pianos I had ever seen. Row after row of black and ivory concert grands sat there waiting for someone with the gift of music in their soul to sit down and play them. I pulled a bench up to one of the pianos, touched the keys and smiled.

"Nice piano," I said to the salesclerk.

"Are you looking for a grand or a baby grand?" He perked up, thinking he had a customer.

"Oh me?" I laughed. "Well, I can't really buy a piano now," I said sheepishly.

My husband walked over and spoke up without hesitation. "Honey, you've been wanting a real piano for years. These are incredible instruments!"

I gave him the you-are-out-of-your-mind look.

"Let me show you a baby grand over here that's really special," the salesclerk said moving us to the back of the store.

My husband followed him excitedly. I trailed behind, dragging my feet, wishing we could just get out of there and save ourselves any further embarrassment. We didn't belong in an expensive music store. I felt like I was trespassing and any minute I was going to be found out.

"This is a brand-new baby grand," the salesclerk gushed. "It's the only one of its kind, and we're clearing it out. It's on sale—and I'll tell you, it's one of the most fabulous pianos I've ever seen."

"Sit down and play it, " my husband urged.

I wished he'd leave me alone. Why should I play it if I couldn't have it? To save face in front of the salesclerk, I sat down at the clean, white keys. They felt like smooth silk and sounded like a symphony. The salesclerk propped the lid open.

"Press the pedals and play hard," he said. "You can't believe how this thing resonates and fills up the whole room."

He was right. It was incredible. It moved and inspired me to just sit and play it in the store. I could have written a song right then and there.

"How much is it?" my husband asked casually—as if he had just won the lottery.

"It lists for ten thousand dollars, but since we're clearing it out, we're giving it away for only five thousand dollars." He grinned.

"Wow!" my husband cheered and turned smiling at me.

Wow yourself, I thought, rolling my eyes. What did it matter if it was five thousand or five million! We were struggling musicians who didn't have the money. I couldn't have this. I was nobody. We weren't the pastors with the big buildings. We didn't have a record company financing our tours. Who was I to spend that kind of money for a music ministry? Still, I wanted that piano, and my husband knew it.

"Let's put some money down on it and hold it," he whispered to me frantically. "If we can't pay for it in thirty days, then we won't get it, but let's take a step of faith and try."

He handed the salesclerk a check for $500.

The salesclerk smiled. "See you in thirty days!" he said, waving goodbye.

As the days passed, I wanted that piano more than anything. Each day on tour I started my day with prayer time, and from somewhere deep down in my spirit, faith rose. Unabashed boldness seemed to come out of nowhere and I talked to God.

"God, if I were a pastor, and I needed one of those million-dollar buildings to share my message, you would provide it without question. If I was a medical missionary, and the 'tool' I needed was an airplane, it would come to me. Well, God, I'm a musician, and that's a God-given calling as worthy and as important as any other calling. I'm not asking for a building or an airplane; I'm just asking for a piano to write my songs. I'm ready to believe that my gift of music is as important to you as the gift of being a pastor or a medical missionary or a brain surgeon. I know you won't fail me because I'm important, too."

Every morning I prayed that prayer and as I did, I began to realize that I was just as "worthy" as anyone else, because God had given me my musical gift. In a few weeks, I believed it wholeheartedly and the doubt that I didn't deserve anything began to fade. I began to tell my friends about the piano I had "on hold."

Our concert tour ended twenty-nine days later. As we pulled into the driveway and started unloading our gear, my parents, who had been watching our house, appeared in the front yard with a letter in their hands.

"Here's the weirdest letter," they said, handing us the stack of mail. "It's addressed to you, honey, but your last name is spelled wrong, and there's no street address. I can't believe it got here."

I stared at the wrinkled, stained envelope with just my name and my small town and state scribbled across it.

I opened it up curiously and saw a yellow check inside. There was no letter or note, just the yellow check. As I unfolded it, I almost fainted. It was for $5,000, and it was made out to me from my great-uncle Britt. I hardly knew him and hadn't spoken to him in many years. My parents looked at the check in shock.

"Honey, what in the world?" my mother gasped.

"My piano," I whispered.

"Uncle Britt did that to me once," my dad laughed. "Sometimes he just likes to start getting rid of all the money he has. I guess your number came up today!" He giggled at his eccentric uncle and hugged me.

The next morning, exactly thirty days later, I called the music store, wired them the full amount of $4,500 and gave the leftover $500 to a worthy ministry. My shiny, white baby grand piano was delivered and placed in the middle of my living room where the sun streamed down on it from a skylight.

There are still times in my life when I feel like "I'm on the outside looking in," and I question whether I'm "worthy" enough. I sometimes wonder if God only blesses big names and big buildings. On those days I sit down in front of the most extravagant concert piano that I have ever played, and I remember that whether anybody else thinks so or not, God believes I am "worth it," and He got a ninety-year-old, eccentric great-uncle to help Him show me.

~Carla Riehl

*Chicken Soup for the Christian Woman's Soul*

# Stories of Faith

## The Power of Love

*It is not how much we do, but how much love we put in the doing.*
*It is not how much we give, but how much love we put in the giving.*
*~Mother Teresa*

# We Are All Jews Now

Viewed from high on the Rimrock cliffs that run along the northern edge of Billings, Montana, the city presents an attractive sight, a thriving metropolis nestling within the great open spaces of the American West. Citizens of Billings say it's a good, civilized place to live. They pride themselves on the quality of their schools and their strong family values.

So it came as a shock to many, when in November 1995, a series of hate crimes took place against minority groups in the city.

Whoever was responsible for these acts must have thought that their victims would be easy targets. Billings is predominantly white; Native Americans, African Americans and Jews make up only a small percentage of the population. But there are just enough of them to frighten and harass—or so the haters must have thought.

They mounted a series of nasty attacks. Graves were overturned in a Jewish cemetery. Offensive words and a swastika were scrawled on the house of a Native American woman. People worshipping at a black church were intimidated. A brick was heaved through the window of a Jewish child who displayed a menorah there.

But the white supremacists, or whoever they were, had reckoned without the citizens of Billings, who had an answer for them—and it wasn't what the hate-mongers were expecting. An alliance quickly emerged, spearheaded by churches, labor unions, the media and hundreds of local citizens.

The results were dramatic. Attendance at the black church rose steadily. People of many different ethnic backgrounds and faiths began to attend services there. Their message was clear: "We may be all different, but we are one also. Threaten any one of us and you threaten us all."

A similar spirit propelled volunteers to come together and repaint the house of Dawn Fast Horse, the Native American woman. This happened at amazing speed. Dawn had awoken one morning to see that her house had been defaced. By the evening, after two hundred people showed up to help, the house had been repainted.

When it came to the incident of the brick being thrown through the window of the Jewish child, an interfaith group quickly had a creative idea. They recalled the example of the Danes during World War II. When the Nazis tried to round up Danish Jews into concentration camps for subsequent extermination, the Danish people worked quickly, within a two-week period, to transport almost every Danish Jew to safety in Sweden until the end of the war.

So the people of Billings organized, and a campaign began. Everyone pitched in, including the local newspaper, which printed a Hanukkah page, including a full-color representation of a menorah. Thousands of Billings residents cut the paper menorah out and displayed it in their windows. By late December, driving around Billings was a remarkable experience. Nearly ten thousand people were displaying those paper menorahs in their windows, and the menorahs remained in place throughout the eight days of Hanukkah. It was a brilliant answer to the hate-mongers: A town that had a few Jews was saying with one collective voice, "We are all Jews now."

The story of what happened in Billings quickly spread, inspiring a national movement called "Not in Our Town." That Jewish child who had so innocently displayed her menorah in the window helped set in motion a chain of events that affirmed all over America the liberating principle of unity in diversity.

Not for nothing does a menorah have many candles flickering on a single stand.

~Bryan Aubrey
*Chicken Soup for the Jewish Soul*

# On the Rocks

*We are here not only to learn about love,*
*but to also support and teach our fellow travelers on this journey.*
*~Mary Manin Morressey*

The view high up in the Colorado Rocky Mountains was breathtaking. All around us the mountains were snow-capped, even though it was July.

I was on an outing, but it was not a pleasant one. My girlfriend, Paula, was upstream; I was downstream. I should have been delightedly skipping flat stones across the stream, but instead I sat on a huge boulder watching the crystal-clear water rushing over the rocks. And that suited me just fine.

Once, it had been so much fun to be together—I thought that I might be falling in love. But today Paula was acting strangely. This was supposed to be a wonderful, exhilarating date—the surroundings were spectacular. Yet I agonized over Paula's silent treatment of me. It seemed that a wall of ice had been building between us, and I couldn't melt it.

Confused and feeling rejected, I pulled a small pocket edition of the Bible from my back pocket. I wanted to read something to get my mind off my pain. The previous day I had stopped reading in the middle of a chapter. Heaving a sigh, I found the place where I had stopped reading. Half-heartedly I continued: "Love your enemies."

Enemies? I perked up as I read. That's Paula. Look how she was acting toward me! It went on to say, "Do good to those who mistreat you." Yes, she sure was mistreating me. Her rotten behavior toward me made me want to withdraw. Who needed that kind of pain?

As I continued reading, this verse really caught my attention: "Give and it will be given to you... for with the measure you use, it will be measured to you."

My focus had been on myself. I felt justified in my anger. Paula had made it plain to me by her coldness that our relationship was over. After all that I had done for her, she was putting our relationship into a deep freeze.

"Give, and it will be given to you." As the mountain stream cascaded over the rocks, thoughts rushed through my mind about the nature of true friendship. Even when hurt or misunderstood, a true friend reaches out to bridge the gap. A true friend is a giver, not a taker.

I was appalled at my own self-pity. My focus had been on "enemies," but now I realized it was better to focus on "love." "Melt that ice—starting from my side of the wall," I mumbled to myself. It would definitely be difficult to begin acting kindly toward Paula. She might totally reject me or hurt me even more. I decided the risk would be worth it.

More than an hour had elapsed since we had parted. As I searched for her, I finally saw her way upstream, sitting on the rocks near the loud, gurgling water. She didn't notice me because she was facing the other way, and the roar of the rushing stream drowned out my steps.

When I got within ten feet of her and looked at the back of her head, I thought, I am too nervous to open my heart to her. I retreated to the trees along the bank. My nervousness was eating me alive.

I tried approaching her a second time, but retreated to the trees again with my self-respect at an all-time low. But the verse kept flooding my mind: "Give, and it will be given to you." That gave me courage, but not quite enough. I knew that if I tried a third time, I would chicken out again. Then it hit me—get her attention from a distance. If she sees me, I will have to go talk with her.

I shouted, rustled some trees and banged some branches. Have you ever tried to make a noise louder than a roaring mountain stream? It's impossible. So I decided to throw some stones—not at her, but near her so she would turn around and see me.

It worked. When she turned and noticed me, I ventured out onto the rocks where she was sitting.

"Hi," I said. The lump in my throat felt as big as the boulder I sat down on next to her. "Mind if I join you for a few minutes?"

"No, I don't mind," she replied with a surprised look on her face.

"What have you been doing?" It was awkward, but I couldn't come up with anything better.

"Oh, thinking. What have you been doing?"

"Reading. May I show you what I read?" I was sure that she could hear my heart pounding in my chest.

"Sure."

I pulled out my Bible and began to read: "Love your enemies." I wanted to make some comment, but I was afraid I would lose my composure. "Give, and it will be given to you." I cleared my throat.

I stammered, "For the past few days, whenever I tried to communicate with you, I felt as if there were a wall of ice between us. You may never want to see me again, but I want to let you know my innermost feelings toward you. I care a lot about you and want to be your friend. If you don't want to date anymore, I'll be disappointed, but I still want to be your friend."

I paused, waiting for an angry rebuttal. What I received was a surprise.

"Would you like me to tell you what I have been thinking?" Paula asked.

"Yes! What have you been thinking?"

"I have started to like you, but I was afraid that you would reject me. My former boyfriend really hurt me, and I did not want to go through that kind of pain again. So, to protect my heart, I have been keeping you away. I'm sorry. Will you forgive me?"

Right there on the rocks we began to break through our barriers of fear. The wall of ice melted. Oh, how easy it is to think the worst about someone, and so difficult to think the best. Building the foundation of a close relationship takes courage, but the lesson I received next to that mountain stream was this: Seek to be a trusted friend, and keep taking the risk to communicate with honesty and humility.

Our experience on the rocks was wonderful. So wonderful that six months later, sitting in a romantic restaurant in Atlanta, Georgia, I asked Paula to marry me—to be my best friend for life.

On our wedding day, we exchanged rings. Inscribed inside each of our rings are the words, "Give, and it will be given to you."

Whenever I look at my ring, I am reminded to be a giver, not a taker. And that simple thought has made all the difference in our sixteen years of marriage.

~Dick Purnell
*Chicken Soup for the Single's Soul*

# The Racking Horse

The first time Bart told me about his horse, Dude, I knew their bond had been something special. But I never suspected Dude would deliver a wonderful gift to me.

Growing up on a one-hundred-year-old family farm in Tennessee, Bart loved all animals. But Dude, the chestnut-colored quarter horse Bart received when he turned nine, became his favorite. Years later when Bart's father sold Dude, Bart grieved in secret.

Even before I met and married Bart, I knew all about grieving in secret, too. Because of my dad's job, our family relocated every year. Deep inside, I wished we could stay in one place, where I could have deep, lasting friendships. But I never said anything to my parents. I didn't want to hurt them. Yet sometimes I wondered if even God could keep track of us.

One summer evening in 1987, as Bart and I glided on our front porch swing, my husband suddenly blurted out, "Did I ever tell you that Dude won the World Racking Horse Championship?"

"Rocking horse championship?" I asked.

"Racking," Bart corrected, smiling gently. "It's a kind of dancing horses do. Takes lots of training. You use four reins. It's pretty hard." Bart gazed at the pasture. "Dude was the greatest racking horse ever."

"Then why'd you let your dad sell him?" I probed.

"I didn't know he was even thinking about it," Bart explained. "When I was seventeen, I'd started a short construction job down in Florida. I guess Dad figured I wouldn't be riding anymore, so he sold

Dude without even asking me. Running a horse farm means you buy and sell horses all the time.

"I've always wondered if that horse missed me as much as I've missed him. I've never had the heart to try to find him. I couldn't stand knowing if something bad...."

Bart's voice trailed off.

After that, few nights passed without Bart mentioning Dude. My heart ached for him. I didn't know what to do. Then one afternoon, while I walked through the pasture, a strange thought came to me. In my heart, a quiet voice said, "Lori, find Dude for Bart."

How absurd! I knew nothing about horses, certainly not how to find and buy one. That was Bart's department.

The harder I tried to dismiss the thought, the stronger it grew. I did not dare mention it to anyone except God. Each day I asked him to guide me.

On a Saturday morning, three weeks after that first "find Dude" notion, a new meter reader, Mr. Parker, stopped by while I was working in the garden. We struck up a friendly conversation. When he mentioned he'd once bought a horse from Bart's dad, I interrupted.

"You remember the horse's name?" I asked.

"Sure do," Mr. Parker said. "Dude. Paid twenty-five hundred dollars for him."

I wiped the dirt from my hands and jumped up, barely catching my breath.

"Do you know what happened to him?" I asked.

"Yep. I sold him for a good profit."

"Where's Dude now?" I asked. "I need to find him."

"That'd be impossible," Mr. Parker explained. "I sold that horse years ago. He might even be dead by now."

"But could you... would you be willing to try to help me find him?" After I explained the situation, Mr. Parker stared at me for several seconds. Finally, he agreed to join the search for Dude, promising not to say anything to Bart.

Each Friday for almost a year, I phoned Mr. Parker to see if his sleuthing had turned up anything. Each week his answer was the same. "Sorry, nothing yet."

One Friday I called Mr. Parker with another idea. "Could you at least find one of Dude's babies for me?"

"Don't think so," he said, laughing. "Dude was a gelding."

"That's fine," I said. "I'll take a gelding baby."

"You really do need help." Mr. Parker explained that geldings are unable to sire. He seemed to double his efforts to help. Several weeks later, he phoned me on a Monday.

"I found him," he shouted. "I found Dude."

"Where?" I wanted to jump through the phone.

"On a farm in Georgia," Mr. Parker said. "A family bought Dude for their teenage son. But they can't do anything with the horse. In fact, they think Dude's crazy. Maybe dangerous. Bet you could get him back real easy."

Mr. Parker was right. I called the family in Rising Fawn, Georgia, and made arrangements to buy Dude back for three hundred dollars. I struggled to keep my secret until the weekend. On Friday, I met Bart at the front door after work.

"Will you go for a ride with me?" I asked in my most persuasive voice. "I have a surprise for you."

"Honey," Bart protested, "I'm tired."

"Please, Bart, I've packed a picnic supper. It'll be worth the ride. I promise."

Bart got into the Jeep. As I drove, my heart thumped so fast I thought it'd burst as I chatted about family matters.

"Where are we going?" Bart asked after thirty minutes.

"Just a bit farther," I said.

Bart sighed. "Honey, I love you. But I can't believe I let you drag me off."

I didn't defend myself. I'd waited too long to ruin things now. However, by the time I steered off the main highway and onto a gravel road, Bart was so aggravated that he wasn't speaking to me. When I turned from the gravel road to a dirt trail, Bart glared.

"We're here," I said, stopping in front of the third fence post.

"Here where? Lori, have you lost your mind?" Bart barked.

"Stop yelling," I said. "Whistle."

"What?" Bart shouted.

"Whistle," I repeated. "Like you used to... for Dude... just whistle. You'll understand in a minute."

"Well... I... this is crazy," Bart sputtered as he got out of the Jeep.

Bart whistled. Nothing happened.

"Oh, God," I whispered, "don't let this be a mistake."

"Do it again," I prodded.

Bart whistled once more, and we heard a sound in the distance. What was it? I could barely breathe.

Bart whistled again. Suddenly, over the horizon, a horse came at a gallop. Before I could speak, Bart leapt over the fence.

"Dude!" he yelled, running towards his beloved friend. I watched the blur of horse and husband meet like one of those slow-motion reunion scenes on television. Bart hopped up on his pal, stroking his mane and patting his neck.

Immediately, a sandy-haired, tobacco-chewing teenage boy and his huffing parents crested the hill.

"Mister," the boy yelled. "What are you doing? That horse is crazy. Can't nobody do nothing with 'im."

"No," Bart boomed. "He's not crazy. He's Dude."

To the amazement of everyone, at Bart's soft command to the unbridled horse, Dude threw his head high and began racking. As the horse pranced through the pasture, no one spoke. When Dude finished dancing for joy, Bart slid off of him.

"I want Dude home," he said.

"I know," I said with tears in my eyes. "All the arrangements have been made. We can come back and get him."

"Nope," Bart insisted. "He's coming home tonight."

I phoned my in-laws, and they arrived with a horse trailer. We paid for Dude and headed home.

Bart spent the night in the barn. I knew he and Dude had a lot of catching up to do. As I looked out the bedroom window, the moon cast a warm glow over the farm. I smiled, knowing my husband and I now had a wonderful story to tell our future children and grandchildren.

"Thank you, Lord," I whispered. Then the truth hit me. I'd searched longer for Dude than I'd ever lived in one place. God had used the process of finding my husband's beloved horse to renew my trust in the friend who sticks closer than a brother.

"Thank you, Lord," I whispered again as I fell asleep. "Thank you for never losing track of Dude—or me."

~Lori Bledsoe

*Chicken Soup for the Unsinkable Soul*

# Letters of Hope

*Hope is some extraordinary spiritual grace that God gives us to control our fears, not to oust them.*
*~Vincent McNabb*

"Love is patient, love is kind.... It always protects, always trusts, always hopes, always perseveres." (1 Corinthians 13:4,7). Our Gran Lindsay, who lives in Burlington, Ontario, has this scripture printed on a magnet on her fridge. To visitors it is only a magnet; to our family it is a gentle reminder of a cherished family story.

It all began with a message in the town newspaper: "For Lindsay—Darling, I am well. Hope you and the children are fine." The year was 1943. A ham radio operator had picked up the fragmented message and directed it to the small-town newspaper.

Martha Lindsay had waited thirteen long months for word from the Red Cross that her husband, William Lindsay, had survived the sinking of the HMS Exeter on March 1, 1942. She did her best to stay busy with the children, always keeping William in her prayers. One afternoon, the Red Cross finally contacted her with the news that she had been praying for—a William Lindsay had been located and was currently a prisoner of war.

Martha's heart soared: William was alive! She had never given up hope. The Red Cross told Martha to begin writing messages to William—short messages, no more than twenty-five words, on a plain, white postcard—and forwarding them to Geneva. From there, the Red Cross would try to get the postcards to William.

Only one postcard a month was permitted. Martha began by telling William about the antics of their children, Billy and Catherine, who had been babies the last time he saw them. She also did her best to express her love and devotion to her husband on the small, white postcards. In just twenty-five words, she kept reminding him that he was loved. Two and a half agonizing years came and went without receiving an answer from William, but Martha's faith and hope never faltered.

One September morning in 1945, as Martha was getting ready to take the children to school, the mail carrier delivered a small scrap of paper through the mail slot. It had no envelope and no stamp. As she turned the paper over her heart began to pound. Soon her eyes filled with tears as she recognized William's handwriting: "Martha, I've been released. I'm coming home."

On a beautiful day in October 1945, William Lindsay returned home to his family. After their tears and joy had subsided, Martha asked William if he had received her cards. Sadly, she learned that not one card had found its way to him in the prisoner-of-war camp.

Shortly after William's return home, there was a knock at the door one day. Martha answered and found a young sailor standing in the doorway.

"Excuse me, are you Martha Lindsay?" he asked.

"Yes I am," she replied.

"Was your husband a prisoner of war?"

"Yes," she whispered.

With tears in his eyes, he introduced himself. "My name is William Lindsay. I was a prisoner of war, too." He reached into his pocket and, very gently, handed her thirty tiny white postcards tied in a ribbon.

"I received one of these every month," the sailor told her. "They gave me the hope that helped me to survive. From the bottom of my heart I thank you."

Martha just as gently placed the cards back in his hands, and he held them to his heart.

"Love is patient, love is kind.... It always protects, always trusts, always hopes, always perseveres" (1 Corinthians 13:4,7).

~Shelley McEwan
*Chicken Soup for the Canadian Soul*

# The Temples Are Burning

In June 1999, I was vacationing on a quiet little island in Croatia with a former college roommate. It was the first vacation I had taken since my ordination and appointment as assistant rabbi at Congregation B'nai Israel in Sacramento.

For Shabbat, my Catholic friend and I did candles, Kiddush and motzi over dinner, and we were going to spend the rest of Shabbat sitting on the beach. (There were very few synagogues in Croatia.)

At midnight, I decided to call a congregant of mine in California, where it was three o'clock in the afternoon. She was ill, and I wanted to check on her welfare. But the conversation we had that night was not what I had been expecting.

"The temple's been firebombed," she said.

"What?"

"Ours and two others—Beth Shalom and Kenesset Israel. I don't know any more yet. It happened in the middle of the night. My husband's at the congregation now trying to find out more."

Shock hit me like a tidal wave. Three synagogues firebombed? In America? I couldn't believe it! Early the following morning, I learned that the attacks had started at about 3:00 A.M. at Congregation B'nai Israel in Land Park. This was followed within forty-five minutes by fires set at Congregation Beth Shalom and Kenesset Israel Torah Center.

In addition to the damage to the temples, the seven thousand-volume library at B'nai Israel had been utterly destroyed. Many of the books were rare and irreplaceable.

I was devastated, even more so when I was told that my own office had been burned down. I had a small collection of prayer-books from pre-World War II Germany and Hungary, some of which were given to me by a former landlord who was a Holocaust survivor. I also had my grandparents' Judaica library in my office. I was horrified that books given to me to protect had been destroyed in a hate crime.

It was horrible to hear all this news when I was sitting on an island in the middle of the Adriatic, so far from home. I felt lonely and desolate, and I could hardly imagine what everyone at home was experiencing.

I made immediate plans to return. During the long, lonely journey from Europe I leaned more—that the damage to all three synagogues was estimated at around two and a half million dollars, with two million of that damage having been down to B'nai Israel alone. I also learned that while the FBI was investigating, at that time there were still no suspects.

There was one moment of elation: I learned that my office had not in fact been burned down, although it had suffered severe smoke damage. Another piece of news that cheered me was that in spite of the devastation, not a single Torah in any of the three temples was destroyed. The Aron Hakodesh, the Ark of the Covenant, the chest that holds the scrolls, had held firm.

I arrived only half an hour before a community service was due to begin. I'd just gone twenty-eight hours without sleep, but nothing would stop me from attending.

I entered the Sacramento Community Theater having no idea what to expect. When I walked out onto the stage, what I saw took my breath away. Over 200 people sat on the stage. It was like a Who's Who of Sacramento and beyond: there were state officials and legislators, city council members, the chief of police, representatives from the ATF and the fire department, people from the governor's office, and clergy from every faith and ethnic background in the entire Sacramento community.

Then the curtain opened, and I was even more astonished. The theater was packed! About 4,500 people were in attendance, including those who crowded into overflow rooms, where they watched on a big screen.

In the crowd were Hispanic Americans, Asian Americans and African Americans; Muslims, Catholics and Protestants from many different denominations; Buddhists and more, as well as people who might have called themselves non-believers, but who believed that victims of cowardly attacks in the night should not suffer in isolation.

It was the most inspiring program I have ever experienced. The outpouring of love and support was overwhelming. Speaker after speaker rose to express their concern, their sorrow and their hope. Each was met with thunderous applause and a standing ovation. Everyone in that theater that night was standing shoulder to shoulder with the Jews of Sacramento, and saying, each in his or her own way, "You are not alone."

That night when I came home, I saw signs in my neighbors' windows that said, "United We Stand." That gesture touched me deeply. As I thanked each of them, I found out that up to then they hadn't even known I was a rabbi. It was a small sign of how the community was coming together in new, positive ways as a result of the tragedy.

When I was finally able to get into my office, I broke down and cried for the first time. The smell was suffocating. Everything was covered with a thick layer of smoke and ash.

But I was deeply moved that people drove in from as far away as Tahoe, the San Francisco Bay Area and Bakersfield to deliver donations and books and to express sympathy.

Although the work has been endless, our congregation and community are optimistic. Money and offers of help have poured in from all across the country. When the Secretary of Housing, Andrew Cuomo, came to visit, he urged us to rebuild bigger and better. And that is what we intend to do. We will not hide. We will continue to teach, to worship and celebrate our Jewish heritage. It was because of these great waves of support that I and my congregants soon came to see the frightening attacks as an isolated event and not reflective of the larger community. Whoever had perpetrated them had zero support in the community. And the attacks weren't like so much of the anti-Semitism of the past. Following this incident, the U.S. government was quick to help. Congress unanimously passed a resolution condemning the attacks; the government promised low-interest loans, and money was promised for programs in Sacramento that would build understanding between different faiths and ethnic groups.

It may sound corny, but because of what happened, I feel proud to live in America. I am deeply grateful for the astonishing outpouring of support from non-Jews. It is overwhelming to me that so many would care, and so deeply. I am grateful also to be a rabbi. You get to see the best in people—my congregation, and the entire Sacramento community, have been so wonderful, jumping in to rebuild and do whatever else they can.

In quiet moments now, I reflect that although people who are filled with hatred may burn down temples and libraries, the human heart, in its capacity to love and to reach out to others in distress, will always endure. As I was taught as a child, love is a more powerful weapon than hate.

~Rabbi Mona Alfi as told to Bryan Aubrey
*Chicken Soup for the Jewish Soul*

# A Gift from the Woman in White

*I have found the paradox that if I love until it hurts,*
*then there is no hurt, but only more love.*
*~Mother Teresa*

Jim Castle was tired when he boarded his plane in Cincinnati that night in 1981. The forty-five-year-old management consultant had put on a weeklong series of business workshops, and now he sank gratefully into his seat ready for the flight home to Kansas City.

As more passengers entered, the plane hummed with conversation, mixed with the sound of bags being stowed. Then, suddenly, people fell silent. The quiet moved slowly up the aisle like an invisible wake behind a boat. Jim craned his head to see what was happening, and his mouth dropped open.

Walking up the aisle were two nuns clad in simple white habits bordered in blue. He recognized the familiar face of one at once—the wrinkled skin, the eyes warmly intent. This was a face he'd seen in newscasts and on the cover of *Time*. The two nuns halted, and Jim realized that his seat companion was going to be Mother Teresa.

As the last few passengers settled in, Mother Teresa and her companion pulled out rosaries. Each decade of the beads was a different color, Jim noticed. The decades represented various areas of the world, Mother Teresa told him later, and added, "I pray for the poor and dying on each continent."

The airplane taxied to the runway, and the two women began to pray, their voices a low murmur. Though Jim considered himself a ho-hum Catholic who went to church mostly out of habit, inexplicably he found himself joining in.

By the time they murmured the final prayer, the plane had reached cruising altitude.

Mother Teresa turned toward him. For the first time in his life, Jim understood what people meant when they spoke of a person possessing an aura. As she gazed at him, a sense of peace filled him; he could no more see it than he could see the wind, but he felt it just as surely as he felt a warm summer breeze. "Young man," she inquired, "do you say the rosary often?"

"No, not really," he admitted.

She took his hand, while her eyes probed his. Then she smiled. "Well, you will now." And she dropped her rosary into his palm.

An hour later Jim entered the Kansas City airport, where he was met by his wife, Ruth. "What in the world?" Ruth asked when she noticed the rosary in his hand. They kissed and Jim described his encounter. Driving home, he said, "I feel as if I met a true sister of God."

Nine months later, Jim and Ruth visited Connie, a friend of theirs for several years. Connie confided that she'd been told she had ovarian cancer. "The doctors say it's a tough case," said Connie, "but I'm going to fight it. I won't give up."

Jim clasped her hand. Then, after reaching into his pocket, he gently twined Mother Teresa's rosary around her fingers. He told her the story and said, "Keep it with you, Connie. It may help." Although Connie wasn't Catholic, her hand closed willingly around the small plastic beads. "Thank you," she whispered. "I hope I can return it."

More than a year passed before Jim saw Connie again. This time, face glowing, she hurried toward him and handed him the rosary. "I carried it with me all year," she said. "I've had surgery and have been on chemotherapy, too. Last month the doctors did second-look surgery, and the tumor's gone. Completely!" Her eyes met Jim's. "I knew it was time to give the rosary back."

In the fall of 1987, Ruth's sister, Liz, fell into a deep depression after her divorce. She asked Jim if she could borrow the rosary, and when he sent it, she hung it over her bedpost in a small velvet bag.

"At night I held on to it, just physically held on. I was so lonely and afraid," she says. "Yet when I gripped that rosary, I felt as if I held a loving hand." Gradually, Liz pulled her life together, and she mailed the rosary back. "Someone else may need it," she said.

Then one night in 1988, a stranger telephoned Ruth. She'd heard about the rosary from a neighbor and asked if she could borrow it to take to the hospital where her mother lay in a coma. The family hoped the rosary might help their mother die peacefully.

A few days later, the woman returned the beads. "The nurses told me a coma patient can still hear," she said, "so I explained to my mother that I had Mother Teresa's rosary and that when I gave it to her, she could let go; it would be all right. Then I put the rosary in her hand. Right away, we saw her face relax! The lines smoothed out until she looked so peaceful, so young." The woman's voice caught. "A few minutes later she was gone." Fervently, she gripped Ruth's hands. "Thank you."

Is there special power in those humble beads? Or is the power of the human spirit simply renewed in each person who borrows the rosary? Jim only knows that requests continue to come, often unexpectedly. He always responds, though whenever he lends the rosary, he says, "When you're through needing it, send it back. Someone else may need it."

Jim's own life has changed, too, since his unexpected meeting on the airplane. When he realized Mother Teresa carries everything she owns in a small bag, he made an effort to simplify his own life. "I try to remember what really counts—not money or titles or possessions, but the way we love others," he says.

~Barbara Bartocci
*Chicken Soup for the Working Woman's Soul*

# A Visit from Mom

Several of us were standing around the nurses' station in the surgical intensive care unit (ICU) where we worked, when I asked the question. "Working in ICU, have you ever felt like someone else was in the room when there was no one else there you could see?"

Another smiled and added, "Or smelled perfume in the room of a patient who was dying when no one else had been in there?"

And another, "Or have you passed by someone in the hallway, turned around and there was no one there?"

We all looked at each other and laughed. "I thought I was the only one," I said.

Explanations were offered. Maybe it was because we had to spend so much time around people who were straddling the threshold between life and death—or maybe it was just stress.

"I think it's real," one of the nurses said soberly, "and has something to do with the kind of love that doesn't end when life does." She went on to tell this story:

A man in his early twenties was admitted to the ICU after a large piece of machinery at work had crushed his foot. He needed immediate surgery, and she quickly began to prepare him for the operating room. She had just started to go through her preoperative procedures when an anxious woman entered the ICU, asking about the young man.

"Is he all right?" the woman asked.

"He's stable and sleeping quietly," the nurse replied.

"Is he in pain?" the woman cried.

"No," the nurse reassured her. "They gave him some very strong medication in the emergency room when he first arrived."

"Is he going to be okay?" the woman asked, her face still creased with worry.

"He's young and healthy, and he should recover wonderfully after the surgery," the nurse assured her.

The woman looked somewhat relieved but asked to see him. "I'm his mother," she explained.

The nurse gave the woman a sympathetic look. "I understand your anxiety, but I have to prepare him for surgery. If you give me five minutes, I promise to let you see him before he is taken to the operating room."

"But he's all right?" the mother repeated. "He's going to be all right?"

"He's going to require a lot of physical therapy, but he looks like a hard worker and I'm sure he will do great."

Relief filled the woman's face. "Thank you so much for taking such good care of my son," she said. "I'll wait outside."

When the nurse had finished her duties, she walked down to the waiting room as promised to get the mother. No one was there. She checked the bathrooms and the vending machines, but still there was no sign of the woman who had been so anxious to see her son. The nurse was about to have the woman paged when a group of the man's coworkers walked up to ask about their friend.

"You can go in and see him for just a few minutes," the nurse replied. "I have to find his mother."

"Ma'am, he doesn't have a mother," one of the men said, looking at her strangely.

"But a woman was here who said she was his mother. I just talked to her," the nurse insisted.

"You don't understand," another coworker said. "His mother died a few years ago. All he has is a cousin. We called him and told him what happened, but we didn't call anyone else."

The nurse was baffled but went back to her work. A little while later, while the young man was in surgery, his cousin arrived and asked about him. The nurse updated him, and then, as he turned to leave, she called:

"By the way, a woman came by and asked about him. She said she was his mother."

The cousin stood motionless for a moment. "What did this woman look like?" he finally asked, and as the nurse described the lady, he slowly shook his head and smiled in disbelief and wonder. "Thank you," was all he said, and left.

When the nurse asked her coworkers later about the woman who had come into the ICU, no one remembered seeing her at all. She never showed up again.

For a minute, we were all silent, reflecting on the nurse's story. Was it possible? Who can really say? All I know is that from my experience as a nurse, I no longer doubt that love goes beyond death. Or that a mother looks out for her children for as long as she lives—and longer.

~Patricia A. Walters-Fischer
*Chicken Soup for the Mother's Soul 2*

# Heaven's Very Special Child

*If you don't like something change it; if you can't change it, change the way you think about it.*
*~Mary Engelbreit*

We were on our way to visit an institution in 1954 with our three daughters: Mary, twelve, Joan, nine, and Ruth, eighteen months old. Because of little Ruth, handicapped since birth, we were making this sad and silent trip. We had been advised to place her in a special home. "It will be less of a burden," "Ruth will be better off with children like herself," "Your other children will have a home free of the care of a disabled person."

To break the silence, I flipped on the car radio and heard the voice of a former classmate. I remembered him as a boy without legs. He was now president of an organization employing persons who are disabled.

He told of his childhood and of a conversation with his mother. "When it was time for another handicapped child to be born," his mother explained, "the Lord and his counselors held a meeting to decide where he should be sent... where there would be a family to love him. Well, our family was chosen."

At this, my wife Edna leaned over and turned off the radio, her eyes shining with unshed tears. "Let's go home," she said.

I touched Ruth's tiny face. She looked like a beautiful symbol of innocence. I knew at that moment Ruth was given to us for a purpose. How miraculous it was that the voice of a friend, with whom I'd had no contact for twenty years, should that day speak to me. Mere coincidence? Or was it God's unseen hand helping us hold on to a little girl who would enrich our lives immeasurably in the years that followed?

That night, Edna awoke at three o'clock in the morning with thoughts that demanded to be written. A pad was on the night table, and in the morning we pieced her notes together into the poem, "Heaven's Very Special Child":

*A meeting was held quite far from Earth;*
*"It's time again for another birth."*
*Said the angels to the Lord above,*
*"This special child will need much love.*
*Her progress may seem very slow.*
*Accomplishments she may not show,*
*And she'll require extra care*
*From the folks she meets way down there.*
*She may not run or laugh or play,*
*Her thoughts may seem quite far away.*
*In many ways she won't adapt,*
*And she'll be known as handicapped.*
*So let's be careful where she's sent,*
*We want her life to be content.*
*Please, Lord, find the parents who*
*Will do a special job for you.*
*They will not realize right away*
*The leading role they're asked to play,*
*But with this child sent from above*
*Come stronger faith and richer love.*
*And soon they'll know the privilege given*
*In caring for this gift from heaven.*
*Their precious charge, so meek and mild,*
*Is heaven's very special child."*

~John and Edna Massimilla
*Chicken Soup for the Unsinkable Soul*

# Family

*The drama of birth is over. The cord is cut, the first cry heard: A new life begun.... The mother—seeing, hearing, perhaps touching her baby—scarcely notices the world around her, let alone how much her body aches. She just participated in a miracle.*

*~Carrol Dunham*

# You Can Be Right

*What is a friend? A single soul dwelling in two bodies.*
*~Aristotle*

Earl once told his younger sister, Liddy, "If you can hang on my back pocket, you can go anywhere I go, too." So Liddy, six years younger, always tagged along, even on Earl's dates. She once stowed away in the dusty back seat of his truck and popped up when he and his date arrived at the drive-in theater. As Liddy grew into a young beauty, Earl made sure all her suitors met his personal approval.

Even after their marriages, Earl and Liddy remained close. Years later, Liddy's husband, Kirby, when diagnosed with terminal cancer, said, "I won't worry about Liddy as long as Earl is alive."

After Kirby's death, Liddy withdrew from everyone, even Earl. He and his wife, Sue, recognized this as Liddy's way of grieving, but gradually their contact with Liddy diminished. As more time passed, it seemed harder to pick up the phone and call.

One February afternoon, Earl collapsed at work. At the hospital, the doctors told Sue it was a heart attack. They offered what they called a "clot buster" shot to open up the arteries around the heart. The shot worked, and Earl's heart attack lessened. After a successful angioplasty the next morning, the doctors told them, "All is well." Relieved and grateful, Earl and Sue went home to rest and recover.

Within twenty-four hours, Earl's entire body swelled. He returned to the hospital. With sinking hearts, Earl and Sue learned that 1 in

100,000 patients who receive the shot experience a side effect called "cholesterol showering." Instead of breaking up only the clots that caused Earl's heart attack, the medication made all the cholesterol in his body release into his bloodstream. The overload was causing all his organs to slowly shut down. One doctor on the medical team said they would have to amputate one limb at a time to try to save him. "I began wondering how much longer I had to live," says Earl. "Emotionally, Sue and I hit bottom. We were both so scared, we didn't know how to comfort each other."

At home a few days later, Sue and Earl received a special phone call. It was Earl's sister Liddy. "I heard about Earl.... I wish I knew what to do. If only Kirby were here...." Liddy's voice broke with little sobs. "May I come over to see you? I'd understand if you said no.... Would you ask Earl?"

Sue gently replied, "I don't need to. We both want to see you—as soon as you can get here." Liddy surprised Earl and Sue by arriving at their home with all her children and grandchildren. Sue hugged each one as Earl watched from the couch where he lay. When Liddy greeted him she said, "It's been a long time, brother." Earl replied, "Give me a hug!" Receiving his hug, he whispered to her, "Can we put lost time behind us?"

"I'd like that," Liddy responded softly, tears brimming over her eyelids and streaming down her cheeks. She sat on the footstool beside him. "Can you forgive me for staying away for so long?"

"You know I can, Sis. I just want us to be brother and sister again, especially now," Earl said, reaching out his hand to wipe away her tears. Liddy grasped Earl's muscular, yet swollen hand and simply said, "I sure missed you."

In the following days, Earl's spirits were up. Not able to leave the house, he had time to rethink what was really important to him. "I realized that if I was going to die, I didn't want anyone I left behind to be angry with me," he says. He began calling friends and cousins he had not seen for years. Some had drifted out of his life for no particular reason. Others, though, carried grudges or hurt feelings. One man, for example, had not talked to Earl for twenty years because of a misunderstanding. Earl called him on the telephone and said, "I don't remember what we disagreed about, but whatever it was, you can be right. I don't want there to be any negative feelings between us." Every person he called came to visit him. One woman, suffering from severe physical pain of her own, came in a wheelchair to visit him during one of his hospital stays.

After many trips to the local hospital for tests and treatment, with only a medical file as thick as a phone book to show for it, Earl and Sue decided to travel to a nearby city to discuss Earl's case with a renowned kidney specialist. The specialist gave Earl a month to live.

Soon after, Earl's niece Ronda, one of Liddy's daughters who worked in the medical field, asked another famous kidney specialist his opinion of what her uncle was going through. This doctor offered a glimmer of hope. He instructed, "Tell your uncle to go to bed; it may take two years, but total rest might allow the cholesterol to filter out of his system naturally." Having exhausted all other options, or so it seemed, Earl agreed to stay in bed for as long as it would take.

Though they had no one to talk to who had survived this rare "cholesterol showering," Earl and Sue found comfort in the renewed friendships that Earl had initiated. Phone calls of support came daily. And since medicine offered no answers, everyone they knew agreed to pray.

Late one night, after months of resting and waiting, Sue begged Earl to try something new. She told him, "We've prayed for your health many times, but I've noticed that the Bible also talks about anointing sick people with oil and asking others to pray over them. Could we at least try?" She nervously awaited his answer, knowing that the Earl she knew before this ordeal would have never agreed. But, she hoped that with all he'd been through, he might be willing.

Sue was not disappointed. With Earl's approval, she called the minister at their church and asked him to come and anoint Earl with oil and pray for him. Though it was nearly 3:00 A.M., the minister and a deacon arrived, ready to do as Sue asked.

The next evening, the entire deacon board came. The members gathered around the bed where Earl was confined, and each took a turn praying. After everyone left, Earl and Sue knelt by their respective sides of the bed to continue praying.

On his knees, Earl realized, "What am I doing out of bed? I'm better!" His arms and legs no longer ached, and the swelling was gone. "When it dawned on us what had happened," Earl says, "we got so excited, we went into our backyard in our pajamas and danced together under the stars!

"I knew in my heart that I had a lot to celebrate: first, all my friends, and now, my health, too!"

Several years later, Earl, now in his late sixties, is in excellent health. More important, though, he says, "Facing death, I realized more than ever how deeply I care for my friends. And I no longer need to be 'right.' Standing by what I believe will always be important, but it doesn't mean I have to insist that everyone agree with me.

"Reaching out, forgiving and telling others, 'Look, you can be right,' didn't cost me a thing. It gained for me one of the greatest treasures this life offers: old friendships. And I got back my sister, too."

Now Earl and Sue talk to Liddy nearly every day. She is hanging on his back pocket again after all these years.

~Amy Seeger
*Chicken Soup for the Golden Soul*

# Missing the Boat

*The Lord is not slow in keeping his promise, as some understand slowness.*
*He is patient with you, not wanting anyone to perish,*
*but everyone to come to repentance.*
*~2 Peter 3:9*

In 1910, Abraham Bank, my great-grandfather, was impressed into the Russian army. At the time, he was twenty-one years old and had lived near Vilna in Latvia for his entire life. He was a qualified rabbi, shochet, and mohel.

The prospect of twenty-five years of mandatory military service was unthinkable to Abraham. So he decided to pack a few clothes and personal belongings and leave his hometown during the night. He promised his girlfriend, Rebecca, that he would write.

Abraham traveled via Finland to Stockholm, Sweden, where he worked for a while as a stevedore. He earned his passage to London where he continued to work. His goal was to earn enough money to follow in the footsteps of his brother, who had already emigrated to America.

Two years after leaving his home in Latvia, Abraham was finally able to buy a ticket on a ship leaving from Southampton that would take him from England to America.

Abraham ran into two difficulties. The first was the knowledge that he would not be able to get kosher food in the steerage class of the ship. The second was the trouble he would have in getting from

London to Southampton over Passover, as the holiday ended on the night before the ship would be boarding.

Finally, Abraham decided not to use his ticket. He remained in London for a few months and then emigrated to South Africa, where eight years later Rebecca joined him. It was not until 1987 that Abraham's descendants—his grandson (my father) and his family—made the move to America that Abraham had come so close to making seventy-five years earlier.

I have good cause to be grateful to Zeida for deciding not to use that ticket all those years ago. In fact, it might well have been the best decision he ever made. The name of the ship that steamed into the Atlantic that day was the Titanic.

~Tanya Bank
*Chicken Soup for the Jewish Soul*

# I'm Right Here with You, Honey

When I was a girl, if I'd had a difficult school day, my mother would call me into her bedroom shortly after I returned home. She'd be sitting on her bed, patting it and smiling at me until I sat down. She'd offer me a Hershey's Almond Joy bar from her secret cache (in her bottom-left lingerie drawer) and tell me that when I wanted to talk, she'd be there to listen. "I'm right here with you, Honey," she'd say.

And she was. Through grade school, high school, college, and into my twenties and thirties. Even when she was dying from ovarian cancer. I remember asking her in a moment of fear, "If there's a hereafter, will you find a way to stay in touch with me?"

She laughed and said, "What if you go first? I'll agree if you agree."

"Okay," I said, humoring her while still looking for reassurance. "Whoever goes first will contact the one left behind, but without scaring them, like turning on the lights without warning."

"Fine," she said. "But if you decide to turn on the lights for me, remember to turn them off before you float out of the room. You know how your father hates it when anyone leaves the lights on."

Three days after she died, I reflected on that conversation while I sat at my computer, writing in my journal. I smiled as I remembered her wacky sense of humor and then cried knowing I'd never hear her laugh again. My thoughts drifted. The next words I typed were a question, "Where are you, Mom?" As I sat there, the strangest thing happened: I heard my mother's voice inside my head, and felt her presence as if she were standing right next to me. I was scared, but equally curious, so I typed what she said as fast I could: "I'm right here with you, Honey. We have a book to write together. Whenever you're ready to write, I'm prepared to help."

When her voice faded back to my own thoughts, I sat there dumbfounded. I wasn't sure what to think; overwhelmed, I decided that I just missed her a lot and this was my mind's way of comforting me.

A year after Mom died, I moved from Milwaukee to San Diego. With the moving and rebuilding of my speaking business on the West Coast, I didn't write in my journal as often and forgot about the book idea until I woke up from a dream in the middle of a summer night two years later. In the dream, Mom and I were sitting at her kitchen table. She said to me, "It's time to start writing the book. It will be a book of questions that daughters will ask their mothers to help them know their mothers better and to help them make healthier choices so they don't end up like me. I will help you write it." Startled and equally excited by the clarity of her message, I wrote down the dream. As I fell back asleep, I shook my head, thinking how preposterous it all sounded. I'd heard countless stories of how near-impossible it is for an unknown first-time author to find a publisher. Now add to that a real ghostwriter. No one would take me seriously—except my mother!

My first phone call of the morning was from my friend Laurie, whom I hadn't talked with for quite a while—who also just happened to be a literary agent. What a wild coincidence! When she asked, "What's new?" I told her about the dream.

Laurie said, "I think it's a great idea. I've been trying to record my mother's history with her all summer. I could use that book. If you write the proposal, I'd love to sell it."

I hung up the phone and burst into tears. I was thrilled that Laurie believed in me enough to suggest I write a book, but I wasn't sure it was a book I could write. My mother wasn't alive, and I wasn't even a mother. Who would take me seriously? "Mom!" I cried out in frustration.

"Write the book," I heard back in my mind.

My mother's idea continued to nudge me; I continued to question it while encountering a far bigger challenge than writing a book. After my annual fall checkup, my gynecologist told me I had cervical cancer and would need a hysterectomy. I was forty-three years old. I thought about dying. I thought about my mother's ovarian cancer. I thought about my mother's hysterectomy when she was only thirty-eight.

Why didn't I think to ask her about that? Why didn't we ever talk about it? If only I'd known more...

What irony, I thought. I need this book I'm supposed to write!

As I recovered from surgery with no sign of cancer, I felt a new appreciation for my mother and her health challenges that previously I had dismissed—her headaches, her mood swings, her fears about being ill. Now I had them all. I began incorporating my experience and insights into my speaking engagements. Women seemed to identify even more strongly with what I was saying about making healthier choices. I continued to share more memories of love and healing between my mother and me. One story in particular, "Squeeze My Hand and I'll Tell You That I Love You," seemed to touch women in a special way. I heard my mother's voice gently encouraging me, "Write the story down."

I wrote the story and sent it to *Chicken Soup for the Mother's Soul*. After submitting it, tired of being all talk and little action, I made an agreement with my mother's spirit and said, "If this story is accepted in *Chicken Soup*, I'll write the book you've been telling me to write. But if it isn't accepted, I'm letting this idea go and moving on with my life." I thought this was a good compromise. I'd been told that *Chicken Soup for the Soul* books receive thousands of submissions, so I knew the odds were not in my favor; it would take a miracle for my story to be published.

To my great surprise, nine months later, that miracle arrived. On April 11, 1997, while sitting at my office desk, I received a phone call from the Chicken Soup for the Soul office — my story had been accepted! Now, this alone was enough to send chills up and down my spine, but what was even more amazing was when I looked at my calendar. That day, April 11, was the sixth anniversary of my mother's death! I glanced at the framed photo sitting next to my computer, of Mom smiling. I realized then that writing "our" book was not an option — it was a calling.

It's been three years since "Squeeze My Hand and I'll Tell You That I Love You" was published in *Chicken Soup for the Mother's Soul*. Many more challenges, gifts, divine guidance and miracles have arrived, including the publication by a major publisher of our book, *My Mother, My Friend: The Ten Most Important Things to Talk About with Your Mother*.

I have come to believe that on a spiritual level, *My Mother, My Friend* completes a contract I made with my mother to help me and all women respect, appreciate and trust ourselves and our mothers, and to remember that their guidance is always with us — in life or in death. What a blessing.

~Mary Marcdante
*Chicken Soup for the Mother's Soul 2*

# Lavender Roses

"I can't get these lavender roses to grow," Papi complained to me one afternoon.

My father had been working all morning cultivating his rose garden, which in the bright light of this warm July day looked almost too lovely to be real.

"Don't worry about it, José," my mother advised him. "You already have so many beautiful shades of roses."

My mother worried about Papi's constant preoccupation with the perfection of things; my father's high blood pressure and fifty years of smoking his beloved handrolled Cuban tobacco gave her reason to be alarmed.

"I promised your mother lavender roses for her birthday," he explained to me. "I've been promising her for the last five years, but aquí no brota nada... nada de nada..."

My father was not a perfect man, but he was a man de palabra, a man who kept his promises. He had promised my mother lavender roses for her birthday, and Papi had little time left to work. He swore he would grow the lavender roses for my mother if it was the last thing he did.

Papi and Mami had come to this country from San Juan, Puerto Rico, in 1927. When Papi told my mother that he wanted to move to the United States, she put up quite a fight (family legend has it that she smashed all her wedding plates the night before they left Puerto Rico; she hides a smile when she hears this story but denies it and claims that the plates were stolen). But Mami eventually gave in to her husband's will, as women of her time were raised to do, and she reluctantly said goodbye to her life on the island.

In San Juan, my mother was an avid rose grower, and she was famous for her prized lavender roses, which everybody said were the prettiest in the region. One of the promises my father made to her before they left the island was that she would be able to have a rose garden in the United States. But for many years Papi's promise went unfulfilled.

They spent the first thirty years in their new country in the frigid concrete of New York's inner city, and only when I got married and moved them to Southern California with me did they get a chance to have a garden. But after ten years of trying to reproduce her rose garden, my mother gave up on the lavender roses. Although all the conditions were right, she just couldn't get them to bloom. So my father, who had never been the slightest bit interested in gardening—or in roses for that matter, took it upon himself to make them grow. This was the fifth year that he worked in the yard, and even though he didn't like to admit it, he had come to love weeding, pruning bushes and cultivating the soil around the flowers. I think that working in the garden for my mother was one way that my otherwise cantankerous father could show his love for her.

Sadly, the growing season came and went that year, along with my mother's birthday, but the roses never bloomed. Months later, on a crisp winter morning, my father got up at his usual hour, brushed his teeth and washed his face. He sat down at the kitchen table, and my mother served him his customary huge bowl of oatmeal. But as he raised the first spoonful to his lips, he turned to me and Mami, and, with a somewhat surprised look on his face, said, "No me siento bien." And with that brief announcement, "I don't feel well," he toppled to the floor.

Mami ran over to his crumpled body, and frantically tried to revive him. But it was no use. He was gone.

Mami spent the next few months grieving and getting her new life in order, sorting through Papi's things and distributing them among the family, answering sympathy cards, talking to relatives in Puerto Rico and Cuba who called with regularity to ask about her. She put the little house that they had shared for ten years up for sale, and made plans to come to live with us. The house sold rather quickly, and on the day of my mother's sixtieth birthday, the young couple who had bought the house stopped by to deliver some papers. When Mami answered the door, she was startled to see the young woman holding out a lavender rose. Mami thought it was a birthday present and was touched at the kind gesture of the young woman.

"Thank you so much!" Mami exclaimed. "You must have known it was my birthday!"

"I didn't know," answered the young woman. "I just wanted to bring you one of these lovely roses from your garden."

"From my garden?" Mami asked, with a look of disbelief.

"Yes," the young woman said, as she stepped aside and gestured toward the rose garden.

My mother looked out the front door and tears filled her eyes. In the middle of her garden bloomed the most spectacular field of lavender roses that she had ever seen.

"Ay, José, bendito..." Mami gasped, calling out my father's name as she wiped the tears from her eyes.

"They must be a birthday present from above," the young woman said.

My mother just smiled.

~Caroline C. Sánchez
*Chicken Soup for the Latino Soul*

# Forwarded Prayer

*Our prayers should be for blessings in general,*
*for God knows best what is good for us.*
*~Socrates*

Like every other Tuesday morning, after driving my middle son to the high school, I returned home at 8:00 to read my e-mails before waking the younger children for school. A woman from our church had sent me a prayer, with the request to pass it on to all those I thought might need it. I sent it to my best friend, a new Christian; to an ill woman in my writer's group; and to my sister, who had just recently acknowledged her belief in the power of prayer. The last person I sent it to was my oldest son, Scott. Just twenty years old, he lived in his own apartment a couple of miles away and was a part-time inexperienced mate on a lobster boat. Scott balked at my fears of him fishing or lobstering. I knew he was at work but would find my e-mail with the prayer when he returned home.

As my day progressed, so did my workload, and I ran errands for most of the morning. When I returned home around noon, I found Scott sitting on our couch with one foot wrapped in plastic and duct tape. He stood up and gave me the biggest hug I'd ever received. I felt him trembling. "What's happened?"

He plopped back on the couch with his arm still around me. "My captain and I went out at three o'clock this morning to pull traps. Around eight, I was in charge of throwing the lines of traps over the side of the boat while he was at the helm. I had no idea my foot was tangled in the line when I threw it." His voice quaked as he recounted the weight of the traps pulling him over the side of the boat, fighting with all his strength to hold on, feeling the icy cold of the black water below, knowing that without immediate help, death was looming.

The captain, oblivious to the situation, had continued steering the boat along its course. After a few minutes, he peeked around the corner to shout to Scott.

"Oh, dear God!" he exclaimed as he hurried toward my son, dangling over the side of the boat. He frantically cut the line holding the traps and pulled Scott to safety.

As I praised God and hugged my son closer, I understood what so many fishermen had told me about respecting the sea, that it was unmerciful to those who failed to learn its power.

After Scott returned to his apartment, I received an e-mail from him. "Mom, the prayer you forwarded came at eight o'clock! That was the same moment I was holding onto life with all my might!"

The moment when God's strength had provided his.

~Kimberly Ripley
*Chicken Soup for the Mother and Son Soul*

# The Secret of Grandma's Sugar Crock

World War II had recently been declared. On the surface, there appeared to be little change in Grandma's ranch. Grandpa worked the fields and orchards every day, just as he had done before, and Grandma tended to the chores and harvesting as usual. But in fact, there had been a big change in the old homestead. The ranch was without the manpower of their five youngest sons, who were now on active military duty somewhere in the Pacific. Both Grandpa and Grandma would have to work twice as hard now to compensate for the absence of their five strong sons.

During World War II, a government-issued flag, imprinted with five blue stars, hung in the front window of my grandparents' old farmhouse. It meant that five of their sons were off fighting in the war. Without the boys to work the land, the ranch was shorthanded. Grandma worked doubly hard now to harvest a bountiful fruit crop. During that time, every member of the family pitched in to help, including grandkids like myself. Even so, it was a difficult time for Grandma: Rationing was in effect, there was little money for luxuries, and worst of all was the constant worry over whether her five sons would come home safely to her.

The old ranch was a lovely place, especially in the spring when the orchards were white with plum blossoms, and the song of the meadowlarks filled the fields and rolling hills of the surrounding valley. It was this beautiful ranch and returning to Grandma and Grandpa that their five sons focused on all during the war years.

In the summertime, while the rest of the family harvested the plum crop, Grandma was in the kitchen cooking up delicious fine Italian dinners. We would all sit on blankets spread out on the orchard ground, enjoying not just the wonderful food, but also the satisfaction of being part of such an important family effort.

To encourage the ripe fruit to fall, Grandpa used a long wooden pole with an iron hook at the top to catch a branch and shake the plums loose from the trees. Then the rest of us would crawl along, wearing knee pads that Grandma had sewn into our overalls, and gather the plums into metal buckets. We dumped the buckets of plums into long wooden trays, where the little purple plums were soon sun-dried into rich, brown prunes.

After a long, hard day I would walk hand-in-hand with Grandpa through the orchards while he surveyed what had been accomplished that day. I'd enjoy eating fresh plums off the trees, licking the sweet stickiness from my fingertips.

On each of these walks, Grandpa would stoop down and pick up a handful of soil, letting it sift slowly and lovingly through his strong, work-calloused hands. Then with pride and conviction he would invariably say: "If you take good care of the land, the land will take good care of you." It was this respect and belief in the soil that helped bolster his generation.

As darkness fell on the ranch, we'd all gather together on the cool, quiet veranda of the front porch. Grandpa would settle comfortably into his rocker, under the dim glow of a flickering moth-covered light bulb, and there he'd read the latest war news in his newspaper, trying to track the whereabouts of his five young sons.

Grandma always sat nearby on the porch swing, swaying back and forth and saying her perpetual rosary. The quiet squeak of Grandma's swing and the low mumbling of her prayers could be heard long into the night. The stillness of the quiet ranch house painfully reflected the absence of the five robust young men. This was the hardest part of the day for Grandma; the silence of the empty house was a painful reminder that her sons were far, far away, fighting for their country.

On Sunday morning, Grandma was back out on the porch again, repeating her rosary before going into the kitchen to start cooking. Then she and Grandpa sat at the kitchen table, counting out ration slips for the week ahead and what little cash there was to pay the bills. Once they were finished, Grandma always took a portion of her money and put it in the sugar crock, placing it high on the kitchen shelf. I often asked her what the money in the jar was for. She would simply say, "A very special favor."

Well, the war finally ended, and all five of Grandma's sons came home, remarkably safe and sound. After a while, Grandma and Grandpa retired, and the family farm became part of a modern expressway.

I never did find out what the money in the sugar crock was for until a week or so before last Christmas. Completely on impulse, perhaps feeling the wonder of the Christmas season and the need to connect with its spiritual significance, I stopped at a little church I just happened to be driving past. I'd never been inside before, and as I entered the church through the side door, I was stunned to come face-to-face with the most glorious stained-glass window I'd ever seen.

I stopped to examine the intricate beauty of the window more closely. The magnificent stained glass depicted the Holy Mother and child. Like an exquisite jewel, it reflected the glory of the very first Christmas. As I studied every detail of its fine workmanship, I found, to my utter amazement, a small plaque at the base of the window that read, "For a favor received—donated in 1945 by Maria Carmela Curci-Dinapoli." I couldn't believe my eyes. I was reading Grandma's very words! Every day that Grandma had said her prayers for her soldier-sons, she'd also put whatever money she could scrape together into her sacred sugar crock to pay for the window.

Her quiet donation of this window had been her way of saying thank you to God for sparing the lives of her beloved five sons.

The original church in which the window was placed had long ago been torn down. Through the generations, the family had lost track of its existence. Finding this window at Christmastime, more than half a century later, not only brought back a flood of precious memories, but also made me a believer in small but beautiful miracles.

~Cookie Curci
*Chicken Soup for the Grandparent's Soul*

# A True Christmas

*You don't choose your family. They are God's gift to you, as you are to them.*
*~Desmond Tutu*

I plopped the last of the ready-made cookie dough onto the cookie sheet and shoved it into the oven. These standard-issue chocolate chip cookies would be a far cry from the bejeweled affairs I'd baked for twenty-six years, but the only reason I'd even summoned the effort was because my youngest son, Ross, had opened and re-opened the cookie jar four times the previous night, saying with fourteen-year-old tact, "What? No Christmas cookies this year?"

Since today was the twenty-third, and his older siblings, Patrick and Molly, would be arriving Christmas Eve, Ross informed me that they would be "big-time disappointed" if there wasn't "cool stuff" to eat. This from the same kid who had never watched a Christmas TV special in his life and who had to be dragged into the family photo for the annual Christmas card.

I never considered a family picture this year. A big piece of the family was now missing—or hadn't anybody noticed?

All my friends had been telling me the same thing since the day of the funeral:

"Pam, the first year after you lose your husband is the hardest. You have to go through the first Valentine's Day without him, the first birthday, the first anniversary..."

They hadn't been kidding. What they hadn't told me was that Christmas was going to top them all in hard-to-take. It wasn't that

Tom had loved Christmas that much. He'd always complained that the whole thing was too commercial and that when you really thought about it, Easter seemed to be a much more important Christ-centered celebration in the church.

The phone rang. Molly was calling collect from the road. She and two dorm buddies were driving home after finals.

"Do you know what I'm looking forward to?" she said.

"Sleeping for seventy-two straight hours?" I asked.

"No." She sounded a little deflated. "Coming home from Christmas Eve services and seeing all those presents piled up under the tree. It's been years since I've cared what was in them or how many were for me — I just like seeing them there. How weird is that?"

Not weird at all, my love, I thought. I sighed, took a piece of paper and penciled in a few gift ideas for Ross, Molly, Patrick, his wife Amy and my grandson, Shane.

And then I snapped the pencil down on the counter. A part of me understood that the kids were in denial. Tom's sudden death eleven months earlier had left them bewildered and scared. And now at Christmas, their shock was translated into exaggerated enthusiasm. The Cobb family Christmas traditions provided a sense of normalcy for them. Patrick had even asked me last week if I still had the old John Denver Christmas album.

But as far as I was concerned, there just wasn't that much to deck the halls about. Tom was gone. I was empty and unmotivated. At worst, I wished they'd all just open the presents and carve the turkey without me.

When the oven dinged, I piled two dozen brown circles on a plate and left a note for Ross: "I don't want to hear any more complaining! Gone shopping. I love you, Mom."

The complaining, however, went on in my head as I elbowed my way through the mob at the mall.

Tom was right, I thought. This is all a joke.

It really was everything he hated: canned music droning its false merriment, garish signs luring me to buy, tired-looking families dragging themselves around, worrying about their credit card limits as they snapped at their children.

Funny, I thought while gazing at a display of earrings I knew Molly wouldn't wear. All the time Tom was here pointing this out to me, it never bothered me. Now it's all I can see.

I abandoned the earring idea and took to wandering the mall, hoping for inspiration so Molly would have something to look at under the tree. It wasn't going to be like years past—I should have told her that. She wasn't going to see a knee-deep collection of exquisitely wrapped treasures that Tom always shook his head over.

"You've gone hog-wild again," he would always tell me—before adding one more contribution. Instead of buying me a gift, he'd write a check in my name to Compassion International or a local food pantry, place it in a red envelope, and tuck it onto a branch of our Christmas tree.

"This is a true Christmas gift," he'd tell me. "It's a small demonstration that Christ is real in our lives."

I stopped mid-mall, letting the crowds swirl past me.

Tom wasn't there, a fact that the rest of the family didn't want to face or discuss. But he could still be with us, maybe just a little.

I left the mall and quickly found a Christmas tree lot. The man looked happy to unload one very dry tree for half price. He even tied it to my roof rack.

Then it was off to Safeway, where I bought a twenty-four-pound Butterball turkey and all the trimmings. Back home, the decoration boxes weren't buried too deeply in the garage. I'd barely gotten them put away last year when Tom had his heart attack.

I was still sorting boxes when Ross emerged from the kitchen, munching the last of the two dozen cookies.

"Oh, I thought we weren't going to have a tree this year," he said between mouthfuls.

"Well, we are. Can you give me a hand getting it up?"

Two hours later, Ross and I stood back and admired our Christmas tree. The lights winked softly as I straightened a misshapen glittery angel Molly had made in second grade and Ross's first birthday Christmas ball.

I wanted to cry.

The house sprang to life when everyone arrived Christmas Eve. In the middle of our church service, however, my spirits sagged. There was no lonelier feeling than standing in the midst of one's family singing "Silent Night"—surrounded by a vivacious college daughter; a sweet, gentle daughter-in-law; a handsome, successful twenty-five-year-old son; a wide-eyed, mile-a-minute three-year-old grandson; and an awkward teenager whose hugs were like wet shoelaces—and being keenly aware that someone was missing.

Back at home everyone continued to avoid the subject.

"The tree is gorgeous, Mom," Molly said. She knelt down and began hauling gifts out of a shopping bag to add to my pile.

"I love what you did with the wrappings, Pam," Amy said. "You're always so creative."

"I forgot to buy wrapping paper," I told her. "I had to use newspaper."

It was Christmas as usual—easier to pretend everything was normal than to deal with harsh reality. Ross and Patrick sparred over whose stocking was whose, and Shane parked himself in front of a bowl of M&Ms. They all got to open the customary one present on Christmas Eve, and after doing so, they schlepped off to bed.

But there was one more thing that had to be done. I went over to Tom's desk, found a red envelope in the top drawer, and stuck into it a check made out to the American Heart Association. It seemed appropriate.

"I know the kids—and even I—have to go on with our lives, Tom," I whispered. "But I wish you were here."

It occurred to me as I tucked the red envelope midway up the tree that one of the kids would say, "Oh, yeah—I remember, he always did that," and then there would be an awkward silence and perhaps sheepish looks.

I hoped so.

Morning, or at least dawn—came way too soon. Shane was up before the paper carrier. I dragged myself into the kitchen and found it already smelling like a Seattle coffeehouse.

"This is what we drink at school," Molly told me and handed me a cup.

"Is anyone else awake?" I asked.

She nodded her head, and for the first time I noticed a twinkle in her eye that was unprecedented for this hour of the morning. "What are you up to?" I asked.

"Mom!" Patrick yelled from the living room. "You've got to see this!"

"At this hour of the..."

What I saw was my family perched on the couch like a row of deliciously guilty canaries. What I saw next was our Christmas tree, dotted with bright red envelopes.

"Man, it got crowded in here last night," Ross said. "I came down here about one o'clock and freaked Amy out."

"I almost called 911 when I came down," Patrick said, "until I saw it was Molly and not some burglar."

I had never heard a thing. I walked over to the tree and touched each one of the five envelopes I hadn't put there.

"Open them, Mom," Molly said. "This was always the best part of Christmas."

From Patrick, there was a check to Youth for Christ, to help kids go on mission trips like the one Dad supported him on to Haiti five years earlier. From Amy, a check to our church for sheet music, because some of her best memories of her father-in-law were of him helping the children's choir. From Molly, several twenty-dollar bills for the local crisis pregnancy center, "because many of the women who go there have probably never experienced the love of a husband like Daddy," she said. From Ross, a twenty-dollar bill for a local drug program for kids, "since Dad was all freaked out about me staying clean."

The last envelope was lumpy. When I opened it, a handful of change spilled out.

"Mine, Gamma," Shane said, his little bow-mouth pursed importantly. Amy finished his thought. "He wants this to go to the animal shelter—you know, for lost dogs. Like the one he visited with Dad just before he died."

I pulled all the envelopes against my chest and hugged them.

"You know what's weird?" Molly said. "I feel like Daddy's right here with us."

"Yeah, that's pretty weird," Ross said.

"But true," Patrick said. "I feel like he's been here this whole time. I thought I'd be all bummed out this Christmas—but I don't need to be."

"No, you don't, my love," I said. To myself, I added, Neither do I. I have my family, and I have my faith.

~Nancy Rue
*Chicken Soup for the Soul Christmas Treasury*

# The Face of God

*God's interest in the human race is nowhere better evinced than in babies.*
*~Martin H. Fischer*

In my years, I have seen the vastness of the Grand Canyon, the splendor of the Alps, the purple mountains' majesty of the Smoky Mountains of Tennessee and the seeming endlessness of the Pacific Ocean. Yet, nothing I have seen, or ever expect to see, compares with what I once witnessed in a dark-paneled, antiseptic birthing room. Then and there, the power and love of God enveloped me.

I was on the last night of my clinical rotation as a nursing student on the labor and delivery floor, and I had yet to see a birth. When my children were born, fathers were relegated to the labor waiting room. Now, at 7:00 P.M. on my last student shift, my nursing instructor suggested I check into labor room four to see if I could watch the birth. With some trepidation, I knocked on the door, stuck in my head, and asked the young couple if I could possibly observe the birth of their baby. They gave me permission. I thanked them and found myself a spot in the room that kept me out of the way but still gave me a good view of the birth. Then I stood with my hands behind my back, studiously looking around the room at the preparations being made by the nurses.

The young mother, covered with blue sterile drapes, lay in the most uncomfortable and exposed position imaginable and was sweating profusely. Every minute or so, she would grimace, groan and push with all her might. Her husband stood beside her, coaching her breathing and lovingly holding her hand. One nurse dabbed her forehead with a cool washcloth, while another encouraged her to rest when she could. The doctor worked on a low stool to ease the birth as best he could. I stood apart, proud of my unemotional, clinical detachment.

The nurse assisting the doctor said, "Here she comes!" I looked and was amazed at what I saw: the top of a head covered with black hair began to appear. I instantly lost the ability to call this wondrous occurrence something as medical as "crowning." Then the doctor began gently but firmly to turn the shoulders of the new life and pull. Transfixed to my spot, I am sure my mouth was agape. The doctor continued to turn and pull; the mother pushed; the husband encouraged; and an event that had taken nine long months of preparation was over in just a few seconds. At the sight of the infant's beautiful face, I felt such wonder that I truly believe angels sing at such times.

My professionalism and clinical detachment had deserted me, replaced with a warmth that surrounded me. At a loss for words—congratulations seemed such an empty and trite thing to say to these two blessed people at that moment—I nonetheless offered my congratulations anyway. After leaving the room, I walked around the corner into a deserted hallway and allowed my tears to flow.

That night some of my fellow students, all of whom were women and many of them mothers, asked me about the birth. Each time, I welled up again with tears and choked out that it was the most beautiful experience I had ever had. They would hug me or pat my shoulder, and with a gleam in their eyes say, "I know." Days passed before I could speak of the birth in any medical light. Even now, as I review that night, I continue to be in awe.

I have seen many sights in my life. Before my life is over, I will see many more. But none can ever compare to the night I saw the love, hope and beauty of God in the face of a newborn child.

~Tony Collins
*Chicken Soup for the Mother's Soul 2*

# Life, What a Beautiful Gift

It was the first week in December. My daughter Julie and I had decided to go Christmas shopping. We have always been extra close, and I always looked forward to this special time together. We would do some "serious" shopping, go out for lunch, and catch up on what was happening in each other's lives.

Over lunch, we discussed what gifts we would buy our relatives and friends. I always felt this was a real chore, as I was always worried about treating all five of my children equally, finding something they didn't already have. Julie, on the other hand, is a person who always seems to find the perfect gift for everyone. Everything has to be the perfect color, the perfect size, the perfect scent! She goes back and forth, from store to store, to get the best bargain.

That day, while eating, our conversation somehow switched from Christmas gifts to life's blessings. This made both of us think of my illness. Although I had been extremely sick several times, for the most part, I still considered myself truly blessed. In fact there had been several times when my M.S. or lupus were out of remission, and my doctor said it was indeed a miracle that I was still alive. Maybe it was a miracle, or maybe God just had other plans for me.

Realizing how lucky I was, when Julie asked me what I wanted for Christmas, I tried to tell her without ruining her Christmas spirit, that I didn't expect or even want a present. I explained just getting together with my beautiful family was all I could hope for.

Julie looked disappointed in my reply. "Oh, Mom," she said, "you are always so darn practical! There has to be something little you want."

I repeated what I had said, "I have a fantastic husband, beautiful children, and now two beautiful granddaughters. I have it all! What more could anyone want in one life?" I was speaking with my entire heart. I truly felt that way. I loved my family so much that little else was important. Each day I thanked God for giving me yet one more twenty-four hours to share with them.

Suddenly, without even thinking, I added, "I know this is selfish, but you know, I really would love to have a grandson before I die! Now that would be neat!"

Julie just shook her head, and said, "I give up!"

"Well, you asked what I would like, didn't you? I have always wanted a grandson! I love little boys! I'll never forget how happy I was to have your brother after all you girls! Oh, I love all of you equally, that is for certain, but there is something very special about little boys! Now if you can find a way to get me a grandson before Christmas, I will take him and love him without complaining!"

"You're impossible!" Julie added. "Let's finish our shopping. You won't accept a little gift, yet you ask for the world! Mothers!"

Hours later, Julie dropped me off at my house. Exhausted from shopping, I hugged her and promised to let her know if I thought of anything "easier" for her to get for me.

When I went in the house, the first thing I did was check our new answering machine for messages. The blinking red light indicated there were several.

The first message was another daughter whose voice assured me that she was concerned because I had gone away for that long without first obtaining permission! I thought it was ironic remembering the times my children had forgotten to call me when they were going to be late. Funny how time changes roles. The second message was to remind me of an upcoming craft auction at church, and the third to confirm a dental appointment. Who needed to be reminded of such things? I started to walk out of the room, when I heard the last voice, that of my husband. He sounded more than a little confused.

"Barb! Are you home? If you are home, then pick this thing up! Can't you hear me? I need to talk to you... Q-U-I-C-K!" Frustrated, when at last he realized he was talking to an electronic piece of equipment, he lowered his voice and said, "Please, Honey, when you get home... CALL ME!"

Wow! This was so unlike the cool man I was used to! What could be wrong? I knew I had to call him back at once.

Call I did. It was not only a shocking call, but also an unplanned answer to a prayer, and that something little I had wanted for my Christmas gift. About the same time I was telling Julie that I would like a grandson before my life was finished, a young girl in a nearby town had called my husband at work to tell him that she was the mother of a little grandson we had never met! We were both in shock. This woman explained she had a brief relationship with our son, had gotten pregnant, and had a little boy who was now seven months old! She said she had pleaded with our son to tell us about the baby. However, he was afraid we would be disappointed in him if we knew, so he had made her promise not to tell.

For some unknown reason that day, she had decided that it was unfair to us to keep this grandchild a secret any longer. Since our home number was unlisted, she had called the place my husband worked and told him the story.

My husband gave me the woman's number, and said she had told him I was free to make arrangements to meet our little grandson if I liked. Grandson! Liked? I was a doubting Thomas. I had to see for myself. I called the woman, and within an hour, I was on the way to see this baby. If she was telling the truth I had a grandson! No matter how complicated the details of his conception were, I knew I would love him. I was happy, sad, excited and tearful all at the same time.

When I arrived at the given address, I was met at the door by the woman and her other children. I sensed all of them were trying to evaluate me, and this made me feel terribly uncomfortable. My first impulse was to turn and run. Something within me told me I had to stay. I offered her my hand; she took it. She invited me inside. Walking ahead of me to a nearby table, she picked up an envelope and handed it to me. "Here are the paternity papers," she said. "Here's proof that Toby is your grandson!"

I had just learned something else: Her baby's name was Toby. I questioned the baby's last name, and I was told he had received my son's last name the previous day in court.

Nearly collapsing, I lowered myself to the nearest chair. I didn't realize the girl had left the room until I saw her return, carrying a little boy. She walked up to me, placed the most beautiful little baby into my arms, and said, "Son, I think it is time you meet your grandma!" Toby looked right up at me and gave me the biggest smile... I cried.

At that moment, little Toby became a very important part of my life. My son and the baby's mother had made a big mistake. However, God himself had created little Toby, and God doesn't make mistakes. I had a grandson! A beautiful bundle of joy! What a precious Christmas gift!

Later that evening, my husband and I had a long talk with our son. We told him we knew about Toby, and I was hurt that he could even think for a moment that his father and I could have loved him less for having made a mistake. I told him if we only love our children when they live their lives the way we feel they should, then that isn't really love. He told me that when Toby's mother first discovered she was pregnant, she had considered an abortion, and we cried together, thanking God she hadn't. Later, we even laughed a little over the speedy way in which God seemed to answer my Christmas gift request!

Since then many Christmases have passed. Toby spends a lot of time with his father and with us, as well. Every day, but especially on Christmas, I am so thankful for this very special gift I received eight years ago.

~Barbara Jeanne Fisher
*Chicken Soup for the Grandparent's Soul*

# The Miracle Baby

He was born six and a half weeks prematurely on a hot, August day in 1967 and was quickly whisked away to a waiting incubator. At a mere four pounds, eleven ounces, and looking like a partially inflated doll, he was still the most beautiful baby she had ever seen.

The baby's father, Dr. Carter, tried to tell his wife, Donna, not to expect too much—their baby was severely jaundiced. More than anything in the world, he had wanted to tell her their little baby was just fine, especially after three miscarriages, and all the sadness they'd felt and tears they shed. But their baby wasn't fine.

In spite of all his medical training and experience, Dr. Carter choked on the words. But he knew he'd have to tell her that the baby they had wanted so badly for years was probably not going to live—maybe forty-eight hours at the most. He had to prepare her for what was to come.

She immediately named the baby Jeffrey, after her husband. As the baby's jaundice grew worse, fellow physicians came by to console them. They shook their heads and tried their best to offer some encouragement. But they knew the odds were not good. Even if he lived, unless little Jeffrey's liver began functioning soon, the jaundice would produce permanent brain damage.

Donna told everyone he was going to be all right. She knew her baby was going to live. The nurses felt sorry for her since her baby was probably going to die anyway, and so they let her hold him.

When she touched his tiny, fragile body and whispered that he was going to grow up to be a strong, healthy man, little Jeffrey smiled. She told the nurses what had happened, and they looked at her sadly and said that babies have involuntary smiles and she needed rest. They did not have the heart to tell her more.

The extended family discussed burial arrangements with her husband and the parish priest. They finally came in to speak with Donna. She started crying and asked everyone to leave the hospital room. Her baby was not going to be buried. He was going to go home, jaundiced or not. She would not even think of burial!

At sixty-two hours, the baby's blood count was checked again. The jaundice was considerably better! Little Jeffrey began eating every two hours. Donna asked to hold him as much as possible, and she talked to him. Since he didn't need oxygen, the nurses humored her. At the next check, the count had dropped another two points. Donna began planning his homecoming party.

Jeffrey did go home almost three weeks after birth. That, however, was not the end of the story.

Six weeks later, at his first checkup, the pediatrician told Donna he thought the baby was possibly blind or had eye damage. She said this was nonsense since he followed her with his eyes. After a few tests, it proved to be a false scare. Yet, the first year, the baby did not do much. He had routine checkups, but Donna knew he seemed far behind in his development. Had he suffered severe brain damage from the jaundice?

At thirteen months, Jeffrey suddenly had a small seizure. They rushed him to the hospital, and he was diagnosed with a possible brain tumor. After several tests and X-rays the neurologist said Jeffrey was hydrocephalic (water on the brain), and they would have to operate immediately to put a permanent shunt inside his head. At this time, a shunt operation was still rather experimental. It was the only procedure known to keep these children alive.

Once again, Donna did not fully accept the diagnosis. If he was hydrocephalic, why did it just now develop? Her friends told her she was in denial. She'd better listen to the doctors.

Of course, she would do whatever was necessary to help her

son, but she also made her own plan of action. Three days before the operation, she called everyone she knew in several states and asked them to pray at 7:00 P.M. each night before the operation. She asked them to ask others to join them if they could.

When the operation day arrived, she felt calm. Friends in seven states had been praying for their son. Later, to her astonishment she learned that her friends had called people, who then called other people, and that ultimately hundreds of people had been gathered to pray at 7:00 P.M. on three successive nights. Even a group of people in Israel were among those praying! And all for a tiny child none of them even knew!

The operation started very early. Donna and her husband paced the floors of the hospital. After what seemed only a short time, the neurosurgeon came running out, wildly waving X-rays. He was grinning from ear to ear. "It's a miracle! We didn't have to do anything. We did the last test through the baby's soft spot, and there was nothing there. He is not hydrocephalic!"

They all started to cry and laugh at the same time. The neurosurgeon said he did not know what to think. He had no explanation for it.

So Jeffrey came home once again to a jubilant crowd of friends and family. All the people who prayed for him were notified of the results and thanked for their prayers. He never had another seizure again.

Still, according to everyone else's timetable, his development was very slow. At Jeffrey's three-year pediatric checkup, the doctor looked sternly at Donna and asked if she and her husband had given thought to institutionalizing him. Donna was stunned. Institutionalize him? How could anyone do that? She refused, and it was never discussed again.

Instead, Donna set up the family basement playroom like a Montessori school. Jeffrey wasn't really learning language so she worked with him by engaging learning techniques that involved all his senses—sight, smell, touch, taste and hearing. Donna believed Jeffrey was normal and just didn't follow other people's timetables.

She taught him colors using M&Ms. He quickly learned the

names of colors and of other things, too. And, while not speaking much more than a few words here and there until he was three and a half years old, his first full sentence was "Pass the ketchup!" He progressed quickly when he learned anything new—not little by little as his sister did, but in giant spurts, all-at-once kind of steps. This became a pattern in his life.

When Jeffrey was four, Donna wanted him to go to real preschool just like his sister. The first year he played with the water fountain—all year. He turned the water off and on, endlessly. The teachers said it was a waste of money to send him to school. He would be better off in "special school." They said he was "slow," and one teacher in exasperation said that Jeffrey was retarded and she ought to know—she'd been teaching for twenty-five years!

Donna remained firm. Would they mind as long as she was paying for it, to keep him another year? They reluctantly agreed but only if he was not allowed to play with the water fountain. She agreed to the terms.

The next fall, he began preschool again. This time he began building intricate architectural structures. He also began examining all the plastic dinosaurs and knew their names, classifying them by types. He found new interests in doing the math blocks, talking and asking question after question after question. He was more social and didn't play with the water fountain. The teachers couldn't believe it. He actually seemed bright!

However, at his pediatric checkup, his new doctor said he thought Jeffrey needed testing. He felt he had developmental delays. After testing, the pediatrician, who is now distinguished nationally in his field, said Jeffrey was autistic. Donna decided she'd had enough! Since birth, Jeffrey had been "diagnosed" as possibly (1) blind, (2) hydrocephalic, (3) epileptic, (4) retarded and now finally (5) autistic. If she and her husband had listened to experts, well-meaning friends and even some family members, Jeffrey would be in an institution. Donna was polite but said that she did not think Jeffrey was autistic at all. He was in preschool and was going to start first grade on time.

Other than being very uncoordinated and not having well-developed motor skills, Jeffrey's elementary years were not unusual. His learning ability was completely on track. He became an Eagle Scout, an honor student, a presidential scholar in his senior year, won two academic scholarships for college and was in all gifted classes. His SAT scores shocked everyone.

But even this is not the end of the story.

After graduating from college with honors, Jeffrey was encouraged to go to medical school. Donna always told him she had faith that his life had a special purpose and that he was here to help people. After graduating medical school, Jeffrey was accepted at a prestigious clinic for his residency program.

One day, while he was doing a rotation in the emergency room, an older man burst in. He was suicidal and, as a last-ditch effort, one of his friends had brought him in to talk to someone. Jeffrey saw him and asked about his life. The man told him about how sad he was about his recent divorce and being downsized out of a job he had held for years. He felt hopeless, that his life was over and nothing he had done had mattered. Jeffrey talked to him a while and, after giving him some tests, gave him a prescription that would help him for the next few days. Jeffrey also got him approved for a caseworker to follow him up for the next month.

Suddenly the patient looked at the doctor's badge and said, "Jeffrey Carter? Is your mom's name Donna?"

Jeffrey answered, "Why, yes. How did you know?"

"You're the miracle baby! You're the miracle baby!" the man cried excitedly. "I prayed for you when you were in the hospital, and now you're a doctor!"

Jeffrey confirmed that he had been born in Minnesota and now he'd returned "home" to complete his medical training.

The old man smiled and just gazed at his new doctor as if examining every inch. Then he told Jeffrey the story.

"Were you really one of the people who prayed for me?" Jeffrey asked him.

"Oh yes, three nights a week at 7:00 P.M. for years. We were only supposed to do it until the operation, but some of us just kept going for a while."

"You prayed for me all that time?"

As the man nodded, tears began to form in his eyes. Jeffrey reached out to embrace his patient—a man who only hours before had thought of taking his own life because he had lost all faith.

"Thank you, for praying for me... for caring about me. You see, I'm here because of you."

Faith had come full circle for both men.

~Ronna Rowlette
*Chicken Soup for the Mother's Soul 2*

Chapter 7

# Stories of Faith

## Making a Difference

*The best portion of a good man's life is his little, nameless, unremembered acts of kindness and of love.*
*~William Wordsworth*

# The Little Black Book

Many years ago I worked for a man whom today I call a great American funeral director. His lifelong motto was "Families first, no matter what," and he lived this with a consistency that few men ever achieve.

The funerals he conducted were flawless, and people genuinely admired and respected him. He was a grand person. However, one of the most interesting mysteries which accompanied this man was his "little black book." It was a small black book with a lock on the cover. It looked as if it was very old, and it was his constant companion.

If you went to his office, you would see it lying on his desk. At funerals, he would pull the black book out and scribble brief notations in it. If you picked up his suit coat, you could feel the black book in his coat pocket.

You can imagine the gossip by the staff and speculation around the funeral home coffee room as to precisely what was in the black book. I remember on the first day I worked, I very seriously asked the embalmer what the book was for, and he responded with a very mysterious glance, "What do you think is in the book?"

I was not the sharpest knife in the drawer and very innocently I said, "I have no idea."

"Oh, come on, farm boy," the embalmer replied. "He keeps his list of girlfriends in there." I was stunned!

Later I asked the receptionist about the black book. Her response was that it was where he kept the list of the horses he bet on at the race track. Again, I was stunned. My employer was a womanizing gambler! I could not believe it.

For nearly three years the mysterious saga of the little black book continued—all the time, the stories, gossip and intrigue getting more and more spectacular and ridiculous.

Then suddenly one day, while conducting a funeral, my boss, this great funeral director, had a massive heart attack and died.

Four days later, we had a grand funeral for him—he was laid out in a solid bronze casket, flowers were everywhere, and when we took him to the church, the place was packed and the governor was in the front row.

I was standing in the back of the church protecting the church truck (that was my job), sobbing as the minister went on about what a great man my boss was and how just knowing him made us all better people. I couldn't have agreed with the minister more.

Then the minister asked my boss's widow to come up and talk about her husband's character. I thought, "Now this will be beautiful," as she rose to walk to the pulpit. It was then I saw she was carrying his little black book! My tears of grief instantaneously turned to sweats of terror.

She walked to the pulpit, stood with complete dignity, looked at the assembly and said, "Thank you all for being here today. I want to share with you a secret about my husband's character."

I thought, "Oh God, here it comes!"

She continued, "You see this small book. Most of you know he carried it with him constantly. I would like to read to you the first entry of the book dated April 17, 1920—Mary Flannery, she is all alone. The next entry August 8, 1920—Frederick W. Pritchard, he is all alone. The next entry November 15, 1920—Frieda M. Gale, she is all alone. You see when he made funeral arrangements or saw somebody at a funeral that he knew was all alone, he would write their names in this book. Then, every Christmas Eve, he would call each person and invite them to share a wonderful Christmas dinner at our house. I want you all to know that this was the true character of my husband; he was concerned, compassionate and caring. This is what the little black book is all about, and I also want you to know that this being 1971, he did this for fifty Christmases."

There was not a dry eye in the church.

Now almost a quarter of a century after his death, I look back at the inner spirit that motivated this funeral director to do what he did. May this spirit of warmth and compassion guide each of us in this great profession. Just think of the humanitarian possibilities if every member of the funeral profession developed our own little black books. The results of human kindness would be staggering.

~Todd W. Van Beck
*Chicken Soup for the Christian Family Soul*

# God's Gentle Man

*No man is poor who has friends.*
~It's a Wonderful Life

I was checking out a construction job site in one of the poorer sections of town at lunchtime, so it was deserted of the few workmen there. At this point just three walls were up on the building, which sat back and isolated, away from the main thoroughfare. I was taking a few measurements when a fellow casually walked up from off the street. At first glance I could tell he was not a workman, so I eyed him cautiously while asking politely if I could help him.

He said, "I just started in a new job, and I'm waiting for my first paycheck. My wife and little girl and I are staying in a motel. I worked all night and when I got back to the room they told me that if I don't have payment for tonight right now, they're gonna make us leave."

I asked if he had checked with welfare and charity agencies for help. He replied he had, but they were slow in coming up with any money. After waiting a long time that morning for a return phone call, he felt he had to do something, so he started walking and asking for help.

As a Christian man, I like to think of myself as someone who will help those in need, but in Atlanta these kinds of requests are not uncommon. So sometime back my wife and I had decided that we would give to specific charities qualified to help such families, so that when we were confronted by such requests, we had an answer ready.

I expressed to the gentleman a simple "No."

His response was surprising. "Thank you," he said kindly, and turned and walked back out to the street.

Normally I would not have given it a second thought, but today this was not the case. Maybe it was his response, maybe it was his story, maybe it was the Holy Spirit, but something pulled at me to rethink what had just transpired—that maybe this time my response was wrong; maybe this gentleman had not just wandered up but maybe he was sent to me. It was out of the way, I was the only one here, and he was the only other person on the job site.

I tried to soothe my conscience with my self-righteousness, telling myself that I already help such people, that I cannot just give to anyone who shows up with a sad story. Believing that a certain amount of stewardship goes into handling our gifts normally justifies my reluctance to give to those who just walk up on the street and ask for money—but not this time.

I stayed on at the site for a few more minutes, finishing up what I had come to do, but the presence of this gentleman and the wrongness of my response kept gnawing at me. Finally, as I got into my truck to leave, I turned to what some of my friends had taught me—I prayed about this. Then I thought, "Let's check this out. Let's see if there really is a place nearby where he could rent a room for a family; if so, he'll be there and then I'll know I should help."

After driving down the street in both directions and not finding any such place, I convinced myself that I was right; it was all just a story to get some cash and I could leave now knowing I had done right. So why did it feel so wrong?

Finally, after stopping once again in a parking lot, I put God to the test. "Okay," I said out loud, "if You want me to help this gentleman, then You show him to me. If I see him I will help him."

Convinced I had solved the problem, I started to pull out onto the street, squeezing between two buildings and pulling out across the sidewalk to see oncoming traffic. I looked right—nothing was coming. I looked left—and right into the eyes of the gentle man looking into my truck window. I'm sure he saw the shock and amazement on my face as he looked in at me in puzzlement. It took a second or two to regain my composure, but I finally found the button to lower the window. "Still need help?"

"Yes."

"Where's this place you're staying?"

"Just down the road."

"Get in." It was a short ride and I had to make a few turns, but sure enough there was the motel, just as he'd said. As I drove up we saw his wife and daughter sitting in the lobby.

He said, "After working all night and walking all morning, I'd given up and was on my way back to get them when you picked me up."

I gave him what cash I had, enough for one night and a meal for his family. He thanked me profusely, then said, "What can I do for you?"

I just said, "Keep me in your prayers, as I will you."

Little did he know he had already done more for me than I for him.

~Richard Duello
*Chicken Soup for the Christian Soul 2*

# The Cookie Lady

*What a lovely surprise to finally discover how unlonely being alone can be.*
*~Ellen Burstyn*

Rain droned against the office window, matching my mood. I should have known that my new job at the hospital was too good to be true. Throughout the day, rumors warned that the newest employee from each department would be laid off due to a drop in census. I was the newest one in the training department.

My boss appeared at the door of my cubicle, interrupting my thoughts. "Got a minute?"

My neck chilled as if he'd shoved ice under my collar. I figured a minute would be all he needed to say, "You're fired!" Would it matter if I told him about my roof leak and overdue notices?

"You probably know we're cutting back," he began. "Administration wants us to offer outplacement classes to help those employees find other jobs. Show them how to write a resume, make a good impression in an interview and so on."

Apprehension made a fist in my stomach. I might as well have been an executioner sharpening her own ax. "Fine," I mumbled, not knowing what else to say.

After he left, I decided to go home early. If someone saw my tears, I'd pretend I had allergies. Through my blurry eyes, I noticed a paper plate of peanut butter cookies, crisscrossed with fork marks, on the secretary's desk.

"Who brought the cookies?" I asked.

"Some lady leaves them every Friday," she said. "Help yourself."

I blotted my eyes with the back of my hand before taking two. "Life's so ironic," I thought. I was expected to teach a job-hunting class before I got my own pink slip, while some rich volunteer donated cookies so she wouldn't feel guilty about not having to work. Her maid probably baked them.

"See you tomorrow," I said, wondering how many more times I'd have the chance to say that.

In the hall, the elevator door opened, revealing a gray-haired woman about the height of a third-grader. Only her head and the top of her green apron were visible over the cart loaded with cleaning supplies. At least she had a job!

All the way home, I fought self-pity, finally giving in to the tears when I reached my driveway. I couldn't remember feeling so alone. And scared.

The next morning, I considered telling my boss to teach the classes himself. I didn't have the nerve, though, so I drove to the library for books to help me prepare my classes.

Later at the hospital, when anyone mentioned my leaving, I joked about taking early retirement and living in the barn on my father's farm.

I kept up the pretense of not caring for the next two weeks until the Friday of the final meeting with the personnel staff in the basement. Personnel employees handed out final paychecks and collected office keys while I waited at a table with my class schedule for those interested in help. Laid-off workers formed a line at the door, most of them crying. I'd be just like them in a couple of weeks.

The chaplain took the seat next to me, probably so he could comfort those who wanted to talk. He opened his Bible, worn and marked with yellow highlighter.

While he greeted the first employee to reach us, I glanced over to see what he'd highlighted. It was Romans 12:5: "...so we, though many, are one body in Christ, and individually members of one another. Having gifts that differ according to the grace given us, let us use them." I read the rest of the passage before he reached for the book. "He, who teaches, in his teaching."

It was one thing to have a gift; another to have the chance to use it, I thought. My throat tightened against the tears that threatened.

Out of the corner of my eye, I noticed a woman in a green apron shuffling to the table. The chaplain leaned over and whispered, "Good heavens! I can't believe our Cookie Lady is being laid off. We'll miss her as much as we'll miss her peanut butter cookies on Fridays."

Cookie Lady? I stared at the woman, noticing that her fingers were crooked, probably from arthritis. She certainly didn't fit the description of the wealthy volunteer I'd imagined.

Settling in the chair in front of us, she folded her hands in her lap like an obedient child waiting for instructions. When the chaplain spoke to her in Spanish, I knew my classes were useless for her.

She smiled and reached into the pocket of her apron to offer us cookies from a paper sack.

"Gracias," I mumbled, wishing I knew more of her language. Suddenly, my self-pity turned to shame as I realized how much better off I was than this poor woman who still thought of others despite her problems. The cookies seemed to emphasize the words from Romans—we belong to each other and each needs the other.

I knew I had to do something for her, even before I examined the classified section of the newspaper for myself.

At noon, the last of the workers filed past our table. I grabbed the cookies, all I planned to eat for lunch, and returned to my cubicle.

Grateful for the midday silence, I wrote and revised until I was satisfied I'd expressed how I felt about the unselfishness of the Cookie Lady who needed a job. Finally, I slid my article into an envelope and asked the boss for permission to leave for awhile, not explaining I was headed for the newspaper office.

Maybe my efforts wouldn't work, but at least I tried. This would be my cookie for her, I thought as I pulled into the newspaper building's parking lot.

After I located the appropriate office, the features editor agreed to see me for just two minutes because he was on deadline.

"I don't know if you print freelance material," I told him. "And I don't expect to be paid for this if you use it...."

"I'll look at it later," he promised, then returned to his work, so I knew my time was up.

Days went by and no story appeared. Why had I felt so sure that my story would interest the editor who had plenty of staff to write features? Several times I started to telephone but decided that if God wanted it to happen, it would.

I scanned the classifieds daily, but found no jobs I felt qualified for. Then after I decided that my article never would be published, I found it by accident.

Obviously, I wasn't the only one who noticed it; messages were in my slot on the secretary's desk. One was from the bakery down the street.

I held my breath as I dialed the bakery's number. This had to be a job for the Cookie Lady.... Within minutes, I had an appointment to bring her in for an introduction to the bakery's owner. Excitement turned to anxiety when I realized I shouldn't have been so presumptuous.

Footsteps startled me and I glanced up to see the chaplain, newspaper in hand, and the Cookie Lady behind him.

"Good piece," the chaplain said. "Just wanted to tell you before we went to the employment agency."

"Maybe you can skip that," I said, smiling. "The bakery down the street has an opening. The owner read my article and thought she.... Will you take her down since I can't translate for her?"

He grinned. "Be happy to, but she won't need a translator. Those folks are from Mexico, so she'll fit in just fine."

After they left, I couldn't concentrate on my search through the classifieds, wondering if she got the job. After all, she taught me to think of others in spite of my own problems.

I took the other messages from my pocket. At least I could answer the rest of my calls before I left. One seemed so unlikely that I read it twice. "An editor of a local magazine liked your piece and wants you to call her next time you're looking for work. Here's her number and the name of her magazine."

Surely I couldn't have found a job so easily before I'd even mailed out a resume. No question about it—we are all one in body with Christ and I intended to remind others, just as the Cookie Lady had reminded me.

~Kathryn Fanning
*Chicken Soup for the Christian Family Soul*

# Drawn to the Warmth

Factoring in the wind chill, I knew the temperature was below zero. The bitter cold cut through my Californian sensibilities, as well as my enthusiasm as a tourist, so I ducked through the nearest door for warmth... and found myself in Washington, D.C.'s Union Station.

I settled onto one of the public benches with a steaming cup of coffee—waiting for feeling to return to my fingers and toes—and relaxed to engage in some serious people-watching.

Several tables of diners spilled out into the great hall from the upscale American Restaurant, and heavenly aromas tempted me to consider an early dinner. I observed a man seated nearby and, from the longing in his eyes, realized that he, too, noticed the tantalizing food. His gaunt body, wind-chapped hands and tattered clothes nearly shouted, "Homeless, homeless!"

I wondered how long it had been since he had eaten.

Half expecting him to approach me for a handout, I almost welcomed such a plea. He never did. The longer I took in the scene, the crueler his plight seemed. My head and heart waged a silent war, the one telling me to mind my own business, the other urging a trip to the food court on his behalf.

While my internal debate raged on, a well-dressed young couple approached him. "Excuse me, sir," the husband began. "My wife and I just finished eating, and our appetites weren't as big as we thought. We hate to waste good food. Can you help us out and put this to use?" He extended a large Styrofoam container.

"God bless you both. Merry Christmas," came the grateful reply.

Pleased, yet dismayed by my own lack of action, I continued to watch. The man scrutinized his newfound bounty, rearranged the soup crackers, inspected the club sandwich and stirred the salad dressing—obviously prolonging this miracle meal. Then, with a slow deliberateness, he lifted the soup lid and, cupping his hands around the steaming warm bowl, inhaled. At last, he unwrapped the plastic spoon, filled it to overflowing, lifted it toward his mouth and—with a suddenness that stunned me—stopped short.

I turned my head to follow his narrow-eyed gaze.

Entering the hall and shuffling in our direction was a new arrival. Hatless and gloveless, the elderly man was clad in lightweight pants, a threadbare jacket and open shoes. His hands were raw, and his face had a bluish tint. I wasn't alone in gasping aloud at this sad sight, but my needy neighbor was the only one doing anything about it.

Setting aside his meal, he leaped up and guided the elderly man to an adjacent seat. He took his icy hands and rubbed them briskly in his own. With a final tenderness, he draped his worn jacket over the older man's shoulders.

"Pop, my name's Jack," he said, "and one of God's angels brought me this meal. I just finished eating and hate to waste good food. Can you help me out?"

He placed the still-warm bowl of soup in the stranger's hands without waiting for an answer. But he got one.

"Sure, son, but only if you go halfway with me on that sandwich. It's too much for a man my age."

It wasn't easy making my way to the food court with tears blurring my vision, but I soon returned with large containers of coffee and a big assortment of pastries. "Excuse me, gentlemen, but..."

I left Union Station that day feeling warmer than I had ever thought possible.

~Marion Smith
*Chicken Soup for the Soul The Book of Christmas Virtues*

# Mother Teresa, the Wino and Me

*Now abideth faith, hope, charity, these three;*
*but the greatest of these is charity.*
*~1 Corinthians 13:13*

I will never forget the day I met Mother Teresa. More than that, I will never forget what she taught me about loving other people, especially the poor.

She wasn't nearly as famous in the late seventies as she is now, but she already had hundreds of thousands of admirers around the world. I was the editor of a Catholic newspaper in Rhode Island, and when I heard she would be speaking in Boston, I decided to go.

I arrived at the auditorium early to get a good seat, but I discovered that I'd already been granted a seat in the press section. As I waited for the lecture to begin, I passed the time by chatting with another reporter, who turned out to be, like Mother Teresa, a native of Albania. As we were talking, a priest walked over and said to my companion, "Mother Teresa would be happy to meet you right now."

With uncharacteristic boldness, I rose to my feet and tagged along. So did a handful of other reporters. We were ushered into a room where a little old lady wrapped in a blue-and-white sari was chatting with the Cardinal Humberto Medeiros, then archbishop of Boston.

I couldn't believe how tiny she was. But what I remember most is her smiling, wrinkled face and the way she bowed to me, as if I were royalty, when I was introduced.

She greeted everyone that way. I thought that if Jesus Christ walked into the room, she would greet him in exactly the same manner. The way she did it conveyed a message that said, "You are holy."

But meeting her wasn't as memorable as what she taught me about loving people. Until that day, I had always thought of charity as simply being nice to people. For Mother Teresa it was much more.

During her talk, she told us how she and the members of her order, the Missionaries of Charity, seek to recognize Christ in the poorest of the poor.

She told a story of how one of the sisters had spent an entire day bathing the wounds of a dying beggar who was brought to them from the streets of Calcutta. Mother Teresa's voice dropped to a whisper as she told the hushed auditorium that, in reality, the nun had been bathing the wounds of Jesus.

She insisted that Christ tests the love of his followers by hiding in grotesque disguises to see if we can still see him.

A few nights later, I was leaving my office after dark when a drunk accosted me. He was dirty and ragged and smelled bad.

"Did the bus leave yet?" he asked.

The only bus that ever stopped on that corner was a van that carried street people to a soup kitchen.

"You've missed it," I told him. Then I thought about Mother Teresa. I didn't exactly buy the idea that this old bum was God in disguise, but I could see a person in front of me who needed a meal. The soup kitchen wasn't very far out of my way.

"C'mon, I'll drive you," I said, hoping that he wouldn't throw up in the car.

He looked surprised, delighted and a little stunned. He studied me with bleary eyes. His next words floated to me on the smell of cheap wine and they seemed to confirm everything Mother Teresa had taught me.

"Say," he said, "you must know me."

~Robert F. Baldwin
*Chicken Soup for the Christian Family Soul*

# An American Beauty

*A bit of fragrance always clings to the hand that gives roses.*
*~Chinese Proverb*

In the 1930s, after the death of her husband, a middle-aged woman named Marguerite left Germany to make a new life in America, away from Hitler and the Third Reich. Marguerite's younger brother, Wilhelm, stayed behind with his Jewish wife and family to protect their assets, unaware of the horrors to come.

In her adopted country, Marguerite lived on a small pension and supplemented her income by raising a variety of roses, which she sold to local florists and hospitals. She sent some of the earnings from her roses to help support her brother in Germany. And, as the war advanced, she also sent money to help Jews escape from Germany.

Marguerite's neighbors viewed her as a quiet, unassuming woman who spent most days in her garden or greenhouse. Not much was known about her, nor did the community try to befriend the foreign-born woman. But when the United States entered the war against Germany, Marguerite became suspect. While her neighbors and shopkeepers had never been friendly or particularly kind, they were now openly hostile. There were mutters and whispers about her being a Nazi, always just loud enough for her to hear.

Without fanfare, Marguerite continued to send money to Jewish families and to her brother in Germany. Then, one day, she received a letter from her sister-in-law with devastating news. Her beloved Wilhelm was dying of cancer. He was praying for a miracle: to be able to come to the United States where he could receive better medical care. At first Marguerite was panic-stricken; she didn't have the extra money. But soon, she was overjoyed when a hospital requested an unusually large order of roses. This was the extra income she needed to make the miracle happen!

For weeks she tended her roses, nurturing and fertilizing them with tender care. Each rose meant another dollar to help bring Wilhelm to America.

In August, Marguerite entered a local contest for the most beautiful roses grown. If she won, the prize money of $25 would ease her financial burden when Wilhelm and his family arrived.

On the day of the festival, she rose early to cut the flowers before they were wilted by the sun. As she stepped into the garden, she nearly fell to her knees with shock. All one hundred rosebushes, lovingly planted and nurtured over the last seven years, lay in shambles before her. Every plant was slashed and chopped to the ground. They all but bled before her eyes. She could barely take it in: her beloved flowers, and her livelihood, gone, possibly forever. And the worst of it was that Wilhelm would not be able to come to America.

Marguerite was devastated, but more determined than ever to show up at the festival. She would not give the hooligans the satisfaction of her absence. She would still enter the contest, even if they had left but a petal. She walked down the garden path to see if she could salvage anything from the debris.

Clinging to life by the back fence, obviously missed by the vandals, was one single red rose. It was an 'American Beauty.' She took the rose into the house, cut the stem on an angle and placed it in the icebox to keep it fresh until the contest. Then, shaking with distress, she cleaned up the ruined rose garden as best she could. When she could do no more, she put on her best hat and took a trolley to the contest, holding the lone rose in her hand.

When Marguerite's turn came to show her entry, she held up her single 'American Beauty.' In her halting English, she proudly described its origin, how she had bred it, and the special fertilizer she had used to enhance the color of its petals. But, when the winners were announced, she wasn't surprised at the absence of her name. Why would they give the prize to a rose from the garden of the enemy? She went home that evening trying to think of some other way she could earn money.

The next day, Marguerite attended church, as was her custom, to pray for strength and guidance. When she arrived home and opened the door, the scent of flowers filled the air. Someone had placed a large vase filled with summer flowers on the entryway table. As she walked toward the kitchen, she saw that every room in her home had more bouquets of flowers in Mason jars and pitchers. It was heavenly!

As she approached the kitchen, she saw a fresh coffeecake in the middle of the table. Under the cake plate was an envelope addressed to "Marguerite." She opened it to find $300 in single bills and a card that said simply, "Many thanks from your friends in town."

Stunned and happy, Marguerite realized that this was the miracle Wilhelm had been praying for! Now she could bring him to America.

The miracle did come to pass. With the $300, Marguerite bought steamship tickets. Within a few months, Wilhelm and his family arrived. Marguerite and his wife cared for him tenderly, and he received excellent medical attention that added years to his life.

For years Marguerite tried to discover who her benefactors were, but without success. Many years later, a local woman was going through the personal effects of her late grandfather, who had been a cantor in the local synagogue. She found his journal—and in it, an entry of particular interest. The journal stated that while attending the rose festival, the cantor had overheard two men in the audience brag about ripping up "the Nazi's" rosebushes. He knew who they meant. Marguerite had never sought recognition for her charity, but many Jews in the community knew that her roses helped Jewish families escape the nightmare of the Holocaust.

That day the cantor set about calling on members of his synagogue, explaining about the vandalism and the financial loss Marguerite had suffered. The men and women in the synagogue gave with their hearts and pocketbooks to the "rose lady." Several women who shared Marguerite's love of gardening gathered flowers from their own gardens to honor her for all she had done for their people. Rather than have her feel an obligation, they took an oath to remain anonymous until death. They all kept the promise.

With patient love and care, Marguerite's roses bloomed again. And Marguerite bloomed as well. She made many friends in town in the years following the war, never knowing that many of them were her secret benefactors. And she continued to send money to Germany to help Jewish families until her death in 1955.

~Arlene West House
*Chicken Soup for the Gardener's Soul*

# You Got Another One, Joey!

*Things do not pass for what they are, but for what they seem.*
*Most things are judged by their jackets.*
*~Baltasar Gracian*

I couldn't believe it. Of all the times for this to happen—a flat tire! But when is a good time? Not when you are wearing a suit and you have been traveling for nearly five hours, and, added to this bleak picture, nightfall is approaching. Wait! Did I mention I was on a country road?

There was only one thing to do. Call the local automobile association. Yeah, right. The cell phone I bought, for security and protection from moments like these, wasn't in range to call anyone. "No service," it said. No kidding!

I sat for a few minutes moaning and complaining. Then I began emptying my trunk so I could get at the tire and tools needed to get the job done. I carry a large, plastic container filled with what I call "just-in-case stuff." When I am training or speaking, I love to have props with me. I hate leaving anything home so I bring everything... "just in case."

Cars buzzed by me. A few beeped sarcastically. It was as if the horns were saying, "Ha, ha."

Darkness began to settle in, and it became more difficult to see. Thank goodness it was the tire on the passenger's side, away from the traffic—but that only made it more impossible to benefit from the headlights of passing cars.

Suddenly, a car pulled off the road behind me. In the blinding light, I saw a male figure approaching me.

"Hey, do you need any help?"

"Well, it certainly isn't easy doing this with a white dress shirt and suit on," I said sarcastically.

Then he stepped into the light. I was literally frightened. This young guy was dressed in black. Nearly everything imaginable was pierced and tattooed. His hair was cropped and poorly cut, and he wore leather bracelets with spikes on each wrist.

"How about I give you a hand?" he said.

"Well, I don't know... I think I can..."

"Come on, it will only take me a few minutes."

He took right over. While I watched him, I happened to look back at his car and noticed, for the first time, someone sitting in the passenger seat. That concerned me. I suddenly felt outnumbered. Thoughts of carjackings and robberies flashed through my mind. I really just wanted to get this over and survive the ordeal.

Then, without warning, it began to pour. The night sky had hidden the approaching clouds. It hit like a waterfall and made it impossible to finish changing the tire.

"Look, my friend, just stop what you're doing. I appreciate all your help. You'd better get going. I'll finish after the rain stops," I said.

"Let me help you put your stuff back in the trunk. It will get ruined," he insisted. "Then get in my car. We'll wait with you."

"No, really. I'll take care of everything," I said.

"You can't get in your car with the jack up like that. It will fall. Come on. Get in!" He grabbed my arm and pulled me toward the car. Crack! Boom! Lightning and thunder roared like a freight train. I jumped into his car. *Oh, God, protect me,* I prayed to myself.

Wet and tired, I settled into the back seat. Suddenly, a kindly, frail voice came from the front seat. "Are you all right?" a petite old woman asked as she turned around to face me.

"Yes, I am," I replied, greatly relieved at seeing the old woman there. I suspected she was his mom.

"My name is Beatrice, and this is my neighbor, Joey," she said. "He insisted on stopping when he saw you struggling with the tire."

"I am grateful for his help," I responded.

"Me, too," Beatrice laughed. "Joey takes me to visit my husband. We had to place him in a nursing home, and it's about thirty minutes away from my residence. So, every Monday, Wednesday and Friday, Joey and I have a date." With a childish grin she looked at Joey.

Joey's whimsical remark, "We're the remake of *The Odd Couple*," gave us all a good laugh.

"Joey, that's incredible what you do for her. I would never have guessed, well, you know...." I stumbled with the words.

"I know. People who look like me don't do nice things," he said.

I was silent. I really felt uncomfortable. I never judge people by the way they dress, and I was angry with myself for being so foolish.

"Joey is a great kid. I'm not the only one he helps—he's also a volunteer at our church. He also works with the kids in the learning center at the low-income housing unit in our town," Beatrice added.

"I'm a tutor," Joey said modestly as he stared at my car.

I reflected for a few moments on what Joey said. He was right. What he wore on the outside was a reflection of the world as he saw it. What he wore on the inside was the spirit of giving, caring and loving the world from his point of view.

When the rain stopped, Joey and I changed the tire. I tried to offer him money, and he refused.

As we shook hands, I began to apologize for my stupidity. He said, "I experience that same reaction all the time. I actually thought about changing the way I look, but then I saw this as an opportunity to make a point. So I'll leave you with the same question that I ask everyone who takes time to know me. If Jesus returned tomorrow and walked among us again, would you recognize him by what he wore or by what he did?"

Joey walked back to his car. As they drove off, Beatrice was smiling and waving as she began to laugh again. I could almost hear her saying, "You got another one, Joey. You got another one."

~Bob Perks
*Chicken Soup for the Volunteer's Soul*

# Letters to a Stranger

*The Lord helps those who help others.*
*~Anonymous*

On a bitter January evening in 1992, the phone rang and my fifteen-year-old son Tajin hollered, "Mom, it's for you!"

"Who is it?" I asked. I was tired. It had been a long day. In fact, it had been a long month. The engine in my car died five days before Christmas, and I had just returned to work after being out with the flu. I was feeling overwhelmed by having to purchase another vehicle and having lost a week's pay due to illness. A cloud of despair hung over my heart.

"It's Bob Thompson," Tajin answered.

The name didn't register. As I walked over to pick up the phone, the last name seemed vaguely familiar. Thompson... Bob Thompson... Thompson? Like a computer searching for the right path, my mind finally made the connection. Beverly Thompson. In the brief time it took me to reach the phone, my mind replayed the last nine months.

As I drove to work last March, some patches of snow were still on the ground, but the river, winding on my left, had opened up and was full of swift-moving water. The warm sun shining through my windshield seemed to give hope of an early spring.

The winter of 1991 had been a hard one for me as a single working mother. My three children were in their teens, and I was finding it hard to cope with their changing emotional needs and our financial needs. Each month I struggled to provide the bare necessities.

I faithfully attended church and a Bible study but had very little time for anything else. I longed to serve the Lord in a way that had some significance. So that day I again apologized to him that I had so little to give back to him. It seemed I was always asking him to meet my needs or answer my prayers.

"Lord, what can I do for you? I feel like I'm always taking from you because my needs are so great." The answer to my own question seemed so simple. Prayer.

"Okay, Lord, I will commit this time that I have during my drive to work to prayer. Will you give me some people to pray for? I don't even have to know their needs, just let me know who they are." My heart lifted as I continued to speak to him during the remainder of my forty-five-minute trip from New Hampshire to Vermont.

I arrived at work and proceeded to open the mail and prepare the deposit. I was in charge of accounts receivable for the Mary Meyer Corporation, a company that makes stuffed animals. I opened one envelope and attached to the check was a note that said, "I'm sorry this payment is late. I have been seriously ill. Thank you, Beverly Thompson."

I can't explain it, but I instantly knew that this was the person the Lord had given me to pray for. "You want me to pray for her, don't you Lord?" I asked him silently. The answer came in a feeling of peace and excitement combined—I knew he had just answered my prayer from less than an hour ago!

So began my journey of prayer for Beverly Thompson. At first I found it very awkward to pray for someone I didn't even know. I did know one thing besides her name. She owned a bookstore in Presque Isle, Maine, and she ordered bulk quantities of our plush animals to sell. I didn't know how old she was. Was she married, widowed, single or divorced? What was wrong with her? Was she terminally ill? Did she have any children?

The answers to these questions weren't revealed as I prayed for Beverly, but I did find out how much the Lord loved her and that she was not forgotten by him. Many days I found myself in tears as I entered into prayer for her. I prayed that he would give her comfort for whatever she would have to endure. Or I pled for strength and courage for her to accept things that she might find hard to face.

One morning, as my wipers pushed the spring rain off my windshield, I saw muted tones of browns and grays. I prayed that the Lord would give Beverly eyes to see that the same drab landscape would be transformed into the greens and yellows of spring by a single day filled with sunshine. I prayed she could find hope, even though it might seem covered up in the muted tones of her life, and rely on a God who can transform winter into spring.

In May, I felt that I should send her a card to let her know I was praying for her. As I made this decision, I knew I was taking a risk. Because I had taken her name from where I worked, I could possibly lose my job. I wasn't in a position to be without any income.

But, God, I told him, I've grown to love Beverly Thompson. I know you'll take care of me no matter what happens. In my first card, I told Beverly a little bit about myself and how I had asked the Lord for specific people to pray for. Then I mentioned how I had come to get her name. I also told her that the Lord knew all about what she was going through and wanted her to know how much he loved her.

I certainly knew how much God loved me. When I first moved into this new town, it had been difficult, especially as a single mom. But only a few weeks after arriving, I bought a Bible for fifty cents at a yard sale. When I got home, I found a folded note inside.

When I opened it, I couldn't believe my eyes.

"Dear Susan," the handwritten note began, "he who began a good work in you will carry it on to completion until the day of Christ Jesus." (Phil. 1:6) Obviously, the writer was encouraging another Susan, since I had randomly picked up the Bible. But for me, it was assurance that God was personally interested in me!

Summer came and went, and I continued to send Beverly cards and notes. I never heard from her, but I never stopped praying for her, even telling my Tuesday night Bible study group the story. They also upheld her in prayer.

At times I had to admit to God that I really wanted a response, I wanted to know what Beverly thought about this stranger and her steady stream of notes. Did she think I was completely crazy? Did she hope I'd stop?

I took the phone from my son's hand and immediately my hand went clammy. I know why he's calling, I thought. He's calling me to tell me to stop bothering his wife. They probably think I'm a religious kook. A million scenarios flew through my mind.

"Hello, Mr. Thompson," my voice squeaked nervously.

"My daughter Susan and I had just been going through my wife's things and found your cards and notes and your phone number. We wanted to call and let you know how much they meant to Beverly and to fill you in on what happened."

My heart loosened as this grieving husband continued to tell me about Beverly's last days.

"While we were going through her things, we found your cards and notes tied up with a red ribbon. I know she must have read them over and over because they looked worn."

Then he said quietly, "My wife had been diagnosed with lung cancer at the age of forty-eight."

I winced at the thought of Beverly's physical setback, but Mr. Thompson's next words comforted me. "She never suffered any pain at all. I know now that this was a result of your prayers."

Then he answered one of the questions I had nagged God about. "The reason you never heard back from her was because she also developed brain cancer," he said.

"Our relationship with God amounted to going to church once in a while, but it was nothing that had much effect on our lives," Mr. Thompson explained. "I wanted you to know that my wife asked to be baptized two weeks before she passed away. The night before she died, she told me it was okay for her to die because she was going home to be with her Lord."

As Bob Thompson continued to share his wife's story with me, the drab landscape of my own life was transformed. As insignificant as my life had appeared to be to me, God used it to shine His love upon another life, resulting in a gift that no one could take away.

The experience increased my faith significantly. God took one of the lowest points in my life and added glints of his glory. It made me realize that when we're willing to be obedient, God works in profound ways.

~Susan Morin
*Chicken Soup for the Christian Family Soul*

# At Face Value

About five years ago, I had a recurring dream. The message was clear and precise, directing me to go to a specific shelter and adopt a particular dog. It was obvious from the dream that I would know the dog by something unusual about its face. But when I woke up, I could never recall what the unique facial feature was. I could only remember it was important for identifying the right dog.

I was very curious and felt compelled to follow the instructions in the dream. So early one Saturday morning, I went to the specified shelter to check the available canine adoptees. After looking carefully at all the dogs, I was disappointed that not one dog had anything unusual about its face. There were lots of cute puppies and just as many appealing older dogs, but I didn't feel a connection to any of them.

On my way out of the shelter, I noticed a box of puppies just outside of view from the main area. My attention was drawn to one puppy in particular, and I decided to take a closer look. The one puppy appeared to have no fur on his face, while the rest of the litter were all black with spots of white. I was worried about the strange-looking pup, and hoped he hadn't been injured. The puppies were a mix of black Lab and Chesapeake Bay retriever, called Chesapeake Labs. Each pup was named after a type of pasta. The one who had captured my interest was Fettuccine. On closer inspection, I realized he did have fur on his face, but it was a very odd shade of gray that made it look like skin. Satisfied that he was okay, I turned to leave the shelter.

And then it hit me: The face—it's the dog with the unusual face! Immediately, I returned to the puppy and picked him up. As I lifted him from the box, his large and clumsy paws reached over my shoulders to cling tightly to my back. We bonded instantly, and I knew we belonged together. I could not leave without him, so I headed for the adoption desk. In that short amount of time, the gray-faced pup had wrapped his paws around my heart.

Meeting with the adoption counselor, I was informed that a family had already selected him. There was, however, still a slight chance since the family had not made their final decision. They were choosing between Fettuccine, the gray-faced pup, and his littermate, a female named Penne. I decided to wait for their decision. I hung around outside, watching the door. After an anxiety-filled hour, I saw the family leaving the shelter carrying Fettuccine. I began to cry inside. Then I realized a member of the family, the mother, was walking straight toward me. They knew I was awaiting their decision, and I was prepared for the worst. My heart pounded and I stood frozen in place as she approached. For a moment she didn't say a word or give any indication of her decision, then, with a broad grin, she said, "Here's your dog."

I was speechless as grateful tears gushed from my eyes. I hugged the puppy to me and again felt those big front paws securely hugging my back. Although I was thankful to have him then, I didn't know how thankful I would be later.

I took the gray-faced pup home and named him Dominic, keeping Fettuccine as his middle name. From the start, he was not at all a typical, rambunctious puppy. He was very calm, serious and didn't play much. However, he was obedient, intelligent and very attentive. We lived happily together, and as Dom grew into a healthy, robust dog, he became my valued companion.

When Dominic was two years old, I was diagnosed with a seizure disorder. I was having full-blown grand mal seizures as well as milder petit mal types. These seizures caused me to collapse into unconsciousness. Upon awakening, I would always find Dom on top of me. At first I was not at all happy to have a ninety-pound dog lying on top of me, until I came to realize he was preventing me from hurting myself by restricting my thrashing movements.

During mild seizures, Dom stood rock solid, so I could hold onto his front legs until the seizure passed. He was also helpful after a seizure. As I began to regain consciousness, I was aware of his "voice." Focusing on his barking became a means to bring me back to full consciousness. I soon came to rely on Dom to warn me before a seizure would take hold, and we'd work through it together, each of us knowing what we had to do till the crisis passed. Dom was my four-legged medical assistant.

During my worst period, I had five grand mal seizures a day. They came without warning, but the force of the seizures and the physical injuries I received were minimized when the vigilant Dom sprang into action. Dominic, the puppy I was led to in a dream, turned out to be a natural-born seizure-assistance dog—a one-in-a-million pup with astounding instincts.

For about a year I had seizures every day, then they gradually started to subside. I am now well, and seizure-free. Dom has returned to his previous daily doggy activities, though still watchful of me and ready to be of assistance.

He finds ways to help out around the house—and I indulge his sense of duty, since that is what he lives for.

Some heroes wear a uniform or a badge; my hero wears fur.

~Linda Saraco
*Chicken Soup for the Dog Lover's Soul*

# A Beacon of Light

*Faith is the pencil of the soul that pictures heavenly things.*
*~Thomas Burbridge*

In Tulsa, everyone who has ever driven downtown at night has experienced the breathtakingly brilliant light glowing from the fifteen-story church tower of Boston Avenue Methodist. The warm beacon of light burns brightly every night. But that was not always the case.

Up until 1950, the tower was lit for only two weeks a year—during the Christmas season—because the cost was so steep. One bitterly cold, windy night of that year close to Christmas, the church's minister, Dr. Paul Galloway, decided to catch up on some paperwork. So, after dinner, he returned to the church. As he walked up to the heavy sanctuary doors, he glanced up at the beautiful building whose art deco style had made the church a landmark since it opened in 1929.

As he unlocked the doors, he looked up at the tower's light glowing in the sky and, as always, felt warmed within.

The minister walked through to his office and began to work. He was soon so lost in thought that he did not hear the sanctuary door open or the footsteps coming through the carpeted church. He was startled when his office door opened, and he looked up to see a young woman in an elegant fur coat close the door behind her and swiftly turned to face him. Framed by wind-blown bleached hair, a bleak despondent face he'd never seen before turned defiant eyes on him. "Are you the pastor of this church?" she demanded, slumping against the door.

"Yes," he answered.

Suddenly she straightened and blurted out belligerently, "What do you have to say to someone who's going to commit suicide?"

Thus a dialogue started which revealed that the woman had come to town to see her brother, a professor at Tulsa University, for the last time. Then she'd rented a room at a downtown hotel where she planned to end her life. But, as she'd started to close the green drapes of her hotel window facing Boston Avenue, a great shining light had caught her attention. She'd stood staring at the beacon of light in the sky. It called to her somehow, as if offering a hope she'd so longed for these last three years.

She'd thrown on her coat and rushed downstairs to the hotel desk. There she'd inquired of a clerk, "Where is that big light in the sky coming from?"

"Boston Avenue Methodist Church," he'd answered.

"How do I get there?"

"Go out the front door, turn right, go to the traffic light and turn left," the clerk said. "That church is only a few blocks away."

Now, sitting in the office of Paul Galloway, she found the heavy-set, graying minister to be a warm, friendly man who did not try to dissuade her from her determined task. Instead, he listened carefully with only gentle comments to her reasons for committing suicide (none of which is known to anyone to this very day except those two). When they had talked together for some time, the minister asked, "Would you be willing to read two little books before you destroy yourself?" After some talk about the books, which spoke of a meaningful life, she agreed.

He handed her a small volume and said, "The other book is at my home. Would you be willing to ride there with me to get it?" After several moments of hesitation, she said, "Okay." The minister was hoping that once they got to his home, his warm caring wife could help him better relate to the young woman.

But, when they arrived at the parsonage on Hazel Boulevard,

she refused to go inside. So the minister went in, got the book, and asked his wife to ride along with him and the woman to her hotel. After they saw the woman into the attractive lobby of her hotel and she left them, the minister told his wife as much as he could (which was little) about the strange encounter.

The next week, Paul Galloway's wife noticed how relieved he looked when he received one of the books in the mail. After another few weeks, the other book arrived.

A year later during Christmas season, a special delivery letter came from the woman. She wrote that the warm reception she'd received on that bitterly cold winter night, when the tower's light had brought her to the church, was so great that she had not only survived her terrible depression, but she had since entered a training school to serve as a medical missionary.

At the next meeting of the church stewards, Dr. Galloway told them the story and asked that the budget include the cost for lighting the tower every night of the year. The stewards enthusiastically agreed after their minister read them the letter's last sentence. The young woman wrote, "I want to serve as a ray of hope to others as your tower's beacon of light reached out to save me that night."

~Jeanne Hill
*Chicken Soup for the Christian Family Soul*

# Miracle Wallet

*Our deeds determine us, as much as we determine our deeds.*
*~George Eliot*

As a military wife of sixteen years, I stay quite busy and have little time for reflection. As a mother of three children and a nurse with a small teaching job, you can guess I don't often think about times past. Over the years, we have traveled and lived in many different places, and there have been many people who have touched our lives in ways that I will never forget. Despite hectic schedules, sometimes a story needs to be shared with others.

We were stationed at Fort Campbell outside of Clarksville, Tennessee, only three hours away from our hometown of Florence, Alabama. My husband was on temporary duty in Africa, and I thought I would take my two girls home for a few days to give them some time with their grandparents. I needed a break, and four-year-old Bethany and ten-year-old Sydney would enjoy the trip.

One crisp, clear spring morning, we set out for home in our small station wagon. After an hour on the road, I pulled off the interstate at Brentwood and stopped at a gas station. A while later, I needed to stop again to buy some snacks for the girls. I reached for my wallet to get change... and it was gone. No!

I thought about the gas station where I had stopped earlier. Okay, I thought, trying to calm myself in front of the children, think! Into the station... bought juice after the bathroom... then out to the car... strapped Bethany in... The wallet! I put it on top of the car beside the luggage rack! Oh no! I already knew the answer but stole a quick look at the top of the car to confirm it wasn't still there.

I did a quick mental inventory. As a military dependent, my identification card was vital to my survival in everyday life, especially with my husband gone. Also, my Social Security card, driver's license and my adopted daughter's green card were in there! I couldn't easily replace that! It was the longest drive to Florence, and I reluctantly told my in-laws about the wallet I left on top of my car.

My father-in-law and I hurried to call the Brentwood police. They hadn't heard of anyone turning in my wallet but promised to look around the gas station and ask the attendants there if anyone had turned it in.

I knew in my mind that there was little to no possibility of my wallet being found, much less returned to me, as I had no current address or phone numbers in it, thanks to our many military moves.

The next day, the phone rang. The girl said she was calling from the Blockbuster Video in Florence. She asked my name and if I had a Blockbuster card in my wallet.

"Yes," I answered, very puzzled.

"Someone has found your wallet and is waiting here at our store. Can you come? They'll be outside waiting for you."

"Of course! I'll be right there!" I scrambled out the door, totally confused, amazed and happy. As I pulled up into the parking lot, I saw a station wagon with three people sitting in the back with the hatch up, two women and a man. I stepped out of the car, and the younger lady came up to me and asked, "Are you Lisa?"

It seems the couple and her mother were on a day trip from Tennessee to the Dismals, a nature park in northwest Alabama. As her mom said, "I have this bad smokin' habit, and I guess the good Lord's tryin' to tell me somethin' 'cause I caught myself on fire as we pulled the car back onto the interstate from Brentwood. I pulled over to jump out and brush off the ashes, and as I was walking behind the car I saw your wallet."

At this point she scolded me. "Honey, you need to promise me to put your address and phone number in your wallet 'cause we couldn't find anything but that Blockbuster card to possibly help us find you!"

This family went out of their way to find the Blockbuster Video with the hope of the store being able to find me. I hadn't used that card, having gotten it in Florence on a previous visit, but the account had a phone number! Luckily for me, the most logical route from Tennessee to the Dismals goes right through... Florence, Alabama.

Of course, I thanked them profusely, but I still regret that I never thought to get their address. That kind act reminded me that there are truly honest people in our world, no matter how bleak things seem when we read the newspaper.

So, to that certain family of three, you seemed more like angels to me. If you are reading this story, I thank you again for your honesty, caring and kindness.

And to the mom in the group: my phone number and address are now in my wallet, updated with every move!

~Lisa Cobb
*Chicken Soup for the Military Wife's Soul*

# Recycling

*The generous who is always just, and the just who is always generous, may, unannounced, approach the throne of heaven.*
*~John Casper Lavater*

Since I had a truck with a trailer hitch, I was the one volunteered to haul the aluminum can trailer to the recycling center after our Bible study on Saturday mornings. It wasn't that big a chore; it took a couple of hours at the most, and sometimes one of the guys from the group rode along with me.

After a couple of trips, the procedure became routine. I would drive up to the scale, weigh my load, back up to the pit and help shovel the aluminum cans out. The attendant would make a few notations, hand me a slip of paper, I'd go back to get weighed again, then take the slip to the cashier. The total was tabulated, the deductions taken and they'd write me a check. Simple enough.

After a few times though, I started having a little problem with their notations and deductions. It was completely guesswork by the attendant, and I had no recourse as he deducted for non-can waste, non-aluminum cans and, of course, my favorite: water content. If it had been raining and the cans were wet, this was usually the largest deduction. The recycling center seemed to think that empty cans could just absorb water, substantially adding to the total weight and our deductions. I had a hard time believing this, but I tolerated it because any money received was a gift to our church fund and graciously accepted. I trusted the Lord could handle any injustice on their part.

One Saturday morning, it was raining and cold—what many would call a raw day. I wanted to wait for another Saturday to haul the cans, knowing how the deduction system would work against us, but the trailer was full. As I suspected, there were no volunteers to ride along this dreary day, so I hooked up and headed down to the center, doing my duty for church and God.

Everything was pretty much normal when I got there. This early Saturday morning, with the cold wind and rain, was especially slow. When I backed up to the pit, the usual attendants were not to be found. After a minute or so I went ahead and started to unload the cans myself, as I had many times before.

About this time a rather large fellow with a cigar and an attitude came around the corner. "What's going on here?" he barked.

I could tell by his white shirt and nametag that he was the supervisor. Poor weather and Saturday morning had combined to deter his help from coming in, so he had to man the station himself, he said. He made it quite clear that he was not happy to be there and seemed determined to make sure I was not happy either. I quickly determined I should simply stay out of the way and make a quick departure.

After we finished unloading, he whipped out the check sheet and started making deductions. He didn't miss a one. It seemed he could find little good with our load of cans as he continued his checkoff. I regretted making a run this day, but it was too late to turn back. When he got to the water deduction, he was especially critical and the deduction cost us dearly. When he finished, he turned to me and asked the name of our organization so he could list it on the sheet.

"Corpus Christi Catholic Church," I said.

He stopped in his tracks. He looked up from his sheet and asked, "What church?"

"Corpus Christi."

He pulled the cigar from his mouth and asked in a gentler tone, "Is that the one by the mountain?"

I replied that it was, a bit surprised that he would know it because it was far from there and few outside of its locale would know much about it.

Standing in the cold wind, he began to tell his story. "When I was in jail, my family needed some help making ends meet. My wife checked with a bunch of organizations for help paying the rent and buying some food for my family. All of 'em turned her down—except you. Yours was the only place that'd help us." I could see tears in his eyes.

His voice choked, "Thank you." At that he reached over and pulled me to him in a bear hug. I'm no small man, but I felt like a child in his embrace. If he could have seen my face as he squeezed the air out of my lungs with his huge arms and his big heart, he would have seen the tears there for him. After a solid slap on the back, he finally released me. I stepped back, breathless, unable to speak. But that was not a problem for him.

He tore the worksheet out of his book and tossed it away. "Let's see here," he said as he filled out a new one, quickly going down the list, checking no deductions. Scrawling Corpus Christi in big letters, he signed it and handed it to me with a big smile and another "Thank you."

After weighing the trailer on the scale again, I took the sheet up to the main desk. The cashier looked at it a little suspiciously but didn't say anything, noting the supervisor himself had signed it.

I drove away feeling warm and happy, knowing our recycling fund had grown a good bit larger that day—more money to help families in need.

~Richard Duello

*Chicken Soup for the Christian Soul 2*

# Ali and the Angel

A few days after Thanksgiving, the pastor of a small church in South Milwaukee, Wisconsin, was shopping at a large mall north of Milwaukee. He wandered into a temporary store set up just for the holiday season, which contained one-of-a-kind statues and sculptures purchased from museums all over the world. Most of the stunning brass and bronze statues were life size. Some were over eight feet tall.

As Pastor Ron wandered down the first aisle, he looked at the prices, thousands of dollars for each. He wondered who could possibly afford to put one of those statues in their home. Certainly no one from my small church, he mused. I doubt if there's a house in South Milwaukee big enough to do justice to one of these enormous statues.

Pastor Ron wandered up another aisle when he saw it. The angel. An incredible angel... approximately four feet tall, cast bronze, with a six-foot wing span and the most beautiful face the pastor had ever seen.

Thinking about the memorial/hospitality room he was dreaming about for the back of his church, he stepped forward and turned over the price tag. He gasped when he saw $7,000 in neat black letters.

"Whew! Too steep for our church," Pastor Ron muttered. His church only had about eight hundred families, mostly blue-collar workers struggling from paycheck to paycheck.

Just then a tall, striking gentleman who seemed to be of Middle Eastern descent walked up.

"May I be of help? The angel, she is beautiful, yes?"

"Oh, without a doubt. The most beautiful angel I've ever seen," Pastor Ron said wistfully. "But unfortunately I need to look at something much smaller."

He followed the dark-haired man to the rear of the store where he pointed out another angel, this one only eighteen inches tall.

"No, this is too small," Pastor Ron said. Even the little angel was beyond the price range for his church.

"We want to build a memorial," Pastor Ron began, "but we don't have that much money to...." He stopped talking when he realized the salesman was no doubt of a different faith and perhaps wouldn't understand.

Pastor Ron followed the man up the aisle toward the front of the store where the first angel, the most beautiful one, stood with arms outstretched. Once more Pastor Ron paused to admire the delicate beauty of the sculpture and the peace radiating from the angel's face. He took a deep breath and started to thank the man for his time, when the salesman spoke.

"Tell me again. What is it you need the angel for?"

"Our church. I'm the pastor of a small church in South Milwaukee. We want to build a memorial, a sort of hospitality room in the back of church. A place where we can remember all of our deceased members. A place to celebrate the living as well. We'll have a bulletin board for photos of weddings, baptisms, confirmations... and I, well, I've been hoping to find an angel to preside over this place of prayer and hospitality."

"I see," said the tall, serious man as he pulled a calculator out of his pocket. "My name is Ali," he said. "I am the owner and manager. We travel all over the country with these exquisite museum pieces."

Ali punched numbers on his calculator. Then he cleared the total and started over.

Pastor Ron felt his shoulders sink as he thought to himself, "Even if he gives us a discount of twenty, thirty or even fifty percent, we still can't afford this angel. What am I doing here in a place where original, one-of-a-kind pieces of artwork are on display?" He began to feel uncomfortable, wishing he'd passed by this store during his visit to the mall.

Finally, Ali finished fiddling with the calculator. "How does this look?" he said as he held the calculator in front of Pastor Ron's eyes. "I will even deliver the angel to your church for you personally," he said.

Pastor Ron's head jerked back a bit when he saw the figure. "Sixteen hundred dollars? Are you sure? You do mean the large angel, this one, the one priced at seven thousand dollars?"

"Yes. The artist signed this cast bronze angel. It is a museum masterpiece."

"But why?" It was all Pastor Ron could mutter.

Ali spoke softly. "Because I, too, am a spiritual man. I am a Muslim. I would rather see this angel in a house of prayer than in someone's home. All I ask is that on the day you put this angel in your church you ask your people to pray for Ali."

On the day Ali and his father delivered the angel to the little church in South Milwaukee, Pastor Ron began to understand a little more about angels. He learned that not all angels are gilded with copper and bronze. Not all of them have wings and small delicate faces. Some of them are tall with dark hair and black mustaches. One of them is a Muslim named Ali.

~Patricia Lorenz
*Chicken Soup for the Christian Family Soul*

# Stories of Faith

## Special Moments

*If I could wish for my life to be perfect, it would be tempting, but I would have to decline, for life would no longer teach me anything.*
*~Allyson Jones*

# The Four Chaplains

*For this is God. Our God forever and ever. He will be our guide.*
*~Psalm 48:14*

In November 1942, four men met while attending Chaplain's School at Harvard University. At age forty-two, George Fox was the eldest. The youngest was thirty-year-old Clark Poling, and the other two, Alexander Goode and John Washington, were both thirty-two.

Reverend Fox, from Vermont, enlisted in the Army the same day his eighteen-year-old son Wyatt enlisted in the Marine Corps. During World War I, Fox—then only seventeen years old—had convinced the Army he was actually eighteen and enlisted as a medical corps assistant. His courage on the battlefield earned him the Silver Star, the Croix de Guerre and the Purple Heart. When World War II broke out, he told his family, "I've got to go. I know from experience what our boys are about to face. They need me."

Reverend Poling was from Ohio and pastoring in New York when World War II began. He determined to enter the Army, but not as a chaplain. He didn't want to hide behind the church, "in some safe office out of the firing line," he told his father.

But his father, Reverend Daniel Poling, knew something of war, having served as a chaplain himself during World War I. He told his son, "Don't you know that chaplains have the highest mortality rate of all? As a chaplain, you can't carry a gun." With new appreciation for the role of the Chaplains Corps, Clark Poling accepted a commission.

Alexander Goode's father was a clergyman, too. While studying to follow in his father's footsteps, Alex had joined the National Guard. When war was declared, he wanted to become a chaplain. He chose to do so as a U.S. Army chaplain.

Mild-mannered John P. Washington left one with the impression that he was not the sort of man to go to war and become a hero. His love of music and beautiful voice belied the toughness inside. As one of nine children in an Irish immigrant family living in the toughest part of Newark, New Jersey, he had learned through sheer determination to hold his own in any fight. Like the others, he wanted to serve wherever his country needed him.

Upon meeting at the chaplains' school, the four men quickly became friends. What makes this fact remarkable is the enormous differences in their backgrounds: Reverend Fox was a Methodist minister, Reverend Poling was a Dutch Reformed minister, Father Washington was a Catholic priest and Goode was a Jewish rabbi.

After graduating from Harvard, the friends were assigned to posts in Europe. The four chaplains said goodbye to their families and reported to New York to board the transport that would take them overseas.

The Dorchester was an aging, luxury coastal liner that was no longer luxurious. Pressed into service as a transport ship, all noncritical amenities had been removed and cots were crammed into every available space. The intent was to get as many young fighting men as possible on each voyage.

When the soldiers boarded on January 23, 1943, the Dorchester was filled to capacity. In addition to the Merchant Marine crew and a few civilians, young soldiers filled every available space. There were 902 lives about to be cast to the mercy of the frigid North Atlantic.

As the Dorchester left New York for an Army base in Greenland, many dangers lay ahead. The sea itself was always dangerous, especially in this area known for ice flows, raging waters and gale-force winds. The greatest danger, however, was the ever-present threat of German submarines, which had recently been sinking Allied ships at the rate of one hundred every month.

The Dorchester would be sailing through an area that had become infamous as "Torpedo Junction."

Most of the men who boarded for the trip were young, frightened soldiers. Many were going to sea for the first time and suffered seasickness for days. They were packed head to toe below deck, a human sea of fear and uncertainty. Even if they survived the eventual Atlantic crossing, they didn't have much to look forward to, only the prospects of being thrown into the cauldron of war on foreign shores. They were men in need of a strong shoulder to lean on, a firm voice to encourage them and a ray of hope in a world at war. In their midst moved the four Army chaplains: Fox, Goode, Poling and Washington.

The crossing was filled with long hours of boredom and discomfort. Outside, the chilly Arctic winds and cold ocean spray coated the Dorchester's deck with ice. Below deck, the soldiers' quarters were hot from too many bodies, crammed into too small a place for too many days in a row.

Finally, on February 2nd, the Dorchester was within 150 miles of Greenland. It would have generated a great sense of relief among the young soldiers crowded in the ship's berths, had not the welcome news been tempered by other more ominous news. One of the Dorchester's three Coast Guard escorts had received sonar readings during the day, indicating the presence of an enemy submarine in "Torpedo Junction."

The Dorchester's captain listened to the news with great concern. If he could make it through the night, air cover would arrive with daylight to safely guide his ship home. The problem would be surviving the night. Aware of the potential for disaster, he instructed the soldiers to sleep in their clothes and life jackets... just in case.

Outside it was another cold, windy night as the midnight hour signaled the passing of February 2nd and the beginning of a new day. In the distance a cold, metal arm broke the surface of the stormy seas. At the end of that arm, a German U-Boat (submarine) captain monitored the slowly passing troop transport. Shortly before one in the morning, he gave the command to fire.

Quiet moments passed as the torpedo silently streaked toward the Dorchester. Then the early morning was shattered by the flash of a blinding explosion and the roar of massive destruction. The "hit" had been dead on, tossing men from their cots with the force of its explosion. A second torpedo followed the first, instantly killing one hundred men in the hull of the ship.

Power was knocked out by the explosion in the engine room, and darkness engulfed the frightened men below deck as water rushed through gaping wounds in the Dorchester's hull. The ship tilted at an unnatural angle as it began to sink rapidly. Wounded men cried out in pain, frightened survivors screamed in terror and all groped frantically in the darkness for exits they couldn't find.

In the darkness, four voices of calm began to speak words of comfort, seeking to bring order to panic and bedlam. Slowly, soldiers began to find their way to the deck of the ship, where they were confronted by the cold winds blowing down from the Arctic. One soldier, reeling from the cold, headed back towards his cabin.

"Where are you going?" a voice asked.

"To get my gloves," the soldier replied.

"Here, take these," said Rabbi Goode as he handed a pair of gloves to the young officer, who would never have survived the trip to his cabin and then back to safety.

"I can't take your gloves," the soldier replied.

"Never mind," the rabbi responded. "I have two pairs."

The young soldier slipped the gloves over his hands and returned to the frigid deck, never stopping to ponder until later when he had reached safety that there was no way Rabbi Goode would have been carrying a spare set of gloves.

Elsewhere on the ship, Reverend Poling guided the frightened soldiers to the deck, their only hope of safety on the rapidly sinking transport. As he led the men, he spoke quietly but firmly, urging them not to give up.

Meanwhile, Reverend Fox and Father Washington tended to the wounded and dying soldiers. Somehow, by their combined efforts, the chaplains succeeded in getting many of the soldiers out of the hold and onto the Dorchester's slippery deck.

In the chaos around them, lifeboats floated away before men could board them. Others capsized as panicked soldiers loaded the small craft beyond limit. The strength, calm and organization of the chaplains, so critical in the dark hull, were still urgently needed. Taking charge, they organized the lifeboat boarding, directed men to safety and left them with parting words of encouragement.

In little more than twenty minutes, the Dorchester was almost gone. Icy waves broke over the railing, tossing men into the sea, many of them without life jackets. In the last moments of the transport's existence, the chaplains were too occupied opening lockers to pass out life jackets to note the threat to their own lives.

Now water was beginning to flow across the deck of the sinking Dorchester. Working against time, the chaplains continued to pass out the life vests from the lockers as the soldiers pressed forward in a ragged line. And then the lockers were all empty, the life jackets gone.

Those still pressing in line began to realize they were doomed; there was no hope. And then something amazing happened, something those who were there would never forget. All four chaplains began taking their own life jackets off and putting them on the men around them.

Then time ran out. The chaplains had done all they could for those who would survive, and nothing more could be done for the others... including themselves.

Those who had been fortunate enough to reach lifeboats struggled to distance themselves from the sinking ship, to avoid being pulled down by the chasm created as the transport slipped under the surface. Then, amid the sounds of fear and pain that permeated the cold dark night, they heard the strong voices of the chaplains.

"Shma Yisroel Adonai Elohenu Adonai Echod."

"Our Father, which art in Heaven, Hallowed be Thy name. Thy kingdom come, Thy will be done...."

Looking back, the men in the lifeboats could see the slanting deck of the Dorchester, its demise almost complete. Four figures were clearly visible as they stood braced against the railings, praying, singing and giving strength to others by their final valiant declaration of faith. Reverend Fox, Rabbi Goode, Reverend Poling and Father Washington linked their arms together and leaned into each other for support.

Then, only twenty-seven minutes after the first torpedo struck, the last trace of the Dorchester disappeared beneath the cold North Atlantic waters, taking with it many men, including the four chaplains of different faiths who had found strength in their diversity by focusing on the love for God—and mankind—they all shared.

~The Chapel of Four Chaplains
*Chicken Soup for the Veteran's Soul*

# A Special Prayer

*Prayer is the universal language.*
*~Author Unknown*

My father is the most unselfish person I know—always thinking of others first before himself. Perhaps that is why he chose to be a rabbi, to serve God by helping other people.

Every Christmas, my father, Rabbi Jack Segal, volunteers at a hospital in Houston so Christian employees can spend Christmas with their loved ones. One particular Christmas he was working the telephone switchboard at the hospital, answering basic questions and transferring phone calls. One of the calls he received was from a woman, obviously upset.

"Sir, I understand my nephew was in a terrible car accident this morning. Please tell me how he is."

After the woman gave my father the boy's name, he checked the computer and said, according to protocol at that time, "Your nephew is listed in critical condition. I'm truly sorry. I hope he'll get better." As soon as my father said "critical," the woman immediately began to sob and she screamed, "Oh, my God! What should I do? What should I do?"

Hearing those words, my father softly stated, "Prayer might be helpful at this time."

The woman quickly replied, "Yes—oh, yes. But it's been ten years since I've been to a church and I've forgotten how to pray," then asked, "Sir, do you know how to pray? Could you say a prayer for me while I listen on the phone?"

My father quickly answered, "Of course," and began saying the ancient prayer for healing in Hebrew, the Mee Shebayroch. He concluded, "Amen."

"Thank you, thank you so much," the woman on the phone replied. "However," she went on, "I truly appreciate your prayer, but I have one major problem. I did not understand the prayer, since I do not speak Spanish."

My father inwardly chuckled and said, "Ma'am, that was not Spanish. I'm a rabbi, and that prayer was in Hebrew."

The woman sighed heavily in relief. "Hebrew? That's great. That's God's language. Now He won't need a translator!"

~Michael Jordan Segal, M.S.W.
*Chicken Soup for the Christian Soul 2*

# Of Moose and Men

*Don't be discouraged. It's often the last key in the bunch that opens the lock.*
*~Author Unknown*

Gardening in the mountains of northwestern Maine has its own peculiarities. Our planting-and-growing season is tucked in between the final thaw and the first killing frost; you may miss it entirely if you have to go out of state for the weekend or take a long nap.

The wildlife is another challenge, but we have learned to manage it. Our dinner guests have gotten used to the delicate scent of insect repellent wafting from the just-picked salad. We've built a chest-high chicken-wire fence to keep out lettuce-happy rabbits. The deer seem to be scared off by our barking dogs, two elderly golden retrievers who wouldn't know what to do with a deer if it lay down for them and poured gravy over its neck. All was well... until the moose came to the buffet table.

There is something about a bull moose. With its way-too-long legs, its huge, nose-heavy head and drooping turkey wattle, its massive rack and hairy body, the moose comes as close to qualifying for Jurassic Park as anything you're likely to see on this continent. Out of season for hunters in the summer, the adult male moose is king. And a king eats when and where he wants.

It was an early August morning that I found the lettuce trampled, several rows of corn nibbled, and those unmistakable hoof prints in the soft soil of our little patch. It appeared that the moose had simply stepped over the fence, chowed down and stepped back into the woods.

We were a little tired of washing lettuce anyway, but we had been looking forward to our corn. I sprang into action. Up went a scarecrow in old overalls, plaid shirt and a felt fishing hat. A rusted BB gun resting against his hip completed the vigilant picture. I went to sleep that night sure that no moose in his right mind would have the nerve to walk into so guarded a garden.

The next morning, of course, proved me dead wrong. New hoof prints circled the scarecrow and wandered away from the corn down to the sugar snaps. As I picked the remaining peas, I racked my brain for another course of action.

I had read somewhere that moose and deer dislike the smell of soap. I ran into the house, grabbed every cake of it, and returned with my trusty pocket knife. Bits of soap were soon sprinkled around the entire perimeter of the garden, giving the area a strangely refined and indoor smell.

But looking more closely, I decided that I had spread my moose repellent too thin. Since we were now out of soap, I came up with what I thought was a wily addition—dog hair. If my dogs weren't man enough to actually attack a marauding moose, maybe their scent would do the trick. I scoured the yard for fallen fur and sprinkled the smelly stuff around the already soapy garden.

Sweet or stinky, I had my bases covered. Or did I? In what I can only attribute to some insane, primal urge, I added my final touch under cover of darkness. After several beers with dinner and two sizeable cups of coffee, I patrolled the garden perimeter before bed, making my mark on every fence post with bladder control my dogs might have envied.

Relieved, I went to bed, satisfied with my personal contribution to protecting what was mine.

Perhaps it was the fact that the soap was Yardley lavender. Maybe the lake had washed the carnivorous smell out of my dogs' coats. Or it could have been that hops are more enticing the second time around. Whatever, the next morning revealed fresh tracks, newly gnawed corn and beans, and distinctly fewer soap flakes. Somewhere out there was a very full, very clean moose.

That day was a gloomy one, with little hope of bathing. By mid afternoon, however, I was barreling back from town with post extensions, a bale of wire, porcelain insulators and a 6,000-volt battery. It was time to show my foe some of the benefits of evolution. I strung two rows of conductive wire above the existing garden fence, topping off at a height of more than six feet. Switching on the current as the sun went down, I felt a little like the warden at Alcatraz going home for the night.

I slept the sleep of the innocent and the deluded. Apparently the crashing, wrenching sounds didn't wake me from my dreams of triumph. The next morning, as I walked out back to the produce penitentiary, I stopped in frozen disbelief at the gate. The entire northwest corner of the fence had been caved in and dragged across a full third of the garden, mowing down every vegetable over three inches tall. The moose, it seemed, had stumbled into my high-tech barricade and only been startled enough by the zap it got to take off posthaste in the direction it was heading anyway. Once the beast had trampled the fence and disconnected the current, it apparently remembered why it had got into such a tangle and stopped to graze in the bottom half of the garden.

Looking back, that final day was an oddly peaceful one. For I discovered that aside from our towering intellect, the other quality which makes us human is our ability to admit defeat.

After a breakfast of half of the remaining strawberries (leaving the other half for my garden's new co-owner), I set to work straightening out what was left of my fence. I hosed the remaining soap shavings into suds. The wind blew the dog hair into the surrounding woods. Finally, I took one more ride into town. I returned the battery to the hardware store as unsatisfactory—they didn't have to know why. Needless to say, when I returned to camp that afternoon, I pulled down the scarecrow.

In its place, I put up something more appropriate... a small statue of Saint Francis of Assisi.

~Peter Guttmacher
*Chicken Soup for the Gardener's Soul*

# The Altar Boy

*Have we not all one father? Hath not one God created us?*
*~Malachi 2:10*

We had made a rapid advance across Northern France from the Normandy beachhead. (Historians say it was the fastest opposed advance in the history of modern warfare.) Now, our 105-millimeter howitzer battalion was bivouacked in an abandoned castle on the outskirts of a small Belgian town. The exact locations of occupied and unoccupied territory were not well known, and due to an error in map reading, we learned at daybreak that we were close to a German infantry unit. Watching our artillery battalion attempting to act as infantry was laughable, but we had no choice. Using our pieces at close range with time bursts, we caused the enemy to retreat.

Later that morning, I ventured away from the castle and observed the local townspeople walking to the center of the village to the sound of church bells. I realized that it was Sunday and people were on their way to a Catholic mass. I followed them.

Inside the church, when the priest appeared from the sacristy, I saw that he was without an altar boy. I was only nineteen years old, not too far away from my own altar boy days in Philadelphia. So almost by rote, I went into the sanctuary, knelt down next to the priest and, still in my uniform, started to perform the normal functions of an acolyte:

"Ad deum qui laetificat juventutem meam" [To God, the joy of my youth];

"Qua to es Deus fortitudo mea" [For Thou, O God, art my strength];

"Confiteor Deo omnipotenti" [I confess to Almighty God].

The priest and I went through the whole mass as if we had done it together many times before: water and wine; lavabo (the ritual of washing hands after the offertory); changing the book; suscipiat (a five-line prayer of acceptance); and the final blessing.

As prescribed, I preceded the priest into the sacristy and, as is the custom, stood apart from him with my hands in the prayer position while he divested. He removed the chasuble, then the cincture. When his arms lifted the alb, I saw that he was wearing a German uniform. My heart stopped: The priest was a German officer!

The man was a German chaplain and though he had realized immediately that he had an American sergeant as an altar boy, during the entire twenty minutes of the mass, he had given no outward sign of recognition.

My German was rather rudimentary, and the only thing I could put together was, "Gut Morgen, Vater" ("Good morning, Father"). Evidently, his English was nonexistent, for somewhat flustered, he only smiled at me. Then, we shook hands, and I left.

I walked back to the castle strangely exhilarated. Two strangers, enemies at war, had met by chance and for twenty minutes, without any direct communication, had found complete unanimity in an age-old ritual of Christian worship.

The memory of this incident has remained with me for over fifty years. It still brings the same elation, for I know firsthand that, even in war, our common humanity—under the same God—can triumph over hatred and division.

~Richard H. Kiley
*Chicken Soup for the Veteran's Soul*

# Cramming for Finals

A ninety-six-year-old lady was a faithful attendant at my women's club Bible studies. She came with her lessons prepared and knew all the answers. One day a tactless member asked her, "Why do you work so hard on these lessons when you're so old and it doesn't matter?"

Little Bess Elkins looked up and said confidently, "I'm cramming for my finals."

~Florence Littauer
*Chicken Soup for the Golden Soul*

# In Better Hands

On the way home from the small Himalayan kingdom of Bhutan, I met with Mother Teresa. Not once but twice.

My friend Laurie and I had flown into Calcutta from Paro in the early afternoon. We had one day in the City of Joy before she would fly on to Bangkok and I would return to Canada via New Delhi, Bombay, and a brief stay with my father in London.

Over lunch, we toyed with the notion of visiting Mother Teresa's orphanage. A taxi ride and a couple of hours later, we were touched by the sight of forty to fifty little kids playing in a small courtyard, half of them running around completely undressed, the others in blue and white striped outfits. As we were leaving, a sister informed us that Mother Teresa's residence was in a building called Mother House, only a few blocks away.

Within minutes we were standing in front of a rather inconspicuous wooden door with a large cross on it. On a small wooden sign to the left of the door, in white lettering, were the modest words, MOTHER TERESA. When asked who we wished to see, we answered simply and in unison, "Mother Teresa." The sister showed us in and, in a short while, informed us that Mother Teresa would meet with us.

We found ourselves waiting nervously on an old bench, trying to figure out what we were going to say. Suddenly, from behind two swinging doors, we saw a white-and-blue sari and two bare feet in open sandals. We gazed in awe as Mother Teresa moved briskly toward us. She sat next to Laurie, took her hand, and got right down to business.

She asked us where we were from and whether we were volunteers. She described the trip she had just taken to Montreal. She told us that she was in a hurry as she was leaving again the next day. With that, she got up, disappeared behind a screen partition and quickly returned with two cards bearing her picture and a small prayer. She signed both: "God bless you. Teresa M.C." and left. Though neither of us was particularly religious, we just sat there, frozen in a state of reverence.

The next day Laurie left for Bangkok and I left for London. Checking in at the Air India counter in Delhi, I couldn't help but hear a woman with jet black hair draped in flowing Indian fabrics shouting at the next counter. In her distinctly Greek accent, she was raging about not getting a particular bulkhead seat. Within seconds, boarding pass in hand, she brazenly marched away from the scene and through the terminal.

A few hours later, when it came time to board, I started towards the gate. As I approached security control, out of the corner of my eye I noticed a pair of sandals and a blue-and-white sari. I looked over and saw a sister of the Missionaries of Charity. And then another. And another—a gaggle of sisters scurrying straight through security. At the very end raced Mother Teresa, carrying nothing but a single book—her Bible. In a glance, she was out of sight.

At the gate, I looked around for a place to sit and spotted the Greek woman, anxiously staring at the departure board. I sat down, and sure enough, she sat right next to me.

We started talking and, when I mentioned meeting Mother Teresa, her mouth dropped. She reached for a cross around her neck and told me how much she had always wanted to meet Mother Teresa. I recounted how I had seen Mother Teresa again only minutes before. My Greek gate-mate struck my arm in disbelief. Oh, how she wanted the chance to meet this living saint!

When we arrived in the Bombay terminal, they told us that our connecting plane was going to be delayed for a "few hours."

Thirty or forty very irate Italian tourists were grabbing their heads, motioning madly with their hands, and screaming at the poor airline attendants and each other. I wandered away from the chaos in search of a place to sleep.

I finally found one of those horrible plastic airport chairs on the other side of the airport, and using my daypack as a pillow, I fell fast asleep.

A couple of hours later, I felt a hand nudge me. Startled, I looked up. It was the Greek woman.

She wanted me to go with her, to follow her. She was very forceful and determined. She explained that Mother Teresa wanted to see me. Of course, I had no idea what this woman was talking about but, after more pleading, I went along. After all, what else did I have to do at four o'clock in the morning?

We got to the door of the business and first-class lounge. She mumbled to the guard that I was with her, and I followed behind.

The room was small and dark. All ten people were sprawled about on couches, fast asleep. The Greek woman motioned to the far corner near a dim light. Sitting there in a hard chair, hunched over, was Mother Teresa, reading. While every other much younger, mortal soul was sleeping, she was wide awake, praying in the middle of the night.

Whispering, the Greek woman prodded me, "You must go and talk to her."

"I can't, she's praying," I replied.

"Just go now!"

"I can't, not until she's finished," I insisted.

We sat down, gazing as she prayed, noting her every movement.

My Hellenic messenger introduced herself as Jenny and related in a soft voice how she and Mother Teresa had talked for a short while earlier on. This was not the same crazy woman whom I had first encountered at the check-in counter in Delhi. She carefully and proudly showed me the necklace of the Virgin Mary that Mother Teresa had given her. She rubbed it and continued.

"She's been praying the whole time," she said, shaking her head in reverent disbelief.

Suddenly, Mother Teresa placed the prayer book down on her lap.

"Go over now!" the Greek woman beseeched.

I got up and inched my way towards the light.

"Mother Teresa, I'm sorry to disturb you but we met yesterday in Calcutta at Mother House."

Her wrinkled face strained upwards to meet my puzzled eyes. "God works in mysterious ways," she quipped. She invited me to sit next to her.

As I sat down, I couldn't wait to ask her about the serendipitous nature of our two meetings. "What does this mean, meeting you again? Is there something I should be doing?"

"What are you doing?" she asked.

"Traveling," I replied impulsively.

She took my hand. "You must look for the truth, and guide others to look for the truth. Time is short. There is so much to do and so little time. You will know what to do."

We talked for an hour, mostly about her missions around the world, before she excused herself to return to her prayers. I withdrew and sat next to Jenny. Together, we studied this winner of the Nobel Prize in the peace of her prayers.

Just after seven o'clock, we heard our flight being called for boarding. As we got up, so did Mother Teresa. She was on our flight.

As soon as the plane took off, I fell asleep. A few hours later, I awoke and went to freshen up.

Leaving the toilet cabin, I heard commotion from the section ahead. I turned the corner, looked up the aisle toward the front of the plane, and glimpsed Mother Teresa's blue-and-white sari just as she was returning to the first-class section. In the brief time that I was in the restroom, she had gone through the whole plane and blessed all of its passengers.

In her wake, the large group of Italians, who only hours before were wound up in a frenzied state of frustration and anger, were now crying and praying, and very, very grateful. Many were down on their knees making the sign of the cross, while others couldn't stop hugging and kissing one another.

Men and women queued from the left side of the plane into a makeshift first-class confessional, emerging moments later on the other side into the embrace of their fellow countrymen and passengers.

The plane stopped in Rome, where the Italians and Mother Teresa deplaned. I read the next day that she had an audience with the Pope.

On my arrival at Heathrow, my father met me, his face ashen. He recounted the morning's news: A plane had crashed in Bombay, around the same time that mine had taken off. He was terrified that somehow I was on that ill-fated flight.

"Well, Dad," I began my story, "if I were, I couldn't have been in better hands."

~Steve Zikman
*Chicken Soup for the Traveler's Soul*

# God's Mountain Garden

*The best place to seek God is in a garden.*
*~George Bernard Shaw*

I grew up on a farm in the mountains of northwest Arkansas. As children, my brother and I roamed every inch of the little mountain facing my parents' house. We knew where every giant boulder and animal burrow was on that little piece of mountain bordering my dad's farm.

One day, my grandpa came to visit from his home several miles away. We sat on the front porch swing looking at the mountain, and he began to tell me a story. It was a delightful tale about him and me living in a little cabin on the mountain.

"Can you see it?" he asked. "It's right there by that big acorn tree. See it?"

Of course I saw it. What eight-year-old child wouldn't see what her imagination wanted her to see?

"We're gonna live in that cabin. We'll catch a wild cow for our milk and pick wild strawberries for our supper," Grandpa continued. "I bet the squirrels will bring us nuts to eat. We'll search the bushes for wild chickens and turkeys. The chickens will give us eggs, and we'll cook us a turkey over the big ol' fireplace. Yep, we'll do that some day."

From that day on, every time I saw my grandpa, I asked when we would go to live in that little log cabin on the mountain. Then he'd once more spin the story of how the two of us would live in the cabin with the wildflowers and wild animals around us.

Time raced on; I grew into my teens and gradually forgot Grandpa's story. After graduating high school, I still saw Grandpa and loved him dearly, but not like that little girl did. I grew out of the fantasy of the log cabin and wild cows.

Before long, I married and set up my own house. One day, the phone rang. When I heard my daddy's sorrowful voice, I knew my grandpa had left us. He had been in his garden behind his house and died there, his heart forever stopped.

I grieved alongside my mother for my dear grandpa, remembering his promises of the cabin in the woods with all its animals and flowers. It seemed I could once again hear his voice telling me the fantasy we shared. I felt my childhood memories being buried with him.

Less than a year later, I went to visit my parents' farm. Mama and I sat on the front porch admiring the green foliage of the mountain. It had been ten months since Grandpa had passed away, but the longing to hear his voice one more time was still fresh in my soul.

I told Mama about the story Grandpa had always told me, of the cabin in the woods, the wild cow, the chickens and turkey. "Mama," I said after I had finished my story, "would you mind if I went for a walk by myself?"

"Of course not," was her reply.

I changed into old jeans and put on my walking shoes. Mama cautioned me to be careful and went on with her chores.

The walk was invigorating. Spring had come to the country, and everything was getting green. Little Johnny-jump-ups were springing up all over the pastures. New calves were following their mamas begging for milk. At the foot of the mountain, I stopped. Where did Grandpa say that acorn tree was?

"Straight up from the house," I thought I heard him say.

I began my journey up the little mountain. It was steeper than I remembered, and I was out of shape. I trudged on, determined to find that tree.

Suddenly the ground leveled out. I was amazed to see what was before me. Soft green moss covered a small, flat clearing. Dogwood trees, smothered in pastel blooms, surrounded it. Off to the side stood a tall oak tree—Grandpa's acorn tree! Scattered among the tufts of moss were vibrant colors of wild wood violets. Green rock ferns and pearly snowdrops were scattered about as well. I could hardly catch my breath.

I don't know how long I stood there—several minutes, I suppose. Finally I came to my senses and sat down on the moss. In all my childhood wanderings on the mountain, I had never seen this magically beautiful place. Was this what Grandpa meant when he pointed out our special spot on the mountainside all those years ago? Did he know this was here?

A squirrel darted in front of me. He had a nut in his mouth. I watched as he scampered up the oak tree. No, I didn't see a wild cow or chickens. But in my heart, I knew they were there somewhere.

I decided to go tell Mama what I had found. She would want to see it, too. Before I left I took one more look. It was the most beautiful place I could have ever imagined.

It didn't take me as long to get back to the house. I burst into the kitchen babbling about the clearing on the side of the mountain. Mama calmed me down enough so she could understand what I was talking about. Daddy heard the conversation and tried to convince me there was no such place up there. He knew the mountain and had never seen anything like that.

On my insistence, he and Mama decided to go see the amazing place I was raving about. Once again I climbed the mountain straight up from the house. Before I knew it, we were at the top.

"We must have missed it," I told my dad.

He just nodded and we retraced our steps. We searched for over an hour for that little place on the mountain. We never found it. I was devastated.

On the way back home, Mama put her arms around my shoulders.

"Sissy," she said, "you know what you saw, don't you?"

"Yeah, I know what I saw, and I know it's there somewhere. We just missed it."

"No, sweetie, it's not there anymore. You saw God's garden. Only special people can see that. Your grandpa loved you so much, and he knew you were grieving inside. Hold that memory in your heart."

I'm fifty-two years old now. Every time I go back to Mama's house and sit on the porch, I remember the secret garden Grandpa told me about. But I no longer go out and look for it. No, I know just where it is.

~Bertha M. Sutliff
*Chicken Soup for the Gardener's Soul*

# The Call

*I would maintain that thanks are the highest form of thought;*
*and that gratitude is happiness doubled by wonder.*
*~G.K. Chesterton*

I'd rarely dealt with residents and interns, and the thought of being responsible for them unnerved me. I resolved to put my best foot forward and be the coolest head in the hospital. Working with them, I was factual, objective and confident. Maybe a bit too confident for the senior resident, who didn't seem to like me.

When I confided this to a coworker, she offered, "You don't make it easy for him, Virginia. Oh, he's impressed, all right, but he's just waiting for you to do something so he can take you down a few notches."

One afternoon, I admitted a seventy-five-year-old man with congestive heart failure. Our new patient was a big, barrel-chested man, about six feet tall, with white hair and large hands gnarled with arthritis. His strong, regal voice boomed through the unit. But he was in trouble. We tried to dry his lungs and pump up his heart, but he grew progressively worse. At 7:38 P.M., he coded.

After we worked on him for about forty minutes with every approved and experimental drug available, his heart was unresponsive. For the umpteenth time, his rhythm wobbled to nothing on the oscilloscope.

Suddenly, I began shouting his name over and over. I didn't even know I was doing it until the resident shook my shoulder and said sarcastically, "Shouting won't bring him back to life. He can't hear you. He's dead."

I cringed at the image of me leaning over the dead man, calling into his ear. I was mortified to realize I was acting like a rookie, especially given the scientific fact that he was no longer alive. I tried to say something in my defense but couldn't explain why it was so vital for me to keep calling his name.

Disgusted, the resident turned away to record the time of death.

Then I saw the heartbeat start up again on the monitor. "He's back!"

Within minutes, to everyone's amazement, the patient stabilized.

I went back to the nurses' desk, still perplexed by my irrational behavior. Apparently my coworker was, too. "Why did you keep yelling at him?"

"I—I don't know. I just had to," I admitted, helplessly racking my brain for a reason. "I just couldn't help it...."

I was even more bewildered the next afternoon when I reported for duty and the day nurse told me the patient had been furious with me all day and wanted to see me the minute I came on duty. I groaned as I walked dispiritedly toward his bed, wondering again what had come over me to make me act so foolishly that I angered this grand, old gentleman.

I pulled back the curtain around his bed to see him glaring at me. "So you're the one who wouldn't let me go!" he challenged.

"Yes, Sir," I said in a low voice.

"Did they tell you I was going to sue you for malpractice?"

"No, Sir."

"Do you think you're God? Why did you think you had the right to call me back?" He held his hand up to keep me from interrupting. "I was on the way out, and it was the most beautiful thing I'd ever known. But someone kept calling me and calling me. I was so mad I hollered at you all night!"

I stammered, "I'm so sorry. I didn't know what I was doing. Will you please forgive me?"

"Oh, my God, yes!" he said huskily. "Without you, I wouldn't have known my granddaughter loved me. See, I thought she never wanted to see me again, but when she heard I was in the hospital she tried all night to get a flight, but couldn't get here until this morning. And," his voice choked, "if you hadn't called me back I would have died thinking she hated me. But she loves me. She told me today. Imagine that. And I have a great-granddaughter, too!" He paused, then added, "All I wanted was to stay in that beautiful light, but I'm glad you didn't let me. I'm glad you didn't give up."

He chuckled at the equal measure of relief and embarrassment chasing across my face. He closed his eyes and said with a sigh, "I guess neither one of us knew what we were doing, eh?"

I nodded in mute acknowledgment.

The grand, old man died later that same night with his granddaughter at his side.

I don't know what overtook my objectivity that evening so long ago when I relied on something beyond science, beyond myself. But I've come to depend on it in a large way—especially when I need to come down a few notches.

~Virginia L. Clark
*Chicken Soup for the Nurse's Soul*

# 7:07 Prayers

*I remember my mother's prayers and they have always followed me.*
*They have clung to me all my life.*
*~Abraham Lincoln*

I sit with phone in hand, watching the minutes click by on the clock. 7:05. 7:06. 7:07. I hit the button and hear the beginning of a ring. My son answers before it is finished. "Hello, Mom!"

"Happy birthday to you. Happy birthday to you..." I finish with my slightly revised version. "...Happy birthday, your mom loves you."

"Thanks, Mom," Aaron says, a smile in his voice. We talk. He has been watching the clock too, waiting for the expected call. I tell him how much I love him. "I love you, too, Mom." We hang up. I say a special prayer for a blessed birthday for him and begin my morning activities. But my thoughts remain with him, my oldest son.

Thirty-six years old! How long have I been doing 7:07 birthday songs and prayers? I guess most of his life. I didn't plan it that way. It just happened. Aaron was born at 7:07 A.M. one cold, winter morning. St. Patrick's Day, in fact.

When he was just a toddler, I would wake him at 7:07 and sing "Happy Birthday" and tell him about the day of his birth. It became a tradition. Even when he was away at college, I would hear a groggy "Hello, Mom" as soon as I called. The only time I missed calling was the first year after his marriage when Aaron and his wife, Amy, took a spring break vacation. Certainly, I wouldn't interfere with this. Later that day, Aaron called.

"Why didn't you call at 7:07?" I could hear the disappointment in his voice.

"Honey, I didn't think it was appropriate, and I had no idea where you were."

He quickly responded, "I told Dad the name of the motel where we would be staying."

Something in my heart began to sing. Our tradition would continue.

But it has become more than a tradition and birthday ritual. Though my prayers are always with Aaron, whenever I look at the digital clock and see 7:07, I know it is a special time to pray for him. No matter the day of the year, whether it be morning or night, I stop everything and say a prayer. Sometimes I awake at exactly 7:07 and immediately begin prayers for him, knowing God has called me to pray at this specific time. Through the years I found that Aaron was in great need of prayer at that particular time. Other times, it remained a mystery. But that's okay. I count it a privilege to pray blessings on my son—any day or night at 7:07.

~Louise Tucker Jones
*Chicken Soup for the Mother and Son Soul*

Chapter 9

# Stories of Faith

## Miracles

*Miracles—whether prophetically or of other sorts—always occur in connection with some message from heaven, and are intended by God as a seal, or endorsement of the messenger and His word.*
*~Aloysius McDonough*

# Lisa

Eight years ago, my big sister received a last-minute invitation from the Lord. Lisa was snowboarding on New Year's Day when she stopped in her tracks. Her boyfriend came up behind her and asked if she was all right. Lisa said, "I saw a vision. Oh my gosh, I saw a vision!" She immediately went into a seizure and was rushed to the hospital. She had suffered a dual cerebral aneurysm which resulted in a stroke. Within twenty-four hours she was brain-dead.

When I received the call from my mother to get to the hospital as quickly as possible, my throat closed up so tightly, I thought I would never breathe again. I didn't know what to pray for. I couldn't even think. I was paralyzed with pain and anguish. All I could do was ask the Lord to get me to my sister's side, quickly and safely.

I endured my journey from my home in Alabama to my sister, hospitalized in her home state of New Jersey. Once all the family members were assembled in the hall, it began to snow. Lisa adored the snow.

I've never experienced deeper heartache than when my parents walked me into my only sibling's hospital room and I saw her body supported by machines, her mind and spirit gone. With irreversible brain damage, she had no possibility of regaining the ability to move, think and feel. My sister had left this world, and I couldn't bear it.

I asked my parents to leave me alone with her. When they stepped out of the room the floodgates of my grief burst into gut-wrenching sobs. I asked her lifeless body, "Why? Why? Why did you leave me?" In the midst of my sobs, I yelled, "I need you!"

Miraculously, my sister's head turned left, then right, signaling, "No, you don't."

I stared in awe and disbelief! But deep inside I heard God saying, "I am here. I will take care of you. Lisa is home now, with Me. Be at peace because we are at peace. With My new angel, we will look after you and always be with you."

Stunned, I yelled out for my mother and father. I called for everybody to come into Lisa's room. But it never happened again. She never moved again. The message was for me.

The next time I went into her hospital room by myself, I walked over to her head. As I stood there, looking at her body, thinking about what had happened previously, something different happened to me. Lisa's presence, her spirit or essence, gathered on my right shoulder. I could feel her there, like an angel on my shoulder, looking at her body with me, letting me know that she was with me, not her body; she was free, she was home and she was happy.

When I told this to Mom, she smiled knowingly. "When I stood beside her, rubbing lotion on her arms and hands, in my mind I actually heard her say, 'I'm free, I'm free and I'm so happy, Mom, don't be sad.'"

I called to tell my husband about this, and he recounted how he had tucked our four-year-old son Jeffrey in for the night. Hours later, Jeffrey woke calling, "Auntie Lisa, Auntie Lisa!"

I couldn't believe it. "And Grandpa too," my mom told me later. "He can't or won't explain it.... All he will say is that he felt Lisa visiting him."

It seems God's newest angel was making her rounds!

We stayed with Lisa's body for the next five days, and it continued to snow... and snow... and snow. The Lord celebrated Lisa's arrival with what became known in the Northeast as the Blizzard of '97. It was a fitting send-off.

I still see and feel Lisa's presence. When I am in need of comfort and guidance, He is there and she is always nearby. She visits me in dreams, and I feel her with me when I need her and least expect it. I'm so blessed to still enjoy and learn from my big sister, God's angel, making rounds.

~Stacie L. Morgan
*Chicken Soup for the Christian Soul 2*

# Stormy Delivery

*Courage is not the absence of fear, but rather the judgment that something else is more important than fear.*
*~Ambrose Redmoon*

It was just an ordinary day. I had tucked our three children in for their naps, fully realizing I needed it more than they did. Plopping into the overstuffed chair, I rubbed my tummy. Only three more weeks and I'd cradle our baby in my arms, not my belly. I whispered, "I can hardly wait." Then I glanced out the window at the blizzard conditions and amended that statement.

I massaged my abdomen again, this time to rub away a subtle uterine twinge. It's nothing, I told myself. The doctor had checked me just the day before and my cervix hadn't dilated a bit. The slight twinges gnawed at me. My first labor was only five hours. My second, just one and a half. My third tied that record. The doctors expected number four to break it. That's why I'd been instructed to call at the earliest sign of labor—that and the fact that I lived forty minutes from the hospital.

As I watched the snow pile higher on the streets, something else gnawed at me. I called my husband Del at work and told him about the twinges. "It's probably nothing, but I think I'll call the office and go in for a checkup before the storm gets too bad. If this isn't early labor, the kids and I will just have dinner with my mom."

Tanya, the office nurse was wonderful as always. She always validated my concerns, though I suspect many of them were unwarranted. In her usual, supportive fashion, she agreed with my cautious plan. So I woke the kids and paraded them to the car, ragged blankets in tow. We inched through the swirling snowstorm for seven miles before the first contraction seized my abdomen. In two minutes, a second contraction—then a third—then a fourth, each more intense, bending me over the steering wheel. The baby's head pressed forcefully down the birth canal. Panicked and pain-stricken, I looked into the rearview mirror at my children, huddled in the back seat.

To six-year-old Timmy I said, "If something goes wrong and our baby comes, you'll have to help Mommy catch it.

"And Danika," I wheezed to my four-year-old daughter, "you just press on the horn and don't stop until somebody comes to help us."

Three-year-old Taylor sat bravely, waiting for her job. "Sweetie, you must sit very still and be quiet."

All three of them followed Taylor's assignment, when they watched my hands grip the wheel as I labored through my Lamaze breathing.

By the time we approached the interstate on-ramp, I knew I couldn't concentrate on slowing a labor and speeding a car, all at the same time.

I pulled over. "Lord," I begged out loud, "we're in big trouble here." I gritted my teeth and panted to keep from pushing. "We need help. Please send a policeman our way."

At that very moment, a patrol car passed us.

Timmy exclaimed, "There he is, Mom! Let's go catch him!" By now the patrolman had pulled on to the interstate, so I put the car in drive again and followed in close pursuit. While the rest of the traffic crawled along at twenty miles per hour, the policeman cruised at thirty. Dangerously, I sped as fast as I dared behind him, honking my horn, flashing my headlights and panting.

The policeman drove on.

I pressed the gas pedal to catch up to him, trying to tap my bumper into his. That caught his attention. He stopped. I stopped. Jumping out of his car, he slammed the door, and tramped to mine. But I was already outside, screaming to him through the sleeting snow. "Contractions, two minutes, baby's coming!"

He looked more terrified than I felt.

He explained that he was on his way to an accident just a few miles down the road. He phoned in my emergency, with little hope for immediate attention. I leaned onto the hood of the car and panted to keep from pushing.

"There's an extra ambulance at the accident site," he exclaimed from his phone. "It'll be here in three minutes!"

"Make it two!" I hollered, wishing the freezing snow could somehow ease the searing pain in my abdomen.

"Can I call somebody for you?" the patrolman asked helplessly.

I shouted my husband's work number to him, but his trembling hands couldn't write it down. He scribbled again and again, and finally just dialed the number as I repeated it a fourth time.

Just then, the ambulance and fire truck screamed across the median and to our aid. Before the paramedics coaxed me onto the cart I went to my children, shivering in the back seat. "Just stay with the firemen," I assured them, unable to force my usual it'll-be-okay-smile. "They'll help you."

I breathed with the rhythm of the ambulance siren, and thanked God I was in the hands of EMTs. Still, I prayed harder that we'd make it to the hospital in time.

Little did I know that my husband was joining me in prayer as he drove too fast down the same interstate. Cautiously, he sped past a fire truck and looked—then looked again at the three little blond heads in the front seat. He waved the fire truck down. "Those are my kids! Where are you taking them?"

The fireman yelled out his window, instructing Del to head on to the hospital; he'd bring the children. Del glanced at the three beaming fire cadets, waving madly from the front seat. He blew them a kiss and jumped back in his car.

The ambulance siren droned as we finally approached the emergency entrance.

"The baby's coming!" I moaned. In a heartbeat, I was on a gurney, with the paramedics jogging alongside, wheeling me into the birthing unit. Dr. Hoffmann greeted me with a nervous smile.

"So, you came special delivery, huh, Debbie?" I could only groan. He squeezed my hand. "Now let's go deliver this baby."

Right on cue, Del ran into the birthing room just as I slid over to the birthing bed. With a gush, my water burst. The only thing scarier than the increased pain was the look on the nurse's face. Dr. Hoffmann's gaze fixed on hers. I knew we were in deep trouble.

"Debbie, the amniotic fluid is badly stained," he said as he worked feverishly over the baby's protruding head. "That means the baby had a bowel movement under all this stress. That's not a good sign." He grimaced as he grabbed the scissors. "And the cord is wrapped around its neck—tight. Don't push, Debbie. Don't push." He turned to the nurse. "I saw a pediatrician in the hall—get him in here—STAT."

As the nurse rushed out, my three kids and the fireman rushed in. I alternated between panting and praying as the fireman talked in a hushed tone to Del, then left.

Dr. Hoffmann said, "Del, I'm going to give Debbie a local anesthetic before the next contraction. You may want to take the kids out of the room."

As Del escorted them to the door, I heard Tim ask, "Daddy, why do we have to leave before the next trash man?"

"No, Timmy," Del chuckled. "He said contraction, not trash man."

So then I was panting and praying and laughing.

Two more contractions, and Del was back at my side as our baby pushed his way into our world. And with no one to watch our children, they watched the birth of their brother.

I wish I could say the moment was joyous, but baby Ty debuted in critical condition. Danika summed it up, "Daddy, I didn't know babies were born purple."

For the next six days, Ty fought for his life in intensive care. The pediatrician shook his head in dismay. "Everything went so wrong," he said sadly.

"I disagree, Doctor," I argued. "Didn't God give me an office nurse who listened to my concerns and told me to come in? And didn't he send a policeman just when I asked for one? And didn't he arrange for an extra ambulance to be just a few miles away? And didn't he see to it that a fire truck was there for our children? And didn't he put you in the hallway when we needed you? And didn't you tell me that if Ty had been born outside of the hospital, he never would have survived? On the contrary, Doctor, I'd say everything went just right."

On the seventh day we bundled little Ty in his brand-new blanket, and took him home, healthy and strong.

We're still in awe of how that Perfect Plan unfolded. The kids will attest to that as they sum up the events of that day. "You'll never believe what happened! We got to ride in a fire truck!"

~Debbie Lukasiewicz as told to LeAnn Thieman
*Chicken Soup for the Nurse's Soul*

# Southbound Miracle

*May the Lord bless you and protect you.*
*~Numbers 6:24*

I was heading south on I-5 from Seattle, joyfully singing along with the contemporary Christian tunes blaring from my car stereo. There were a few hours left on my trip home, so I settled comfortably in my seat, tap-tapping my steering wheel to the beat.

"Our God is an awesome God, He reigns from Heaven above," I sang loudly.

Suddenly a bizarre question flashed through my mind. What would you do if someone in the lane to your left crashed right now and stuff flew into your windshield blocking your vision?

I went silent. Where had that weird thought come from?

Yet I did ponder what I might do in such a case. I counted the lanes on the freeway: one to my left, two to my right. I decided that if such a strange thing were to happen, I'd quickly check my right rearview mirror for traffic, move across the two lanes if they were clear and stop.

I shrugged, then began listening to the music again. Yet I was more keenly alert to my driving.

About five minutes later I heard a tremendous crash to my left. Instantaneously my windshield was covered with debris.

*Oh God, oh God... It's happening, isn't it? Help me!* I prayed. I instinctively looked in my right rearview mirror. As if on autopilot, as if I had been commanded to do so, I crossed the two lanes and pulled over onto the shoulder.

I quickly got out of my car and saw a car crushed against the concrete barrier separating the southbound and northbound lanes. Several other people parked on the shoulder near me, exited their cars, and ran to the mangled vehicle to open the passenger side. Inside a man was crumpled on the floor of his car. My fellow Samaritans pulled him from the wreckage and quickly carried him across the four lanes to where I stood. I fretted a bit as he was carried: If he had a spinal cord injury, moving him might make it worse. Yet our side of the road seemed the only safe place to lay him.

As he was placed on the ground near me, I saw him bleeding from the mouth. I feared the worst. I ran to my car and grabbed a yellow sweatsuit from my suitcase, covered the injured man with my sweatshirt, then rolled up the sweatpants to form a pillow between his head and the roadside gravel.

As I tucked the fabric under his head, he weakly muttered something strange, "No, no. Don't help me. Don't help me."

It suddenly struck me that the man might be suicidal. Could he have crashed on purpose? It seemed a stretch. But since I'd worked for three years on a psychiatric unit with suicidal patients, I didn't rule out the possibility that the accident hadn't been an accident.

A policeman appeared and asked all who had witnessed the accident to describe it. I shared my impression about the man's comments. Finally, there seemed to be little else I could do, so I got in my car and began driving home.

A few minutes later, I started to weep and shake uncontrollably and did so for the following hour. I realized that in the few seconds it had taken for the accident to happen, I could easily have been killed if I'd been surprised and lost control of my own car. But moments before the accident, a still, small voice had entered my head and prepared me, even helping me to create a plan to protect myself. Never before had I had a premonition like that. Why had that happened? Had God allowed that incident to remind me that my time on Earth might be fleeting, that at any moment I could be face-to-face with Christ?

I later realized that situation wasn't all about me.

The officer on duty phoned me at my home about a month later to tell me the injured man, desperately depressed, had indeed attempted to kill himself by driving directly into the concrete barrier. He'd since recovered from his injuries and gotten mental and emotional help. It occurred to me that rarely do officers call bystanders simply to reassure them their perceptions about an accident had been correct.

I began to see a greater picture.

God loved that desperate man and knew he was going to attempt to take his life. While allowing for his free will, God put at the ready someone who would recognize those strange few words, "Don't help me," as the opposite: a cry for help. God made certain that I would be on the freeway at that exact place and time and even be ready seconds before the accident.

I'd love to meet that man someday, but doubt I will this side of heaven. I wonder how he is treating his second chance at life? Does he see how God protected him, as I see He protected me?

~Laurie Winslow Sargent
*Chicken Soup for the Christian Soul 2*

# Afraid of the Night

*For what is it to die, but to stand in the sun and melt into the wind? And when the Earth has claimed our limbs, then we shall truly dance.*
*~Kahlil Gibran*

Death came to call most often in the early morning hours. Sometimes peacefully, taking my patient as he dreamed. Sometimes violently, with a rattle deep in the throat. Sometimes Death came like a refreshing breeze and carried away my long-suffering patient like a buoyant kite cut loose in the wind, leaving her pain behind. Sometimes it was only after much pumping and pounding and fluids and medications and electrical shocking that we allowed Death to come. But, for whatever rationale, it was my personal observation that Death came to call most frequently in the early morning hours, and for that solitary reason I came to dread the night shift.

Until Olga.

Olga was a terminal-cancer patient whose family could no longer endure the hardship of caring for her at home. It was the family decision, with this strong matriarch leading the family, to place her in one of the beds our tiny hospital designated for long-term, palliative care. Olga firmly insisted they pay only for thirty days because she had chosen the Fourth of July to be her "freedom day"—her chosen day to die. Her doctor, on the other hand, stated his expectations. Although she was terminal, she would probably live three to six months, and her demise would be a slow and probably very painful process. He gave orders to provide comfort measures and allow complete freedom for family visitation.

The family came faithfully every day, often staying for hours talking or just sitting with Olga and listening to the radio perpetually playing the Christian music she loved. When the song "I Give You Love" would play, Olga smiled broadly and announced, "That's my favorite song. That's the last song I want to hear when I die."

On the night of July third, I came on duty as charge nurse for the night shift. According to report, Olga's family had been in to see her that evening and left instructions for the nurses not to call them if "it happened," as they had all said their goodbyes. "Please allow Reverend Steve to sit with her," they said. "He wants to accompany her in her passage." With the warped humor only nurses understand, the evening shift joked, "Olga's vital signs are stable and there's nothing physiologically to indicate her death is imminent. Lucky you. You're going to have to deal with Olga in the morning, and boy is she going to be mad that she's still here!"

But, things are different at night. Night is when we are closer to ourselves, and closer to our cardinal truths and ideas. I checked on Olga and, pulling her covers up around her shoulders, whispered, "Good night, beautiful lady."

Olga smiled and whispered back, "Good night and goodbye. You know, tomorrow is my freedom day." A warm sense of calm settled about my shoulders—a strong but strangely comforting awareness that she might be right, even though it went against logic, reason and educated predications. Though her vital signs were unchanged, I left the room feeling Olga was very much in control of her destiny.

Throughout the night, Mary, the other nurse on duty, and I turned Olga and provided care. Reverend Steve sat holding her hand, and together they listened as the radio softly played one song after another. When we returned to her room mid-shift, Olga did not arouse as we gently repositioned her.

At 6:00 A.M., just as the sun cast a warm rosy glow through the windows, Mary and I returned to her room. Reverend Steve requested we wait just a few minutes as he felt Olga was "almost through her passage." As I stood at the foot of her bed watching this young minister accompanying Olga to her journey's door, I was filled with awe and a sense of envy of the mastery this strong and beautiful woman had over her life. Out of habit, I checked my watch and began counting her respirations, one—two—three. At that moment, a song began on the radio and a smile spread over Olga's sleeping face. "I Give You Love"—four—five—six....

Olga accomplished not one, but two of her last life goals. The Fourth of July was her day of freedom from the pain of her disease. And the last song she ever heard was her favorite.

I have often remembered that night over the years and felt that Olga's story should be told. Because this strong and beautiful woman chose not to "rage against the dying of the light," but to accept it—even welcome it—as entry into the light. Because of Olga I have a much deeper appreciation for endings and beginnings, for the cycles of life and death.

And, because of Olga, I no longer fear the night.

~Nancy Harless
*Chicken Soup for the Nurse's Soul*

# They Got In!

I was the younger of two boys and was literally a "mama's boy." Every morning that I was not on the road speaking, I had a routine.... I got up and went to 7-Eleven to get my mother a cup of coffee and a sausage biscuit. Mama loved a good sausage biscuit. If I was on the road, I made it a habit to call her every day no matter where I was in the world. Even in Australia and New Zealand, I got up extra early so I could talk to her awhile before she went to bed. When I got married, I bought a house a mile away from my mama so I could see her every day.

On April 11, 2003, my mother died. I was devastated. She was not only my mother, but also my advisor and my biggest supporter. We had a tremendous home-going celebration for her. It was the day before Easter, and she would have celebrated her seventy-fifth anniversary of being baptized that Easter, so it was fitting that we memorialized her that day. We brought in the best of the best singers and speakers. Les Brown (her almost-son) spoke, and I spoke and sang, and then my brother, Noble, the master musician and evangelist, spoke.

After the funeral I took the rest of the month of April off so my brother and I could get all of Mama's affairs in order. We worked closely every day and even traveled together to Virginia (where Mama was buried) a couple of times to make sure everything was perfect. We leaned on and loved each other, as always.

At the beginning of May, I felt like I was finally ready to get back to work. Then at 8:30 in the morning on May 6, I got a call from my niece saying Noble had collapsed! I rushed to his house and watched as the paramedics worked feverishly on him, and then we followed the ambulance to the hospital and waited for news. Finally a team of doctors came in and reported what we had dreaded. Noble had died of a massive heart attack.

I called my wife and told her to come pick me up because I was too shaken to drive. I got home and just sat at my desk with my head in my hands and cried, trying to fathom the fact that my big brother had died, twenty-five days after my mother. I could not believe this terrible storm was raging in my life; I did not know the storm was not over.

At 5:30 that same day, as I sat at my desk with my head still in my hands, the phone rang. My son picked it up, and I heard him gasp. He turned to me. "Dad, Aunt Rose just called to say that Granddad just died!" Eight hours after my brother and twenty-five days after my mother, my father-in-law, the Rev. Rivers S. Taylor, died. He was not just my wife's father, but my mentor, my friend, my surrogate dad. He had taken the time to talk to me over the years and taught me how to be a good father and husband. He was one of the people I respected most in the world, and now he too was gone. It was unbelievable, unfathomable, yet true.

In less than thirty days I had eulogized three of my closet allies and family members. I didn't know how I would be able to go on. I realized that no matter how positive a person is, death is always painful and always difficult. Yet, it is a road we all must walk sooner or later, so I walked the road and tried to hold on to my faith, even as my heart was breaking. I prayed for strength to somehow make it through this storm. I read the Book of Job over and over again and became acutely connected to him. I understood what it was like to be hit with one loss after another loss after another loss, without time to catch your breath, yet to fight through the pain, hold on to your faith and continue to give God the glory.

About a month after the funerals I was still struggling with the grief and the pain. One day I walked in my office and saw the message light on my phone. It was a voice from the past, the Rev. W. H.

Law, an old friend of my mother's we hadn't seen in many years. I thought it was quite a coincidence that he would call now, because when Mama died, Noble and I tried to locate his number but we could not find it anywhere. So when Noble died I was doubly sad I could not reach him. Yet, here was a message, out of the blue, from Rev. Law. I was so stunned to hear his voice on the message that I could hardly dial the number.

When he answered, I was filled with emotion and said, "Rev. Law, this is Willie Jolley, I... I... am so glad to hear your voice. How are you?"

"Willie, I'm doing fine, son. Are you still doing the work of the Lord and speaking to people around the country?"

"Yes sir, I am."

"Very good, very good! You know, I tried calling your mom's house and got no answer. And then I tried to call Noble and got no answer, so I decided to give you a call and check on how everyone is doing. Tell me how your mother's doing? And how is your brother Noble?"

I was quiet for a few seconds, then managed to speak. "Well, Rev. Law, I hate to tell you this, but Mama has gone on to be with the Lord."

Rev. Law was silent for a second and then said, "What? Are you telling me that your mama got in?"

I swallowed hard. "And Noble passed away twenty-five days after Mama, and my father-in-law, Rev. Taylor, passed later the same day!"

Rev. Law exclaimed, "What? Are you telling me that your mama and your brother and your father-in-law, they all got in?"

Then I heard the phone drop. And in the background I heard this old feeble voice shouting, "Hallelujah! Hallelujah! They got in! They got in! They got in!"

He picked up the phone. "Willie Boy, I'm ninety-four years old, and I am still preaching and teaching and visiting the sick and the shut-in and those in the prisons and sending clothes and money to people all around the world. I get up early and go to bed late, working as hard as I can, doing all that I can to get in! Willie, you need to shout and celebrate, because your mama, your brother and your father-in-law—they got in!"

In those few minutes, it was like someone had lifted the burden and the grief off my shoulders and I was given a new lease on life. In only a few minutes this man had changed my whole perspective and made me realize that my mother and brother and father-in-law had gotten what we all want to get... they got in.

Yet, this is not the end of the story. I asked Rev. Law if he would like to get a copy of the video from Mama's funeral, where Noble gave one of the most powerful sermons I'd ever heard. He was quiet and then said softly, "Ahh... sure. Sure, send me the tape."

I got his address and repeated it to him, and he assured me it was correct and I told him I would get it out immediately. I hung up, addressed the package to him and sent the tape out in that day's mail.

A week or so later I was surprised when the package I sent to Rev. Law was returned to me in the mail. I looked to see why, and the message stated, "Returned to sender...undeliverable as addressed—no forwarding order on file." I couldn't believe it. I was confident I had the right address. I went to the computer and checked the address, and it was correct. So I picked up the phone to call Rev. Law to confirm the address one more time. When I called I heard, "The phone number is no longer in service." I dialed again: "The phone number is no longer in service."

I called the operator and asked her to check the number. She did and said that not only was it disconnected, but that number had not been working for a long time. I couldn't believe it. I had just spoken to Rev. Law at that number a week ago. How could it be?

And then it hit me. God had sent an angel in the form of Rev. W. H. Law to reach out to me and help relieve me of the overwhelming burden of grief I was bearing, and to let me know that all was well with my mother, my brother and my father-in-law. God had sent Rev. Law to let me know that "They got in! They got in! They got in!"

~Willie Jolley

*Chicken Soup for the Christian Soul 2*

# The Rescue

In a cruel jungle in Vietnam, a country that fiercely punishes its foreign inhabitants, a small group of men fought for survival. The sweltering heat tormented the soldiers with every step they took. Surrounded by the enemy, their losses astronomical, they wanted to hold their dying comrades, but they could only watch helplessly as the fallen men's bodies writhed from the mortal wounds. Screams filled the air, "I'm hit, I'm hit. Oh, God."

Bullets whistled by them as the group gathered to form a strategy. Their chances were grim. They were trapped, the ammunition was gone, and the only thing left to do was pray. They were no longer at home, where war was fought in the halls of Congress. They were in Vietnam, in combat.

"Ben, what are we gonna do?" a young soldier named James asked, his voice shaking with fear.

"Somebody will come get us. It shouldn't be long now," Ben replied, but he was filled with doubt. He felt in his heart that it was over, but maybe if he didn't say it out loud, it wouldn't happen. He grabbed the cross that hung from his aching neck and prayed to be anywhere but there. "God, please help us. I'm not ready to go," he pleaded quietly as he dived for cover from the enemy fire. Blood and death surrounded him. He was sure that hell existed because he was in it.

At the same time, approximately twenty kilometers away, I was playing a game of gin with a group of fellow pilots. The winner would be rewarded with a bottle of gin. Quite fitting, I thought. From looking at my hand, it seemed I might have a good chance at sampling that bottle, but in the next instant, I threw down my cards as our flight commander came in shouting, "On your feet! Second Platoon's pinned down by VC. Reported seven left. OPS has the grid coordinates. Get in, get 'em and get out!"

I ran to the UH-1 Huey, my adrenaline rushing. My door gunner, a Texas cowboy named Eric, raced toward the plane, hollering war yells, "Let's rock 'n' roll, boys!"

"Just don't slam your privates in the door," yelled Garret, my copilot. He quickly boarded the bird, ready to go. And off we went, over the deceptively beautiful jungles of Vietnam, wondering what we would find when we reached our destination. We were hoping for the best and fearing the worst.

As we approached the coordinates, we could see the tracer rounds of the VC weapons. Eric released the safety, pulled the gun stock of the weapon tight against his armpit, drew a bead on the closest enemy soldier and opened fire. He continued to fire, struggling to keep the muzzle of his raging machine gun from firing high of its mark. The enemy scattered for cover. We could see the flash from the weapons of the VC as they returned fire.

I spotted a place where it looked like I could touch down, bring the soldiers on board and take off again. I landed the bird, but our soldiers were nowhere in sight. Eric kept up a rack of fire that seemed endless. He was crazy but good—very good.

Finally, we saw a band of six U.S. soldiers running toward the door; they were being shot at from every direction. We saw one take a shot to the gut, and he was gone. Then, just as another reached the tail of the bird, he was hit in the head. The remaining four soldiers safely reached the bird, and as quickly as I could, I flew up to the treetops and skimmed across them, hoping to remain hidden.

In the back of the helicopter, one of the soldiers clapped his buddy on the back, "You were right, Ben."

"Of course I was," Ben told him. Turning to the soldiers who'd saved the group, he said, "I can't thank you guys enough. We were on a routine mission, walked straight into the middle of an ambush! There were forty-seven of us, and they got most everybody within the first five minutes. It was brutal. I really didn't think we'd make it. Sent the transmission and lost the radio, bullet right smack through it. I just didn't know what to do. But we're here, thanks to you. By the way, I'm Lieutenant Ben Brooks." He was still shaking—both from the terror of his ordeal and the shock that he was safe.

"Brooks? We got a Brooks flying the plane. Where ya from, pardner?" Eric asked.

"Iowa."

Eric turned and called to me, "Hey, Bob, ain't you from Iowa?"

"Yeah. Why are you asking me that at a time like this?"

"This guy back here's from Iowa. Name's Ben Brooks."

Ben? I couldn't believe it. Was it possible that I had just saved my own kid brother from the worst kind of combat situation in the middle of a war, what seemed like a million miles from home? It wasn't the first time I'd saved his skin. Growing up, I'd pulled him out of neighborhood fights where he'd stuck his foot in his mouth, but this situation was unbelievable. It couldn't be my Ben. But as the soldier maneuvered his way toward the front of the bird, I turned my head, and sure enough, there stood Ben.

"Well, I'll be damned," I said, shaking my head in sheer astonishment.

"No, I thought I was damned," Ben grinned at me. "You saved our butts back there."

"I only wish it could have been more," I said and watched his smile fade.

"I lost the whole platoon, Bob. We didn't have a chance."

"I know, Brother. I know."

We finished the remainder of the flight in silence, each thinking what might have been, what was. I landed the bird, and we all stepped off. Ben walked over to me. I reached out my hand; he grabbed me and pulled me against him. I patted his back, reassuring him that he was safe.

"Bob, um... I..."

"Yeah. I know."

"Thanks, Bob."

Ben and the other remaining soldiers from his platoon disappeared into the barracks, where they were interviewed and extensive reports were taken.

That fateful day in Vietnam had started out like any other day, and had ended like no other. I'd simply been doing my job. Yet, I didn't just save my little brother's life that day; I saved my own as well. I know if I'd lost Ben, part of my soul would have been lost that could never have been found.

From that day on, whenever I went out on a rescue, I always carried something extra with me. Never again did I go up as though it was another day at the job. I went up with the thought that I was saving somebody's kid brother. I went up knowing I was making a difference.

~Robert E. Brooks Jr. as told to Kimberly D. Green
*Chicken Soup for the Veteran's Soul*


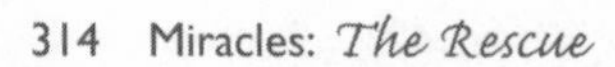

# The Miracle of Medjugorje

*To the immigrant who comes on dreams and bears the mirror that reflects us all. Keep faith—this place is capable of miracles.*
~*Lindalee Tracey,* A Scattering of Seeds

Mom always had a great devotion to the Virgin Mary. She didn't believe that Mary could answer prayers, but that she was an intercessor to her son, Jesus. While my mom was raising eight kids, she likely thought she needed all the interceding she could get!

Each of us had a rosary, and my mother taught us to say the Hail Mary on each bead. A statue of the Blessed Virgin sat prominently on the buffet, and fresh flowers adorned her, especially in May.

Mom read us stories of how Mary had appeared to a young girl in Lourdes, France, and to children in Guadeloupe, Mexico. Then in the 1980s, Mom told her then-grown children new accounts of Mary appearing to youngsters in Medjugorje, Bosnia. Intrigued by the modern-day miracle, my mom bought books about it, subscribed to the Medjugorje magazine, attended seminars on the topic—and bought a ticket to Bosnia.

I've always said that my mother was eighty going on fifty. In spite of several old fractures, numerous surgeries and a mild heart condition, she taught religious education classes, gave slide show presentations of her safari to Africa and drove "old people" to their doctors' appointments.

"I don't know if I can climb the mountain," my mom said, "but I just want to go. I can't explain it—I just need to go. And I'm not going so I can ask for a miracle," she added emphatically.

But many who went, did. There were hundreds of accounts of miraculous healings and faith conversions at Medjugorje.

Her tour group arrived in Medjugorje late one damp November night. The next morning, they learned their scheduled trek had been postponed, due to the rain and slippery slopes. One younger man who had made the trip twice before, said he could wait no longer—he was climbing the mile-long mountain path right then. My mother said, "Me, too."

So with a pin in her ankle, five metal rods in her back and a song in her heart, my mom set off for the climb. She was surprised to see the trail was only jagged rocks. Step by cautious step, she hiked upward—past a woman even older than she, kneeling in prayerful meditation, and past a half-dozen rowdy ten-year-old boys, running and yelping with joy. Soon they raced ahead of her and later she came upon them again, kneeling in quiet prayer.

Within two hours, my mother stood in wonder and awe at the top of the mountain, on the very site the Virgin had appeared. She knelt in the sprinkling rain and did what she always did—she prayed for her children.

The trek down was even more difficult than the ascent. Each step on the rugged rocks jarred her as she struggled to find stable footing. The rain intensified as they wound their way through the foreign streets. Mom returned to the group, soaking wet but marveling that, not only had she made the climb, she had done so without her usual pain. "Maybe that was the miracle," she mused.

The next day was just another day in war-torn Bosnia, but it was Thanksgiving Day in the States—and the tour guide had a plan to make it a day of thanksgiving in Medjugorje, too. On every tour, the staff purchased and distributed groceries and supplies to the most needy in the community. All of the dozen members of my mother's tour group readily offered to contribute to the fund and help with the deliveries.

Their large bus stopped at the grocery store where the ordered bags of goods were loaded into the back. Carefully, the group counted the twenty-four, garbage-sized bags. Local church and government officials had made a list of those in most desperate need, and the bus headed off to share thanksgiving with them.

The first stop was a shanty with the roof partially blown off. Mom and her new friends filed past damaged household furniture sitting on the dirt lawn and entered the one room the family of four occupied. Laughing, smiling and crying, the old couple accepted the food and supplies. Two young boys in clean ragged clothes chattered their gratitude, while their toddler brother clung to his grandma's leg, whining and fussing. Their parents had been tortured and killed by the enemy, the tour guide explained. Yet the family jubilantly hugged my mom and her crew goodbye as they headed off to the next stop.

The bus driver seemed to have the route and stops memorized from the many trips before. At the next run-down house, a wrinkled old woman in a headscarf stood waving from her cluttered front porch. As the group entered, she placed her hands on each of their faces and kissed them, one by one, thanking them in her native tongue. Inside she gathered them in one of the two rooms left standing in her once-three bedroom home. There she prayed, not for herself, but for her guests.

The driver stopped next at a ramshackle house at the end of a lane, and before the tour guide could say, "They aren't on our list this time," a man and two young boys raced toward the bus clapping for joy. At the directive of the tour guide, the bus pulled away.

"Can't we please leave them some food," my mother politely protested as she looked back at the family waving sadly.

"We only had twenty-four bags to start with," the guide explained, her voice thick with sorrow. "We have other families waiting for these—we promised them."

The team sat, despondent, until the driver stopped at yet another war-damaged home. A couple who looked years older than my mom were caring for two grown sons, each suffering from a wasting muscular disease. Yet their faith and joy exceeded even that of the team as they crowded the entire group into their tiny kitchen to pray—then insisted that they all share in the food the old woman had prepared for them.

And so went the day, house after house, family after family, each physically destitute and spiritually wealthy.

"That's twenty-four!" the guide said as she checked the last name off the list after the final stop.

"No, twenty-three," someone corrected. "There is one bag of food left."

Dumbfounded, the group looked in the back of the bus to see one lone bag of food.

"We all counted the bags and the people on the list three times," one member said breathlessly.

"There was no error," the guide said. Then, smiling, she asked, "Are there loaves and fish in that bag?"

The entire team stared at each other—first in confusion, then in awe, then in elation. They cheered, "Let's go!"

The bus returned to the ramshackle house at the end of the lane, and the man and two boys raced out, as if they were expecting them.

~LeAnn Thieman

*Chicken Soup for the Christian Woman's Soul*

# My First Miracle

*Make your own optimism come true.*
*~Author Unknown*

I believe in miracles because I've seen so many of them.

A patient was referred to me who was one hundred and two years old. "There's a sore under my denture," she said. "I told my own dentist it's nothing, but he insisted I come see you."

Her eighty-year-old son accompanied her. He would occasionally attempt to add something to her story but she would say, "Hush up, son!" She wanted to tell it herself. I found a large cancer that extended over much of the roof of her mouth. A biopsy later confirmed the diagnosis—a particularly bad sort of cancer.

During her next appointment, I explained to her the seriousness of the problem. She reached down, clasped my hand in hers and said, "I know you're worried about me, but I'm just fine."

I knew differently. After considerable effort on my part, and kindness on her part because she wanted to please me, she consented to have me refer her to a cancer surgeon. She saw him, but as I expected, declined treatment.

About six months later she returned to my office.

"How are you?" I asked. Her son started to speak, but she told him to hush once again.

"I'm just fine, honey," she said to me. "When can I get started on fixing my denture?"

Surprised to see her at all, I sputtered, "Let me take a look in your mouth and we'll see about it." I was thinking, no way.

I couldn't believe my eyes. The cancer that had covered nearly the entire roof of her mouth was gone—only one small area of redness remained.

I had read of such things happening, but had never actually seen them with my own eyes. I was dumbfounded.

"You see, honey? Like I told you, I'm fine," she said, patting my antiseptically gloved hand.

Now I believed her.

That was my first miracle. Since then I've seen many others, because they keep getting easier to see. In fact, miracles are daily events for me now. Every time I remember to take a slow, deep breath, I think about the miracle of being alive—how the sun rises and the Earth turns, all the while shooting through space at thousands of miles an hour. And people are a miracle, for through them we have a chance to know ourselves, to know God and to love beyond ourselves. We have a chance to show kindness, to provide service, and to see the miracles of one another.

Since my first miracle, I've come to understand that the time and place for a miracle is wherever we choose to find it.

~Dane E. Smith
*Chicken Soup to Inspire the Body & Soul*

# The Making of a Miracle

*We acquire the strength we have overcome.*
*~Ralph Waldo Emerson*

It had been five long years without our little daughter. How can I explain the desperate feeling? The situation seemed hopeless. We'd been in Canada for five years and had just received our fourth rejection letter from the Hungarian government. There was no explanation—as usual—just a short statement: "Your request cannot be fulfilled at this time."

In 1945, while fighting in Hungary against the invading Soviet forces, I was captured and forced to spend the next six years in a Soviet camp doing hard labour. My wife and I had been married only two months when I was captured, so we weren't reunited until April 1951. After my release, I was forced into exile as a state farm worker. Although she did not have to, my wife went with me voluntarily. Our beautiful baby daughter was born on August 15, 1952, while we were in exile.

After Stalin's death in 1953, my exile ended. My wife had a residency permit back in Budapest, Hungary, but as a former deportee, this status was denied to me. So I lived illegally with her in Budapest—where I worked as a bricklayer—in constant fear of being found out and arrested. In order to protect our beloved daughter, we sent her to live with my parents in a town close to the eastern border.

I was a strong supporter of the Hungarian freedom fighters, and in 1956, when they were subdued by the Soviets after a spontaneous uprising, we were suddenly forced to flee. First we headed for my parents' home to get our daughter, but our attempts to reach her failed. The Danube River flowed between Budapest and the town where my parents lived, and all the bridges that would have allowed us to cross the river were guarded as a result of the uprising. Budapest was now under siege, and we were in great personal danger. Despite our terrible despair over leaving our daughter behind, we had to leave.

With the help of some very good people, we made our escape from Hungary to Austria and eventually to Canada and to freedom. We settled in Winnipeg and started a new life. Our beautiful little daughter was only three years old when we came to Canada and began the process of applying for her to come join us in Winnipeg. Little did we know how many years it would take.

When we received our fourth rejection from the Hungarian government, I feared for my wife's emotional health. First she had waited six years for me to return from captivity; she had now been waiting another five years for our daughter to return to us. How much could one person endure? The most frustrating part of it was that with each rejection we were required to wait another six months before making another application.

Another six months! I couldn't bear waiting one moment longer. We had become Canadian citizens and were so very grateful for that, but the seemingly simple matter of reuniting our family remained out of our reach.

One day my wife said to me, "I'm going to pray for the intervention of St. Jude. He is the patron saint of hopeless causes."

"Fine with me," I replied. But I had lost faith in such supernatural intervention long ago. At that time, I was working in the basement of a downtown building in the evening as a sculptor. Day after day, after finishing my regular job, I went to work for a church supplies company for a few extra dollars. The bonus was, I was allowed to use the facilities for some of my own work—and sculpture is an art form that really requires a work space. In the church basement I was surrounded by dusty plaster figures of various saints. My job was to finish them and prepare them for painting. Hollow lifeless figures, I thought to myself. Ridiculous to expect any help from them.

But what did I have to lose? Why not take a chance? One evening I made a sudden decision. I dropped my work pail and went to the heap of wood where I often chose pieces for my own carvings. There I found a nice block of basswood that seemed to offer itself up for the task I was planning.

I began to envision the features of St. Jude. I had to see him first in my imagination. In a sudden flash, I saw a bearded face full of dignity and hope. That's it! I thought. I put my chisel to the wood and started carving like I'd never carved before. The hours slipped away. Usually I arrived home at eight every evening, but on this occasion it was well past ten when I finally entered our little attic apartment.

I realized immediately that my wife was very agitated. "Where have you been?" she cried. "I was anxious to reach you, but there is no phone in that basement!"

"Why, what happened!" I asked.

"Look!" she said excitedly. "A new response from the Canadian government. They put some pressure on the Hungarian government, and they have finally relented. They're letting her go! Our daughter is coming to us in six weeks!"

I was speechless. Suddenly feeling weak, I reached for a chair to sit down. I gently placed my new carving on the kitchen table.

"What is that?" my wife asked.

"Don't you see? It's a statue of St. Jude," I replied. I told her then the reason why I was late, about my sudden impulse to carve and about my vision of St. Jude's face.

We looked at each other. There were no words to express our emotions. Joy, disbelief, shock—all of these and more were wrapped into one.

Six weeks later, my wife and I stood at the Winnipeg Airport waiting for the plane that would bring our daughter home to us, to

Canada and to freedom. Back then, the airport was more like a barn in a large field. We saw the plane land, but it was far away across the field. I could see people disembarking. Guards were placed there to keep the waiting people back. And then, suddenly, I saw her! Our little girl—now almost ten years old! In an instant, I broke free of the guards. I ran to her and in one miraculous moment, embraced her. My heart was overjoyed. Our beloved daughter had finally come home!

~Alex Domokos
*Chicken Soup for the Canadian Soul*

# The Calling

There was nothing spoken. Words seemed unnecessary as I gazed in amazement at the most beautiful face I had ever seen in my life. I wanted to recall every detail of her divine face always. Yet now, when I try to describe it, I have no words, only the feeling of her divine presence. At the time, I didn't even question that this was happening to me. I allowed myself to feel the experience and accept the reality with peace and contentment.

I had just moved out of my parents' house when I saw this affirmation of my prayers, Mary, the Blessed Mother of God. My eyes opened, and I focused on her face. I couldn't believe she was appearing to me, of all people, and in my bedroom. It all seemed so surreal and so unbelievable. Shouldn't Mary, Mother of God, be appearing at the Vatican or some holy shrine? What possible business did she have with me?

A few months later, I was returning from Italy, and as we were preparing to land in New York City a stranger approached me. The middle-aged woman said, "I just returned from a pilgrimage to Medjugorje, and I feel strongly that I need to give you this picture of Mary." You can imagine my shock as the emerald eyes of this compelling woman held me captive. Of the five hundred passengers on board the plane, she had chosen me.

Normally I would have put the picture in my room at home, but for some reason I decided to frame it and place it in my office at work. It sat on my desk for several years. One day a coworker approached me and told me he had always been drawn to the picture, but now he seemed to have a real connection. He said he was worried about his wife. She had been visiting a home in Yonkers, where oil supposedly was seeping from a statue of the Blessed Mother. The poor man thought his wife may have lost her mind.

I said softly, "It could be true." I added that I would be happy to investigate for him.

On my way that bright morning in April, I thought, This place, Yonkers, is near the Bronx. If this miracle is indeed true, shouldn't it be happening in Rome or Jerusalem? But as I drove up to the humble, freshly painted light blue house, I realized that, as usual, anything could happen. I would try to open my heart to the possibilities.

I arrived just before 7:00 A.M., a bit early for a Saturday, but I wanted to be sure that I had the right house, and I wanted time to sit and think about the situation. But before I could even examine the house, a tiny, wrinkled woman with silvery hair and coal-colored eyes approached my car, seemingly from out of nowhere. Her wide grin and quiet whisper assured me she was glad I came at such an early hour. In fact, it almost seemed as if she was expecting me.

As I entered her home, I was taken aback by the dizzying scent. The woman seemed to know. She grabbed my arm and whispered something in my ear. I turned to her as if in a dream and realized she had said "Rose-scented." She motioned me toward a small room off the kitchen, and as I approached I hesitated on the threshold as the scent overwhelmed my senses. I had never experienced anything like it in my entire life—it was sweet yet pungent, light yet powerful. I can still remember how the scent seemed to surround me like a fog, lingering above my head, then flowing downward and around my body like a soft, comforting blanket.

And then I saw it. The statue of Mary was literally oozing with oil. My first instinct was to walk around trying to find the pump or electrical connection. This had to be some kind of hoax. But when I felt the oil, I knew it was real. When you come in contact with the divine, you know—you just know—and it was happening to me.

I made several visits to Muna's house after that. On one particular visit, she informed me that the oil had begun seeping from the walls and furniture as well as from the statue. She said she didn't know what to do about it, so she used cotton to catch some of the oil. She was giving away the cotton-soaked oil and offered me a bag. I accepted it, of course, brought home the precious gift, and placed it on my dresser. Little did I know that I soon would need to use it.

When I got the call several months later, I knew I had to go. I was afraid, but I knew I had to do it. The baby was only three months old when she contracted meningitis, and as I arrived at the hospital and saw all the long faces, I knew the prognosis was not a good one; she was not expected to live. If she did, the doctor said, there would be severe damage. I talked to the family, and every one of them was open to any prayers or any form of healing that might save their baby. I didn't know why or how I had come to be there or who in fact had known that I had the oil, but what I did know was that I had to use it for healing, and I had to do it now.

I walked into the immaculately white hospital room and saw the helpless child lying listlessly on the white linens, tubes coming from what seemed like every part of her tiny body. I had a very strange feeling that I knew exactly what to do. I walked over and touched her spine, gently rubbing the oil into her skin so as not to dislodge the tubes. She didn't move, but I swear I saw a twitch of a smile as I continued to rub the oil up and down her spine.

Two days later, little Eva was alert, nursing and back in her family's arms. The doctor called it a miracle. Today Eva is perfectly fine.

From the silence of that first vision, from the lack of words and the awe, from the feeling of the divine presence come the peace and the contentment in knowing that I have helped to bring joy and comfort to others. That I, an ordinary girl from New Jersey, have been given the gift of grace is still quite unbelievable to me, but I have accepted this calling. And when I am called again, I hope that I will hear and react accordingly, for if I have learned anything from this experience it is the old cliché—that it is in giving that you truly receive. And perhaps that is the true miracle.

~Dawn J. as told to Cheri Lomonte
*Chicken Soup for the Christian Soul 2*

# CPR

*So our human life but dies down to its root,*
*and still puts forth its green blade to eternity.*
*~Henry David Thoreau*

One Sunday morning I heard my minister say if you want results from prayer, pray for thirty days without ceasing. I didn't know why it was thirty days, but I was willing to give it a try. The following became my daily prayer:

*I am available Lord to be used by you each day.*
*Guide me, precious Lord, and lead me in what I say and do.*
*May my words and actions be a witness that you are living in me.*
*To the one that is lonely, may I be a friend.*
*To those with heavy burdens, help me to meet their needs.*
*Lord I do not want fame or fortune.*
*My prayer is that you will use me to glorify your name.*
*I know I don't have much to offer, but I will give you my all.*
*Guide me to be what you want me to be.*
*Amen.*

On the twenty-first day of this prayer, CPR took on a new meaning for me.

I was working an extremely busy twelve-hour night shift in labor and delivery. I had just sat down for my first break when a phone call came from my friend working in the emergency room. I barely recognized her urgent voice. An eighteen-year-old boy had been brought to the ER for alcohol and drug overdose. The young man was very close to death, and they had done all they could do to help him. The father of this boy was requesting a priest or minister, and they were having difficulty locating one who could come to the ER quickly. My friend stated, "We know you're a Christian, and we need you to come and try to comfort this father. Please help."

Reluctantly, I said I would come down. As I waited for the elevator, my thoughts became very judgmental and frustration welled up inside me. Then I remembered the prayer I'd been praying. I walked into the ER and approached the father. Taking his hand, I silently led him to the chapel. Before I could even say, "I am not a minister," this six-foot, 220-pound man sank into the chair and became a brokenhearted child.

Through his nonstop sobbing, he spoke, "Christian, pray for Raymond. I remember the first time I held my boy. I felt so proud, and I just kept saying, 'I have a son.' As the years passed, those tiny feet became bigger and walked away from his family's love and entered a strange, hardened and destructive world. Tonight too much alcohol and an overdose of drugs are taking his life. It's as though he wants to rebel against everything his family stood for. He knew what he was doing was wrong. Sometimes he seemed so afraid, but he wouldn't stop. Now it is too late. Christian, you have to pray for Raymond."

Those large hands trembled in mine and, as I looked into his eyes, I mourned with him. Silence fell between us, as I searched for the words that would comfort this crumbling tower of a man. I felt so inadequate. I wanted to scream, "Lord, it has only been twenty-one days since I began that prayer! I am not ready for this!"

Time was running out, and I knew I couldn't stall any longer. I clutched his hands, now wet with tears, and began to pray. The words came easily, much to my surprise.

I finished praying with him and went to Raymond's bedside. I took his cold, lifeless hand, and once again began to pray. "Lord, I am asking for a miracle, and I know you can do it."

I stayed with them both until Raymond was taken to intensive care. I visited Raymond on a daily basis and continued to pray for him. Eight days passed with little improvement. On the ninth day, I entered the ICU and a miracle had taken place. Raymond was awake and talking with his father.

CPR had taken on a new meaning for me: Christian Pray for Raymond. As I left the ICU with tears falling down my face, I realized, that was the thirtieth day of my prayer.

Now, I not only believe in miracles, I depend on them.

~Johnnie Dowdy
*Chicken Soup for the Nurse's Soul*

# Stories of Faith

## Celebrating Life

*As you grow older, you'll find the only things you regret are the things you didn't do.*
*~Zachary Scott*

# A Second Chance

*When you are ready, come to me. I will take you into nature.*
*In nature you will learn everything that you need to know.*
*~Rolling Thunder, Cherokee Medicine Man*

Sitting up in the hospital bed, Buddy smiled and reassured his wife, Ruth, "I'll be waltzing you across the dance floor again soon." Ruth nodded and squeezed his hand a little tighter. Looking at the man she loved, she knew this ordeal had frightened him much more than he would ever show. But Buddy was not the kind of man to let a thing like a mild heart attack dampen his spirits. Instead, he was making a concerted effort to put everyone at ease. Besides, the doctors assured him that he could go home in a few days. So Buddy's mood was even more jovial than usual, joking and winking at his wife.

That changed in an instant as Buddy's expression suddenly went blank. He called out, "Ruth, everybody, come closer—quick!" He then quietly began to recite his confirmation verse, and continued with the Lord's Prayer, asking everyone to say it with him. Then, Buddy looked up at his family and said, "This is it—I love you all. Goodbye..."

Ruth cried out, "Help him!" as she felt his hand go limp in hers. The room was immediately filled with doctors and nurses, and the panic-stricken family was pushed from the room. Ruth watched helplessly from the hall.

Buddy was watching, too, but not from the hall. Floating above all the commotion, he was looking calmly down at the frantic scene. Suddenly, he felt himself being pulled through a tunnel of brilliant light. He could see the most beautiful view up ahead. It was like nothing he had ever seen before, and he knew it was not a dream.

Ahead, he saw a mountain covered with flowers from the foot to the peak. Each bloom exploded in brilliant color, and not even the tiniest blossom was hidden from view by leaves or stems. At the bottom of the mountain, Buddy saw a figure cloaked in pure light at the center of a group of people. Buddy knew he was in the presence of God.

A little girl wearing a nightgown stood nearby. The child smiled up at him, then walked to the figure whose arms were outstretched to greet her. Buddy began walking toward the shining figure, an overwhelming sensation of peace and joy growing stronger with each step. Then, with only a few feet to go, he could go no farther. The figure put up a hand and spoke, "Stop, it's not time. Go back."

Buddy's eyes fluttered open. For an instant the light still filled his hospital room, but then it was gone. Past the doctors and nurses Buddy could see his worried family, and he smiled. Ruth blew him a kiss, looked up and whispered, "Thank you."

"It was a massive heart attack." That was the doctor's diagnosis the day all Buddy's vital signs had indeed stopped. Triple-bypass surgery was successful a week later, and in time Buddy regained his strength and his health.

But from then on that vision was never far from him, and neither were those words: "Stop, it's not time. Go back."

Ruth and Buddy knew more than ever that each day they had together was a special gift. Dozens of family members and friends were invited to a golden celebration for their forty-fifth wedding anniversary instead of waiting for a fiftieth anniversary to celebrate their long marriage. At the toast, Ruth told everyone, "Buddy and I believe that as long as you are celebrating together, every year is golden."

Buddy enjoyed each day with renewed appreciation. The smell of fresh-cut grass, the taste of iced tea on a hot summer day, the laughter of a friend, offering comfort by letting someone cry on his shoulder—these were things far too precious to take for granted.

Twelve years later, while he was resting in the shade of his favorite tree, Buddy's spirit left his body again. Without a doubt, that shining figure spoke to him in a strong, reassuring voice, "Come with me. Now is the time," and welcomed him home with outstretched arms.

I remember walking in at my dad's funeral and seeing more people in that church building than I had ever seen there before. People were standing in the aisles and outside the doors of the sanctuary. Everyone spoke of the glimpse of heaven Daddy had seen for a moment more than a decade before. The thought was comforting in facing the awful pain of his death, but I noticed something more about life, too.

Although I knew my dad was a special person, I had no idea until his funeral how many other people felt the same way. I realized that a successful life is measured by how you live and love in the time you are given. Daddy was given a second lease on life and made the most of it, not by getting busier, but by enjoying it more fully. And spending it on people. That's what second chances are for.

~Renae Pick
*Chicken Soup for the Golden Soul*

# One More Chance

*Heaven's the perfection of all that can be said or thought—*
*riches, delight, harmony, health, beauty;*
*and all these not subject to the waste of time, but in their height eternal.*
*~James Shirley*

One night in April 1997, my husband Andrew was having a routine evening at work. It was dark and the day's warmth had given way to the coolness of a spring evening. Andy was the supervisor that night for the local emergency medical services that provide advanced life support to most of our county. He was hoping for a quiet end to his shift when a call came over his radio that there was an unconscious person at the local Kmart. He turned his truck in the direction of the strip mall and hit the lights. He would provided back-up and support to the team of paramedics and EMTs that responded ahead of him.

When Andy arrived, a middle-aged man was sitting in the shoe department of Kmart acting somewhat combative and confused. The man talked with the ambulance crew, then became unresponsive, and then began responding again. Within a few minutes however, he was unconscious and on the floor. When the paramedics placed the heart monitor on the man's chest, they saw on the display what they call a fatal heart rhythm, ventricular tachycardia or V-Tach. His heart was beating incredibly fast and not effectively pumping blood to his vital organs. In this state, he wouldn't be able to survive long.

My husband and the team began their work. They quickly

administered the prescribed medications and contacted the emergency department physician to give them orders. Soon, however, it was obvious that the medications had failed to work and the man's condition worsened. Their next step was to defibrillate (or shock) him with an electric current to attempt to get his heart back into a healthy rhythm. By all accounts, this man was clinically dead, or would be soon.

After an initial electric shock, the man came around but then deteriorated and again lost consciousness. His heart returned to that awful rhythm. After another electrical shock, he was brought back to consciousness. But instead of calm and compliant behavior, he was confused and belligerent and was obviously angry with them because, he said, they had "brought him back."

The man was transported to the Emergency Department at the hospital close by and Andy came home from his shift. He told me how interesting the call had been. He was perplexed that the man was angry with them for saving him, while most people are grateful beyond words.

After that, we didn't think much more of the day, it was just another day at work for Andy. That is, until about a month later when a letter arrived at the emergency department, addressed to the ER staff and ambulance crew. The letter was from the man who they'd rescued in the shoe department of Kmart.

In the letter, he thanked everyone for their love and understanding toward him when he needed them. He said that he had since undergone by-pass surgery, and had a device implanted in his heart that would keep the rhythm normal and he was growing stronger every day.

He also apologized for getting angry with the crew when they revived him. The rest of the letter confirmed to Andy why he does what he does:

It read:

> *...I'll never be fully able to thank you for what you've done for me but will try by moving forward with the rest of my life, making*

*it as vibrant and positive as an example to others who may feel it's okay to ignore their health the way I did.*

Then he shared:

*I went to Heaven... at least twice! It was a glorious experience and I still revel in the sense of peace and serenity I experienced in those few, brief moments. I now fully understand and accept that it wasn't my time to go to this glorious place. I know enough now not to fear death, but also enough to love and respect life and to seek the plans I know God still has for me here on earth. For the rest of my life, I have the pleasure of living now with more than a mere belief in my Creator and the place He has waiting for us all, but rather with the fact that these things are all very real and are meant for all who chose to follow Him.*

That truth set his life on a course that will change not only him, but all of us.

~Audrey Gilger
*Chicken Soup for the Christian Soul 2*

# High-Flying Nun

Gumption and prayers have helped me live my dreams for more than seven decades. As an eleven-year-old, I read a news story about a barking dog leading two nuns to a newborn baby abandoned in the bushes. My dream of becoming a nun and helping others was born. Five years later I joined a convent in Mission San Jose.

After serving as a Dominican Sister for thirty-six years, I began to dream new dreams. Pope John XXIII had announced that nuns should consider leading more contemporary lives. In my early fifties at the time, I remember thinking, I could do that. So when I was asked to teach high school science, I wasted no time accepting the offer and tackling the preparation required to teach these courses. I provided the gumption, and I asked everyone I knew to lift up their prayers for me. Despite my "advanced age," I earned two master's degrees, and later finished a Ph.D. at the ripe old age of sixty-seven.

Following the pope's directive ended up being fun. My new "contemporary life" included flying, bungee jumping, sky diving and striving to do other things I had never contemplated. Somewhere along the way I was called "the high-flying nun," and that nickname has stuck.

I took jobs with the Archdiocese in Los Angeles as a curriculum coordinator and then as a director of education for the California Museum of Science and Industry in Los Angeles. A student's comment triggered the beginning of a new dream. The student said, "This is supposed to be a science museum, and there's nothing about space science." My passion for space science was born.

After organizing an Explorer Post Program, I took its sixty-three young members up and down the state of California to visit aerospace companies such as Lockheed and Rockwell. Next came tours on four chartered planes with the museum's docents and their family members to see the astronauts fly into space on Apollo missions from Cape Canaveral.

Another dream was fulfilled when NASA asked if I would teach hundreds of inner-city children about space. With stars and planets twinkling in my eyes, I spent twelve years traveling as an aerospace education specialist, showing children aircraft models, space rockets, astronaut suits and moon rocks, and teaching them about scientific principles from gravity to inertia.

When I was seventy-two, I retired from NASA and refocused. Now I fly just once a month up and down the California coast working for the Jet Propulsion Laboratory to teach elementary students.

Aging hasn't stopped me from doing fulfilling and fun things. With tremendous fulfillment, I traveled to Bosnia and Croatia to help orphans. More recently, I went to Honduras and Guatemala, taking along toothbrushes, toothpaste, T-shirts and learning items such as periscopes and magnifying glasses.

Just for fun when I was seventy-nine, I white-water rafted down the Colorado River, hiked for miles and slept under the stars along the Grand Canyon. And only months ago I accepted the invitation of a pilot at an air show to soar into the sky on a navy training plane to enjoy a few aerobatic twists and turns. He even let me pilot the plane! My only regret is that we didn't turn upside down.

People often ask what has been the most fun and fulfilling dream in my life. Hands down, it's the students. I remember one extremely troubled high school student who was going downhill fast. He wrote me a letter I still have. Evidently my teaching about science and space touched a chord in him, for he wrote, "Sometimes I lie out at night just looking at the stars." When I was eighty, he found out where I lived and came to show me how well he had done. He owned his own company, and he had with him a lovely wife and their baby.

I've loved my career of literally soaring with mind, body and spirit upward to the heavens. But the real thrill has been showing young people how to reach their own stars.

~Sister Clarice Lolich as told to Diana L. Chapman
*Chicken Soup for the Golden Soul*

# How to Be New and Different

*Nobody can make you feel inferior without your consent.*
*~Eleanor Roosevelt*

The year 1993 wasn't shaping up to be the best year of my life. I was into my eighth year as a single parent, had three kids in college, my unmarried daughter had just given birth to my first grandchild and I was about to break up with a very nice man I'd dated for over two years. Faced with all this, I was spending lots of time feeling sorry for myself.

That April, I was asked to interview and write about a woman who lived in a small town in Minnesota. So during Easter vacation, Andrew, my thirteen-year-old, and I drove across two states to meet Jan Turner.

Andrew dozed most of the way during the long drive, but every once in a while I'd start a conversation.

"She's handicapped, you know."

"So what's wrong with her? Does she have a disease?"

"I don't think so. But for some reason, she had to have both arms and legs amputated."

"Wow. How does she get around?"

"I'm not sure. We'll see when we get there."

"Does she have any kids?"

"Two boys—Tyler and Cody—both adopted. She's a single parent, too. Only she's never been married."

"So what happened to her?"

"Four years ago Jan was just like me, a busy single mother. She was a full-time music teacher at a grade school and taught all sorts of musical instruments. She was also the music director at her church."

Andrew fell asleep again before I could finish telling him what little I did know about what had happened to Jan. As I drove across Minnesota, I began to wonder how the woman I was about to meet could cope with such devastating news that all four limbs had to be amputated. How did she learn to survive? Did she have live-in help?

When we arrived in Willmar, Minnesota, I called Jan from our hotel to tell her that I could come to her house and pick her and the boys up, so they could swim at our hotel while we talked.

"That's okay, Pat, I can drive. The boys and I will be there in ten minutes. Would you like to go out to eat first? There's a Ponderosa close to your hotel."

"Sure, that'll be fine," I said haltingly, wondering what it would be like to eat in a public restaurant with a woman who had no arms or legs. And how on earth would she drive? Ten minutes later, Jan pulled up in front of the hotel. She got out of the car, walked over to me with perfect posture on legs and feet that looked every bit as real as mine, and extended her right arm with its shiny hook on the end to shake my hand. "Hello, Pat, I'm sure glad to meet you. And this must be Andrew."

I grabbed her hook, pumped it a bit and smiled sheepishly. "Uh, yes, this is Andrew." I looked in the back seat of her car and smiled at the two boys who grinned back. Cody, the younger one, was practically effervescent at the thought of going swimming in the hotel pool after dinner.

Jan bubbled as she slid back behind the driver's seat, "So hop in. Cody, move over and make room for Andrew."

We arrived at the restaurant, went through the line, paid for our food, and ate and talked amidst the chattering of our three sons. The only thing I had to do for Jan Turner that entire evening was unscrew the top on the ketchup bottle.

Later that night, as our three sons splashed in the pool, Jan and I sat on the side and she told me about life before her illness.

"We were a typical single-parent family. You know, busy all the time. Life was so good, in fact, that I was seriously thinking about adopting a third child."

My conscience stung. I had to face it—the woman next to me was better at single parenting than I ever thought about being.

Jan continued. "One Sunday in November of 1989, I was playing my trumpet at the front of my church when I suddenly felt weak, dizzy and nauseous. I struggled down the aisle, motioned for the boys to follow me and drove home. I crawled into bed, but by evening I knew I had to get help."

Jan then explained that by the time she arrived at the hospital, she was comatose. Her blood pressure had dropped so much that her body was already shutting down. She had pneumococcal pneumonia, the same bacterial infection that took the life of Muppets creator Jim Henson. One of its disastrous side effects is an activation of the body's clotting system, which causes the blood vessels to plug up. Because there was suddenly no blood flow to her hands or feet, she quickly developed gangrene in all four extremities. Two weeks after being admitted to the hospital, Jan's arms had to be amputated at mid-forearm and her legs at mid-shin.

Just before the surgery, she said she cried out, "Oh God, no! How can I live without arms and legs, feet or hands? Never walk again? Never play the trumpet, guitar, piano or any of the instruments I teach? I'll never be able to hug my sons or take care of them. Oh God, don't let me depend on others for the rest of my life!"

Six weeks after the amputations, as her dangling limbs healed, a doctor talked to Jan about prosthetics. She said Jan could learn to walk, drive a car, go back to school, even go back to teaching.

Jan found that hard to believe so she picked up her Bible. It fell open to Romans, chapter twelve, verse two: "Don't copy the behavior and customs of this world, but be a new and different person with a fresh newness in all you do and think. Then you will learn from your own experience how his ways will really satisfy you."

Jan thought about that—about being a new and different person—and she decided to give the prosthetics a try. With a walker strapped onto her forearms near the elbow and a therapist on either side, she could only wobble on her new legs for two to three minutes before she collapsed in exhaustion and pain.

Take it slowly, Jan said to herself. Be a new person in all that you do and think, but take it one step at a time.

The next day she tried on the prosthetic arms, a crude system of cables, rubber bands and hooks operated by a harness across the shoulders. By moving her shoulder muscles she was soon able to open and close the hooks to pick up and hold objects, and dress and feed herself.

Within a few months, Jan learned she could do almost everything she used to do—only in a new and different way.

"Still, when I finally got to go home after four months of physical and occupational therapy, I was so nervous about what life would be like with my boys and me alone in the house. But when I got there, I got out of the car, walked up the steps to our house, hugged my boys with all my might, and we haven't looked back since."

As Jan and I continued to talk, Cody, who'd climbed out of the hotel pool, stood close to his mom with his arm around her shoulders. As she told me about her newly improved cooking skills, Cody grinned. "Yup," he said, "She's a better mom now than before she got sick, because now she can even flip pancakes!" Jan laughed like a woman who is blessed with tremendous happiness, contentment and unswerving faith in God.

Since our visit, Jan has completed a second college degree, this one in communications, and she is now an announcer for the local radio station. She also studied theology and has been ordained as the children's pastor at her church, the Triumphant Life Church in Willmar. Simply put, Jan says, "I'm a new and different person, triumphant because of God's unending love and wisdom."

After meeting Jan, I was a new and different person as well. I learned to praise God for everything in my life that makes me new and different, whether it's struggling through one more part-time job to keep my kids in college, learning to be a grandmother for the first time or having the courage to end a relationship with a wonderful friend who just wasn't the right one for me.

Jan may not have real flesh-and-blood arms, legs, hands or feet, but that woman has more heart and soul than anyone I've ever met before or since. She taught me to grab on to every "new and different" thing that comes into my life with all the gusto I can muster… to live my life triumphantly.

~Patricia Lorenz
*Chicken Soup for the Unsinkable Soul*

# Good Medicine

*The future is called "perhaps," which is the only possible thing to call the future. And the only important thing is not to allow that to scare you.*
*~Tennessee Williams*

As a young boy, I fondly remember my grandfather. He was tall in physical size, but he was also larger than life itself, in my eyes. As a Cherokee Indian, he loved to tell the old stories that had been passed down from generation to generation in the tribe, located in the Great Smoky Mountains of North Carolina. His zest for life and his love of nature was passed on to me through the experience there in the mountains of western North Carolina.

On a warm spring day when I was a young boy, my grandfather and I were sitting on a large rock on the edge of the Oconaluftee River in Cherokee. I was looking into a small puddle of water that was caught in an etched indentation of a rock. The large rocks were worn away by water action, and we would sometimes fish on the rocks and watch the fish travel downstream between the rocks. This particular day, I was more interested in the small minnows moving around the puddle of water that seemed to be caught in the rocks. I must have stared endlessly at the minnows wondering how they would get back to the larger body of water and their parents for safety. After all, I had my grandfather there to protect me. Who would protect them from the warm sun and from being eaten by animals, or other fish? Wow, I thought, I was glad I was not a fish!

My grandfather would glance around every few minutes to see what I was doing. He saw me looking at the small fish and asked, "What do you see when you look into the water?"

Always wanting to please my grandfather to show him how smart I really was, I looked quickly downstream and said, "I see the little fish swimming around, but they have no place to go."

"Are you afraid for them, or yourself?" My grandfather would often ask two questions at once.

"The sun is hot, and I am afraid they will get too hot in the shallow water. Besides, what if they don't get back to their parents in the river?" He softly spoke, "Well, maybe they are all right in this special little pool of water. They might get out into the large river and a larger fish might come by and eat them for dinner."

"Grandfather, what will they eat to stay alive? What if they stay there and grow too big for a little pool of water?" I guess I must have learned to ask two questions, as well, from my grandfather.

"Grandson," he said, "you do not need to worry because Nature will take care of them. Whatever happens is all part of a greater plan of life. It is the Great One's plan."

I am sure I must have looked perplexed by this statement, but I didn't really know what to ask. Even at that young age, I knew he would be quiet to allow me to respond, then he would share more with me.

"What do you see when you look into the water?" asked my grandfather. I would look closely to see the water rushing quickly downstream. My eyes would catch the glimpse of the fish, flies touching the water, the water beetles moving quickly down the river, a piece of wood floating with the movement of the water, and the beautiful green plants. I must have explained all these things to him.

There was a long pause. Then he said, "What else do you see? Look deeply into the water."

I looked as hard as I could, then he said, "Now look at the surface of the water." My eyes began to water as I stared, wanting to make my grandfather proud of my ability to see everything he saw.

"Ah, I see my reflection," I proudly responded. He quietly said, "That's good." A smile came across my face.

"What you see is your whole life ahead of you. Know that the Great One has a plan for you, as well as the little fish in the puddle of water. Sometimes we don't understand why things happen the way they do, but there is a plan."

By this time I had forgotten about the little fish and asked, "What is the Great One's plan for you and me?"

"Well," he replied, "my way is working itself out as I am growing older. I am an elder now, and I am to be the 'keeper of secrets' just for you. You will be the keeper of stories and much that you will experience in life to be a helper to others. You are a keeper of all living things."

As I listened to my grandfather, I got excited. "Even the keeper of the rocks and the little fish?" I exclaimed. "Yes," he said with a grin, "because they are all your brothers and sisters, even the rocks, because they had the same elements of you and me."

That special day seems so far behind me now. Shortly after that day my grandfather was taken to do better work, as he would say, in the "great skyvault above, where all things are perfect."

What I remember most about that day was that he taught me to give thanks every day for all things, even the little fish and the rocks that we sat upon together.

As he said, "Always remember to walk the path of Good Medicine and to see the good reflection in everything that occurs in life. Life is a lesson, and you must learn the lesson well to see your true reflection in the water, as well as in life itself."

~J. T. Garrett, Ed.D., M.P.H.
*Chicken Soup for the Grandparent's Soul*

# Keep Your Fork

*Why not enjoy yourself? Your life is here and now.*
*Birth is not a beginning; death is not an end.*
*~Lama Thubten Yeshe*

The sound of Martha's voice on the other end of the telephone always brought a smile to Brother Jim's face. She was not only one of the oldest members of the congregation, but one of the most faithful. Aunt Martie, as all the children called her, just seemed to ooze faith, hope and love wherever she went.

This time, however, there seemed to be an unusual tone to her words.

"Preacher, could you stop by this afternoon? I need to talk with you."

"Of course. I'll be there around three. Is that okay?"

As they sat facing each other in the quiet of her small living room, Jim learned the reason for what he sensed in her voice. Martha told him that her doctor had just discovered a previously undetected tumor.

"He says I probably have six months to live." Martha's words were certainly serious, yet there was a definite calm about her.

"I'm so sorry to..." but before Jim could finish, Martha interrupted.

"Don't be. The Lord has been good. I have lived a long life. I'm ready to go. You know that."

"I know," Jim whispered with a reassuring nod.

"But I do want to talk with you about my funeral. I have been thinking about it, and there are things that I want."

The two talked quietly for a long time. They talked about Martha's favorite hymns, the passages of Scripture that had meant so much to her through the years, and the many memories they shared from the five years Jim had been with Central Church.

When it seemed that they had covered just about everything, Aunt Martie paused, looked up at Jim with a twinkle in her eye, and then added, "One more thing, Preacher. When they bury me, I want my old Bible in one hand and a fork in the other."

"A fork?" Jim was sure he had heard everything, but this caught him by surprise. "Why do you want to be buried with a fork?"

"I have been thinking about all of the church dinners and banquets that I attended through the years," she explained. "I couldn't begin to count them all. But one thing sticks in my mind.

"At those really nice get-togethers, when the meal was almost finished, a server or maybe the hostess would come by to collect the dirty dishes. I can hear the words now. Sometimes, at the best ones, somebody would lean over my shoulder and whisper, 'You can keep your fork.'

"And do you know what that meant? Dessert was coming!

"It didn't mean a cup of Jell-O or pudding or even a dish of ice cream. You don't need a fork for that. It meant the good stuff, like chocolate cake or cherry pie! When they told me I could keep my fork, I knew the best was yet to come!

"That's exactly what I want people to talk about at my funeral. Oh, they can talk about all the good times we had together. That would be nice.

"But when they walk by my casket and look at my pretty blue dress, I want them to turn to one another and say, 'Why the fork?'

"That's what I want to say. I want you to tell them that I kept my fork because the best is yet to come."

~Dr. Roger William Thomas
*Chicken Soup for the Grieving Soul*

# Grateful Life, Joyous Passage

Thirty-five years go, during a Michigan winter, I shot two rabbits in the woods near my home. When I made the incision to skin the second animal, the room filled with a putrid smell—I literally jumped back from the animal. In the process, I nicked myself with my hunting knife. The small cut on my hand infected me with what the doctors diagnosed as tularemia. Within days, my "cold symptoms" turned into a 105-degree fever. I was rushed to the hospital and zipped inside a plastic body bag filled with ice.

I went into a coma just the same. At that point, the strangest thing happened: I had a clear sense of leaving my body. I observed my physical suffering with divine detachment, taking none of it seriously. I was able to move about freely, but part of me felt attached to my body as though by an invisible thread. I found myself staring into a startlingly bright tunnel of light—the same tunnel described by many in the years since then.

With a sense of quiet exhilaration, I approached the tunnel and saw it opened into endless space. Then I stopped and turned around to see my body, packed in ice. I noticed my father sitting in a chair near the bed, crying. I had never seen my father cry, and it disturbed me. I remember trying to communicate with him, to comfort him. I couldn't figure out at first why he was upset; then I realized my body was dying, my soul withdrawing. From my vantage point, sorrow made no sense. It all seemed entirely natural, simple and ordinary.

The gaunt-looking body in the bed took shallow breaths, and I was able to identify it as my body. I understood that I had a decision to make—to live or to die. It seemed arbitrary at that moment. I felt attracted to the brilliant light, but was drawn back, in part, by sympathy for my father. So, being sixteen at the time, I decided to stick around and find out what life was all about.

Having made the decision to stay, I began a journey I might not have chosen had I known what I was getting into. Upon returning to my body, I found I had to work harder than I'd ever worked before. The body was badly damaged by the disease: My hair had fallen out; I looked like a skeleton; I was blind; and my senses were mixed up. Sounds sometimes manifested as images in my brain; light might translate into physical sensations.

The physical world at that time made only minimal sense.

As months passed, my sight returned and my senses straightened themselves out. But thanks to the "rabbits' revenge," as I now call it, I never again saw life with the same eyes.

My near-death experience was repeated twelve years later after a motorcycle accident. It wasn't until ten years after that scary incident that I seriously asked myself why such experiences were given to me. I was working for a publisher at the time who asked if I'd be interested in editing a manuscript. It turned out to be a book on death and dying, and it was the catalyst for examining my own experiences with death.

Over time, I began talking with what I took to be an imaginary character in my psyche, who introduced himself to me as "Alex." I was an author now (*The Well Body Book* with Mike Samuels), and had earned my Ph.D. By all accounts I was a rational human being, so I treated Alex as my muse, or a foil with whom I could converse and ruminate. Then Alex started making suggestions, such as "Stop here and visit Ann. She's having a difficult time."

Amused by this oddity, I did stop by. Ann opened the door almost immediately and stared at me in disbelief: "I've just been thinking about you," she said. "I was about to call you." Ann told me a mutual friend of ours had died a few days before in a violent accident. "Since he died," Ann said, "it's like he's always here, nagging at me. I don't know what to do."

Alex gave me detailed directions: "The next time her dead friend nags her, Ann should go to a quiet place, sit down and just be with him—talk with him as if he were physically present. Give him permission to leave this life. Ask him if there is any unfinished business he needs her to finish for him."

A week later Ann called to tell me it had worked. Whether my (Alex's) advice was my own subconscious wisdom that helped put her mind to rest, or whether our friend's soul was able to finally let go and leave, I cannot know for certain. But after some of my experiences, it seemed as credible an explanation as any.

Many adventures with the living and dying followed. I will share a special one with you. The evening my mother died, I was holding her hand. My mother's eyes dropped shut, and I decided to close mine as well. As I did so, a tremendous feeling of peace spread over me. Speaking only in my mind, I said, I think it's time for you to go. I opened my eyes. My mother was looking right past me, her eyes alert and happy.

"All right," she said, answering what I had only said in my mind. A coincidence?

"Go toward the light," I said.

She turned her head slightly up, to the right. Her face lit up. I had the clear impression she was greeting someone she was pleased to see. In a soft, calm voice, I repeated these words, "Go lightly, lightly, lightly."

I felt her hand in mine, but she was slipping away, like an airplane fading away, growing smaller, becoming a dot, a blur. Then she was gone. Her soul had left her body—of that I had no doubt. Yet she looked radiant.

I said a little prayer, though I don't recall the words.

My mother's gravestone bears the following epitaph: "A grateful life, a joyous passage." It tells the story well.

And so, I end, as all stories end, with a farewell and a reminder: "Go towards the light. Go lightly, lightly, lightly."

~Hal Zina Bennett, Ph.D.

*Chicken Soup to Inspire the Body & Soul*

# *Salvation in Sarajevo*

*Live simply that others might simply live.*
*~Elizabeth Seaton*

In the autumn of 1941, most of the Jews of Sarajevo were herded onto trains and sent to concentration camps. Some managed to flee; others joined the Partisans. Josef Kabilio, a Jewish artisan, was a close family friend of Mustafa Hardaga, a wealthy Muslim merchant. Not long after the Germans occupied Sarajevo, Mustafa Hardaga went to inspect one of his properties and found Josef Kabilio hiding there. Mustafa Hardaga now faced an excruciating moral dilemma.

If he turned Josef Kabilio over to the authorities, it would be condemning him to death. Yet, if he were caught sheltering a Jew, it would mean certain death for both of them. But this was his friend for many years; what was he to do? His high principles prevailed. He took Kabilio into his home and hid him there. Kabilio made two attempts to flee Sarajevo, and both times he was caught and jailed. On both occasions, he managed to escape from jail and again Hardaga, his Muslim friend, sheltered him in his home.

Zeyneba Hardaga, the merchant's wife, also had a close relationship with Kabilio. On one occasion she spotted him in a labor brigade and risked her life by bringing food to Kabilio and his fellow prisoners. At a later date, she explained her actions. "When Josef left us for the third time, all we could do was pray and hope. Later, when my children asked why I did this, I always answered what my husband said, 'You do not abandon your friends.'"

Miraculously, Kabilio survived the war and returned to Sarajevo in 1945. Finding his home plundered, the Hardagas took him in. In 1948, he left for Israel, promising to write often, as did the Hardagas. Very soon the first letter arrived from Israel to Sarajevo, and they continued like a paper chain for decades.

Over the course of those years, Josef Kabilio married, had children and grandchildren, and became a widower. Similarly, Zeneyba Hardaga in Sarajevo became a widow and then remarried, becoming a mother and grandmother. However, with the passage of the years, in addition to losing her second husband, she also lost all her property and a good deal of her health. Ultimately, a leg had to be amputated, and she could no longer walk. Despite all these woes, she never informed her good friend and correspondent, Josef Kabilio, of her troubles.

All the while, and unbeknownst to her, Kabilio was hard at work in Jerusalem to have her recognized by Yad Vashem, Israel's National Holocaust Museum, as a Righteous Gentile, a non-Jew who went to extraordinary lengths during the Second World War to save Jewish lives. He went many times to the museum to speak to the office in charge of this award and learned that the necessary process of substantiation was exceptionally arduous, and furthermore, this award had never been given to a Muslim.

Kabilio persisted in the face of many obstacles, and when he turned eighty-eight, Zeyneba Hardaga received a letter from Yad Vashem. They informed her of her award and told her that she would be flown to Jerusalem to receive it. Seven months later, Josef Kabilio had the privilege of watching his old friend helped off the plane at Ben Gurion airport. He was shocked to see that she could not walk. His first words were, "You never told me!" With a smile, she scolded him, "You never told me what you were up to, either."

Kabilio died just four years later and never knew how valuable his work would ultimately become in having Zeyneba recognized by Yad Vashem. The war broke out in Sarajevo in 1992. In February 1994, Mrs. Hardaga and her family were given special preference to escape the horrors of war by leaving the city on a convoy of 294

Muslims, Jews, Serbs and Croats, organized by the Joint Jewish Distribution Committee. This Muslim family had their lives saved by a Jewish organization.

Furthermore, Kabilio's family in Israel went to the Israeli authorities and arranged for an El Al plane (Israel's national airline) to be sent to the Sarajevo area to bring Zeyneba Hardaga, her daughter and her family, to Israel. All these miraculous events occurred in large measure because of Josef Kabilio's efforts to properly recognize his friend's heroism during the war. What beautiful symmetry. The Muslim Hardagas saved Kabilio when his life was threatened, and the Jew Kabilio was instrumental in having the Hardagas saved when their lives were in danger.

Isn't this the way the world should always be?

~Rabbi Richard Plavin
*Chicken Soup for the Jewish Soul*

# One Step at a Time

*Heal me, O Lord, and I shall be healed.*
*~Jeremiah 17:14*

Running has always been a great love of mine. For fifteen years I ran five miles a day, four days a week. I had developed a very successful business as a sales representative, and my work required a great deal of travel. Living near Lake Ontario, I covered New York, western Pennsylvania and eastern Ohio. I drove an average of 35,000 miles a year to meet with customers. I was always active, always on the go.

A few years ago, I began to feel a minor irritation in my left eye. Finally, after many months, I decided to see a doctor. X-rays revealed a small growth behind my eye. It didn't appear cancerous, but the surgeons recommended having it removed as soon as possible.

Because my travel was usually very light around Christmas, I scheduled surgery for December 19th. I was not looking forward to the surgery, but at least while recuperating I could stay home and enjoy the company of my wife, Barbara, and our three children: Denise, then nineteen; Jerry, seventeen; and Chuck, twelve.

When I awoke after the operation, nothing seemed clear. Conversations made no sense. I remember experiencing everything as a series of short, dream-like situations. I felt as though I were lost in the hospital and nobody could help me. Wake up, Jerry, I told myself. This dream is scary! Actually, I hadn't been dreaming at all.

During the surgery, a blood vessel that removes blood from the brain had been severed. Although this was a routine procedure, it had devastating effects. My brain tissue began to swell. The next day, I suffered a stroke to the left-front temporal lobe, affecting my speech. I could no longer communicate and the look of terror on my face alerted my daughter to my fears.

My brain continued to swell, and that evening I suffered another stroke, affecting vision. I had lost the right-peripheral vision in both eyes. I was rushed into emergency surgery. The only option left to the doctors was to remove a small portion of my brain which was already damaged by the stroke, in order to make room for any additional swelling. When the doctors finished surgery, they told my wife, "We've done all we can, the rest is in God's hands." They explained to Barbara that I could be paralyzed, blind and unable to speak.

I was hospitalized for three months at St. Mary's Brain Injury Rehabilitation Unit in Rochester, New York. During that time, I was reintroduced to my wife and children, but had no idea who they were. When I returned home for a visit, I stood there shaking, asking my wife, where we were. I recognized nothing. Literally, everything had to be reintroduced to me.

After leaving St. Mary's, I attended their outpatient rehabilitation program for another year. With the wonderful support of the therapists, doctors, family and friends, I began to relearn all the basic tasks of everyday life. During this period, I often used to see a man with long hair and a beard and wearing red-and-white clothing. His arms were outstretched, and there was a glowing heart in the middle of his chest. I loved staring at this wonderful sight. At the time, I didn't know that this man was appearing in the part of my field of vision that was supposed to be blind.

At the school, I would always use the walking machine at break time. My body slowly started to feel the urge to run again. But because of my near blindness, I was discouraged from running. One day during my prayers, I broke into tears at the thought of never being able to run again. All of a sudden I felt a warm hand touch my leg, and I heard the words, "You can run again."

Sustained only by an unyielding faith in those words, I gradually retrained myself to run indoors on the walking machine. That was in February 1996. Little by little I did more and more until, in March, I started running outdoors. My family watched me so I wouldn't get hurt or lost. It was over a year since I had run outside, but my body was adjusting nicely. When I made it down to the lake, I yelled, "Hi, Lake Ontario! It's me, Jerry Sullivan!"

I worked my way back up to twenty miles a week. My friends took me to the St. Patrick's Day Five-Mile Run. What a thrill that was! I could run again, and it seemed life was coming back to me.

Driving was next in line. Although 50 percent blind, I learned to drive again. When I passed my driving test, my mother-in-law gave me a gift—a small religious sticker to place in my car. On the sticker was a picture of a man with long hair and a beard, dressed in red and white. There on his chest was a glowing heart. It was the same man I had seen so often during my recovery.

I don't know what to make of this coincidence. But I do know the extraordinary power of faith. If it can make a blind man run, it can truly work miracles in our lives.

~Jerry Sullivan
*A 5th Portion of Chicken Soup for the Soul*

# What Day Is Today?

*Better to lose count while naming your blessings*
*than to lose your blessings to counting your troubles.*
*~Maltbie D. Babcock*

Sid taught the staff and patients alike that there's room for life and laughter in a hospice. This wonderful man tried hard to cope with a paralysis that left him highly dependent on his family and the nurses. Though this irritated him immensely, he was a born actor with a wonderful sense of theater. Sid knew exactly how to act out his sense of injustice in the face of his terminal illness. Often he played to the gallery—in this case, the three other patients who shared the same room. His roommates tolerated Sid, although "here-he-goes-again" was a much-used refrain.

But Sid was also very religious. One morning, I was giving out the medication in his room when he hoisted himself onto his elbows, looked soulfully across the room and muttered weakly (but loud enough for all to hear), "What day is it today?"

I answered truthfully, "Palm Sunday."

Staring up at the ceiling, Sid blurted dramatically, "Then today is a good day to die." With this he fell back on the bed in such a dramatic fashion, I wondered if he would actually do it then and there! But a few seconds later, he popped opened his eyes, looked at me and sighed.

Later that same week, when I was back in Sid's room, he decided to give a repeat performance. Lifting himself onto his elbows again, he asked, "What day is it today?"

Again telling the truth, I said, "It's Good Friday."

Without looking up from his book, his roommate muttered loudly, "I hope to God he doesn't die today—he might rise again on Sunday!"

~Dennis Sibley as told to Allen Klein
*Chicken Soup for the Nurse's Soul*

# Do Unto Others

*Hope is the thing with feathers*
*That perches in the soul,*
*And sings the tunes without the words,*
*And never stops at all.*
*~Emily Dickinson*

Of all the sadness that came out of September 11th, one story shines like a jewel in the dust. It is a story of giving and receiving—a story of saving and being saved and not knowing which is which—the story of the firefighters of Ladder Company 6 and Josephine.

More than three hundred firefighters perished in the tragedy of the World Trade Center. On September 29th, at a time when the country was desperate for good news, NBC Dateline reported "The Miracle of Ladder Company 6." By the time I sat around their table in the back of the firehouse two weeks later and heard them recount it, the firefighters of Ladder 6 had said these words many times, but every word was still flooded with the vibrant sound of their gratitude.

They had gone to the World Trade Center that day to give. To rescue. That's what firefighters do. They run into burning buildings against instinct and nature, while the rest of us are running out, trying to save our own lives. They had entered the building at Number One, as had so many of their brothers, after the first plane had mortally wounded it. People were streaming down beside them, saying words of thanks and encouragement to them, offering them drinks from the machines and telling them they should get a pay raise.

They, in turn, offered words of encouragement back. "It's over for you," the firefighters said to those lucky enough to be exiting. "Go out through the lobby and go home now. You're okay."

The stairwells were narrow, only room enough for one person to move past another in either direction. Each of the firefighters climbing the steps carried at least a hundred pounds of equipment. At the twenty-seventh floor, some of them learned that the other tower had gone down, and the effort to save the building was rejected for the more pressing job of saving the people. Somehow in all the confusion, somewhere between the twelfth and fifteenth floors, the men of Ladder 6 were entrusted with the safety of a sixty-year-old bookkeeper named Josephine Harris. Josephine worked on the seventy-third floor, and she had been trudging down those sixty flights of steps through smoke and heat until her desire and ability to go on seemed completely exhausted.

Now getting her safely out was their assignment. So, despite her unwillingness to continue down the stairs, the firefighters encouraged her on. They reminded her of her grandchildren, who were waiting for her when she escaped the building. They told her she could do it. They cajoled. They encouraged. They promised to get her out if she would just keep moving.

On the fourth floor, she finally stopped in her tracks. She could not take another step. Would not take another step. She seemed willing to let them go on without her, but she was done walking. Never even thinking about leaving her, the firefighters began looking around for a chair on which to carry her down the rest of the stairs.

They were tired, too, and burdened by the heat and the weight of their equipment, and they were anxious to evacuate the building. But because some of them were not aware of the other building's collapse, and because the towers had always seemed somehow immortal, they did not feel at that moment that there was great urgency.

None of them expected the terrible, otherworldly, thunderous sound; none of them expected the rumble that, in an instant, signaled catastrophe. Time stands still at moments like that. They stretch out long enough to give people pause, to consider what dying would mean. Bill Butler thought, I didn't even get to say goodbye to my wife and kids. Clearly, this was it. They had done their best, and now it was over. They prayed for it to be over quickly; they repented and asked for forgiveness; they thought of loved ones.

And then everything turned to dust around them. One hundred and five floors above them came tumbling down, each crushing the one under it with greater force. Within seconds the proud, shiny tower had been turned to sand-sized pieces of rubble, taking thousands of lives in its shattering wake.

From all vantage points, there was no way for anyone to survive this disaster, and no obvious reason why the staircase at which Josephine had halted should have been spared. But miracles have their own reasons. And as the dust settled, Captain John (Jay) Jonas, Sal D'Agostino, Bill Butler, Tommy Falco, Mike Meldrum, Matt Komorowski and Josephine, thrown wildly through the debris, were left whole, if not exactly standing, seemingly buried alive.

For four hours they were trapped in the rubble, wondering what was happening around them and how long they would be trapped. D'Agostino found a can of Sunkist orange soda, which seemed a drink of the gods to the thirsty team. Josephine was "a trooper," D'Agostino said of her. He offered her a drink and she declined, being brave and stoic. When, after a while, she said she was cold, Falco gave her his coat and even held her hand when she said she was scared. They had no idea what was happening around them; they could only hope that there were efforts being made to find survivors. Little did they know how ecstatic firefighters would be to discover that anyone had survived this disaster. Little did they know that the search for them was frantic and urgent for all concerned—those lost and those desperate to find them.

While they waited, some of them methodically repacked the rope in case they would need it later, a routine that now gave them something to do. A cell phone played a part in the outcome, as it had in the tragedy of Flight 93. This time it was when Butler, who couldn't reach the firehouse through all the chaos of the phone system, called his wife. She called the firehouse and let them know of the plight of the missing men.

Finally, they were found. Rescued.

But it had been an intense time that they had shared with Josephine, and the six were not ready to turn her over to another company. D'Agostino said that when a firefighter finally discovered them there, he was so pumped up that he rushed to take Josephine from them, calling her "Doll" and saying, 'We'll take care of you, Doll. We got you."

But after all those hours of sharing the limbo between life and death with her, it seemed to them inappropriate not to give her the honor due her. D'Agostino said he grabbed the rescuer's arm and explained, "Her name isn't Doll. Her name is Josephine." When he thinks of it now, he shakes his head. Even in the midst of the excitement of recovery and the terrible fright through which each soul had journeyed, the other firefighter recognized the holiness of the moment and apologized, saying, "Sorry, Josephine, we'll take good care of you.'"

Ultimately, because special equipment was required to remove her from the wasteland that Ground Zero had become, Josephine was taken away from the men of Ladder 6 and they parted.

As I sat around the table with Sal and Mike and Bill and Tom and listened to them tell it one more time, I could see that the talking about it was part of the process—that we understand so much through stories. They had a reunion with Josephine at a later date, gave her a special jacket and called her their "guardian angel." While she says that they saved her life, they contend the opposite. They believe that by insisting that they stop there at that spot, at the only place left standing at Ground Zero, holding it as a sacred space, Josephine had saved their lives.

~Judith Simon Prager

*Chicken Soup for the Soul of America*

Chicken Soup for the Soul

# Share with Us

We would like to know how these stories affected you and which ones were your favorites. Please e-mail us and let us know.

We also would like to share your stories with future readers. You may be able to help another reader, and become a published author at the same time. Please send us your own stories and poems for our future books. Some of our past contributors have launched writing and speaking careers from the publication of their stories in our books!

Your stories have the best chance of being used if you submit them through our web site, at:

www.chickensoup.com

If you do not have access to the Internet, you may submit your stories by mail or by facsimile. Please do not send us any book manuscripts, unless through a literary agent, as these will be automatically discarded.

Chicken Soup for the Soul
P.O. Box 700
Cos Cob, CT 06807-0700
Fax 203-861-7194

# More Great Books On Faith

Chicken Soup for the Christian Soul
1-55874-501-7

Chicken Soup for the Christian Family Soul
1-55874-714-1

Chicken Soup for the Christian Woman's Soul
0-7573-0018-9

Chicken Soup for the Christian Teenage Soul
0-7573-0095-2

Chicken Soup for the Christian Soul II
0-7573-0320-X

**Loving Our Cats**

We are all crazy about our mysterious cats. Sometimes they are our best friends; sometimes they are aloof. They are fun to watch and often surprise us. These true stories, the best from Chicken Soup's library, will make readers appreciate their own cats and see them with a new eye. Readers will revel in the heartwarming, amusing, inspirational, and occasionally tearful stories about our best friends and faithful companions — our cats.

**Loving Our Dogs**

We are all crazy about our dogs and can't read enough about them, whether they're misbehaving and giving us big, innocent looks, or loyally standing by us in times of need. This new book from Chicken Soup for the Soul contains the 101 best dog stories from the company's extensive library. Readers will revel in the heartwarming, amusing, inspirational, and occasionally tearful stories about our best friends and faithful companions — our dogs.

**Christmas Cheer**

Everyone loves Christmas and the holiday season. We reunite scattered family members, watch the wonder in a child's eyes, and feel the joy of giving gifts. The rituals of the holiday season give a rhythm to the years and create a foundation for our lives, as we gather with family, with our communities at church, at school, and even at the mall, to share the special spirit of the season, brightening those long winter days.

**Christian Teen Talk**

Devout Christian teens care about their connection and relationship with God, but they are also experiencing all the ups and downs of teenage life. This book provides support to teens who care about their faith but are trying to navigate their teenage years. This book includes 101 heartfelt, true stories about love, compassion, loss, forgiveness, friends, school, and faith. It also covers tough issues such as self-destructive behavior, substance abuse, teen pregnancy, and divorce.

**Christian Kids**

This is the first Chicken Soup book, with 101 great stories from Chicken Soup's library, created specifically for Christian parents to read themselves or to share with their children. All of the selected stories are appropriate for children and are about raising Christian kids twelve and under. Christian parents will enjoy reading these heartfelt, inspiring, and often humorous stories about the ups and downs of daily life in today's contemporary Christian families.

**Living Catholic Faith**

This is Chicken Soup for the Soul's first book written just for Catholics. From the once-a-year attendee at Christmas Mass, to the church volunteer and daily worshipper. 101 spirit-filled stories written by Catholics of all ages, this book covers the gamut, including stories about growing up Catholic to stories about sacraments and miracles. These stories bestow happiness, hope, and healing to everyone in all stages of life and faith.

Family & Faith

Chicken Soup for the Soul®

Who Is

# Jack Canfield?

Jack Canfield is the co-creator and editor of the *Chicken Soup for the Soul* series, which *Time* magazine has called "the publishing phenomenon of the decade." Jack is also the co-author of eight other bestselling books including *The Success Principles™: How to Get from Where You Are to Where You Want to Be*, *Dare to Win*, *The Aladdin Factor*, *You've Got to Read This Book*, and *The Power of Focus: How to Hit Your Business and Personal and Financial Targets with Absolute Certainty*.

Jack has recently developed a telephone coaching program and an online coaching program based on his most recent book *The Success Principles*. He also offers a seven-day *Breakthrough to Success* seminar every summer, which attracts 400 people from fifteen countries around the world.

Jack is the CEO of the Canfield Training Group in Santa Barbara, California, and founder of the Foundation for Self-Esteem in Culver City, California. He has conducted intensive personal and professional development seminars on the principles of success for over a million people in twenty-three countries. Jack is a dynamic keynote speaker and he has spoken to hundreds of thousands of others at more than 1,000 corporations, universities, professional conferences and conventions, and has been seen by millions more on national television shows such as *The Today Show*, *Fox and Friends*, *Inside Edition*, *Hard Copy*, *CNN's Talk Back Live*, *20/20*, *Eye to Eye*, and the *NBC Nightly News* and the *CBS Evening News*.

Jack is the recipient of many awards and honors, including three honorary doctorates and a Guinness World Records Certificate for having seven books from the *Chicken Soup for the Soul* series appearing on the *New York Times* bestseller list on May 24, 1998.

To write to Jack or for inquiries about Jack as a speaker, his coaching programs, trainings or seminars, use the following contact information:


Jack Canfield
The Canfield Companies
P.O. Box 30880 • Santa Barbara, CA 93130
phone: 805-563-2935 • fax: 805-563-2945
E-mail: info@jackcanfield.com
www.jackcanfield.com

## Who Is

# Mark Victor Hansen?

Mark Victor Hansen is the co-founder of Chicken Soup for the Soul, along with Jack Canfield. He is also a sought-after keynote speaker, bestselling author, and marketing maven.

For more than thirty years, Mark has focused solely on helping people from all walks of life reshape their personal vision of what's possible. His powerful messages of possibility, opportunity, and action have created powerful change in thousands of organizations and millions of individuals worldwide.

Mark's credentials include a lifetime of entrepreneurial success. He is a prolific writer with many bestselling books, such as *The One Minute Millionaire*, *Cracking the Millionaire Code*, *How to Make the Rest of Your Life the Best of Your Life*, *The Power of Focus*, *The Aladdin Factor*, and *Dare to Win*, in addition to the *Chicken Soup for the Soul* series. Mark has had a profound influence in the field of human potential through his library of audios, videos, and articles in the areas of big thinking, sales achievement, wealth building, publishing success, and personal and professional development.

Mark is the founder of the *MEGA Seminar Series*. *MEGA Book Marketing University* and *Building Your MEGA Speaking Empire* are annual conferences where Mark coaches and teaches new and aspiring authors, speakers, and experts on building lucrative publishing and speaking careers. Other MEGA events include *MEGA Info-Marketing* and *My MEGA Life*.

He has appeared on *Oprah*, *CNN*, and *The Today Show*. He has been quoted in *Time*, *U.S. News & World Report*, *USA Today*, *New York Times*, and *Entrepreneur* and has had countless radio interviews, assuring our planet's people that "You can easily create the life you deserve."

As a philanthropist and humanitarian, Mark works tirelessly for organizations such as Habitat for Humanity, American Red Cross, March of Dimes, Childhelp USA, and many others. He is the recipient of numerous awards that honor his entrepreneurial spirit, philanthropic heart, and business acumen. He is a lifetime member of the Horatio Alger Association of Distinguished Americans, an organization that honored Mark with the prestigious Horatio Alger Award for his extraordinary life achievements.

Mark Victor Hansen is an enthusiastic crusader of what's possible and is driven to make the world a better place.

Mark Victor Hansen & Associates, Inc.
P.O. Box 7665 • Newport Beach, CA 92658
phone: 949-764-2640 • fax: 949-722-6912
www.markvictorhansen.com

## Who Is

# Amy Newmark?

Amy Newmark was recently named publisher of Chicken Soup for the Soul, after a thirty-year career as a writer, speaker, financial analyst, and business executive in the worlds of finance and telecommunications.

Amy is a graduate of Harvard College, where she majored in Portuguese, minored in French, and traveled extensively. She is also the mother of two children in college and has two grown stepchildren.

After a long career writing books on telecommunications, voluminous financial reports, business plans, and corporate press releases, Chicken Soup for the Soul is a breath of fresh air for Amy. She has fallen in love with Chicken Soup for the Soul and its life-changing books, and found it a true pleasure to conceptualize, compile, and edit the "101 Best Stories" books for our readers.

The best way to contact Chicken Soup for the Soul is through our web site, at www.chickensoup.com. This will always get the fastest attention.

If you do not have access to the Internet, please contact us by mail or by facsimile.


Chicken Soup for the Soul<br>
P.O. Box 700<br>
Cos Cob, CT 06807-0700<br>
Fax 203-861-7194

Chicken Soup for the Soul®

# Thank You!

Our first thanks go to our loyal readers who have inspired the entire Chicken Soup team for the past fifteen years. Your appreciative letters and e-mails have reminded us why we work so hard on these books.

We owe huge thanks to all of our contributors as well. We know that you pour your hearts and souls into the stories and poems that you share with us, and ultimately with each other. We appreciate your willingness to open up your lives to other Chicken Soup readers.

We can only publish a small percentage of the stories that are submitted, but we read every single one and even the ones that do not appear in a book have an influence on us and on the final manuscripts.

As always, we would like to thank the entire staff of Chicken Soup for the Soul for their help on this project and the 101 Best series in general.

Among our California staff, we would especially like to single out the following people:

- D'ette Corona, our Assistant Publisher, who is the heart and soul of the Chicken Soup publishing operation, and who put together the first draft of this manuscript

- Barbara LoMonaco, our Webmaster and Chicken Soup for the Soul Editor, for invaluable assistance in obtaining the fabulous quotations that add depth and meaning to this book

- Patty Hansen for her extra special help with the permissions for these fabulous stories and for her amazing knowledge of the Chicken Soup library

- and Patti Clement for her help with permissions and other organizational matters.

In our Connecticut office, we would like to thank Madeline Clapps, for her wonderful editing assistance, and Leigh Holmes, who keeps everything running smoothly.

We would also like to thank our Creative Director and book producer, Brian Taylor at Pneuma Books, for his brilliant vision for our covers and interiors.

Finally, none of this would be possible without the business and creative leadership of our CEO, Bill Rouhana, and our president, Bob Jacobs.